Amateur Gardening

POCKET GUIDE

A glance at the list of contents and even a cursory examination of the pages which follow will leave the reader in no doubt why this excellent best-selling gardener's guide, now revised, has been so popular with gardeners. A. G. L. Hellyer, the distinguished horticultural journalist and author who was Editor of *Amateur Gardening* from 1946–67, is a gardener writing for gardeners. A plantsman of distinction and with a lifetime devoted to practical gardening, Mr. Hellyer has through his professional duties been given an unrivalled insight into the problems, ambitions and interests of millions of amateur gardeners in this country.

The Amateur Gardening Pocket Guide gives readers the benefit of Mr Hellyer's knowledge in a form which makes reference particularly easy. It has not been overlooked that the gardener in need of information is usually in a hurry, nor that unnecessary verbiage is, at such times, unwelcome. To have this *Pocket Guide* to hand when advice is needed is the next best thing to having an unusually well-informed and articulate professional gardener at your elbow.

Amateur Gardening

POCKET GUIDE

COMPILED BY

A. G. L. HELLYER, M.B.E., F.L.S., V.M.H.

COLLINGRIDGE BOOKS
LONDON · NEW YORK · SYDNEY · TORONTO

Published for Collingridge Books by
The Hamlyn Publishing Group Limited
London · New York · Sydney · Toronto
Astronaut House, Feltham, Middlesex, England

First published in 1941
Fourth revised edition 1971
Sixth impression, fourth edition, 1976

Printed and bound in Great Britain by
Hazell Watson & Viney Limited

CONTENTS

SECTION ONE

WEIGHTS, MEASURES, AND GARDEN CALCULATIONS

WEIGHTS AND MEASURES

1. British Linear Measure.

12 inches	= 1 foot
3 feet	= 1 yard
22 yards	= 1 chain
10 chains	= 1 furlong
8 furlongs	= 1 mile
1,760 yards or 5,280 feet	= 1 mile

2. Square Measure.

144 square inches	= 1 square foot
9 square feet	= 1 square yard
$30\frac{1}{4}$ square yards	= 1 square rod, pole or perch
40 square rods, poles or perches	= 1 rood
4 roods	= 1 acre
640 acres	= 1 square mile

3. Cubic Measure.

1,728 cubic inches	= 1 cubic foot
27 cubic feet	= 1 cubic yard

4. Surveyor's Measure.

7·92 inches	= 1 link
100 links	= 1 chain
80 chains	= 1 mile
100,000 square links or 10 square chains	= 1 acre

5. Land Measure.

62·724 square inches	= 1 square link
2·295 square links	= 1 square foot
20·655 square links	= 1 square yard
625 square links	= 1 rod, pole, or perch
40 rods (poles, perches)	= 1 rood
4 roods (4,840 sq. yards)	= 1 acre
10 square chains	= 1 acre

6. Apothecaries' Measure.

60 minims	= 1 fluid drachm
8 fluid drachms	= 1 fluid ounce
20 fluid ounces	= 1 pint
8 pints	= 1 gallon

7. Measure of Capacity.

5 fluid ounces	= 1 gill
4 gills	= 1 pint
2 pints	= 1 quart
4 quarts	= 1 gallon
2 gallons	= 1 peck
4 pecks	= 1 bushel
8 bushels	= 1 quarter
5 quarters	= 1 load
2 loads	= 1 last

8. Avoirdupois Weight.

16 drams	= 1 ounce
16 ounces	= 1 pound
14 pounds	= 1 stone
2 st., or 28 lb.	= 1 quarter
4 qrs., or 112 lb.	= 1 hundredweight
20 cwt., or 2,240 lb.	= 1 ton

9. METRIC EQUIVALENTS

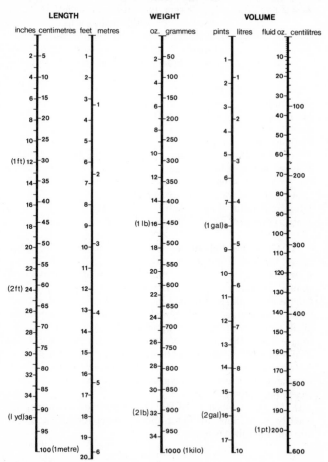

LENGTH				WEIGHT		VOLUME			
inches	centimetres	feet	metres	oz.	grammes	pints	litres	fluid oz.	centilitres

LENGTH

inches — centimetres | feet — metres

2 — 5
4 — 10
6 — 15
8 — 20
10 — 25
(1ft) 12 — 30
14 — 35
16 — 40
18 — 45
20 — 50
22 — 55
(2ft) 24 — 60
26 — 65
28 — 70
30 — 75
32 — 80
34 — 85
(1 yd) 36 — 90
— 95
— 100 (1 metre)

1
2
3 — 1
4
5
6
7 — 2
8
9
10 — 3
11
12
13 — 4
14
15
16 — 5
17
18
19
20 — 6

WEIGHT

oz. — grammes

2 — 50
4 — 100
6 — 150
8 — 200
— 250
10 — 300
12 — 350
14 — 400
(1 lb) 16 — 450
18 — 500
20 — 550
22 — 600
24 — 650
26 — 700
28 — 750
30 — 800
— 850
(2 lb) 32 — 900
34 — 950
— 1000 (1 kilo)

VOLUME

pints — litres | fluid oz. — centilitres

1
2 — 1
3
4 — 2
5 — 3
6
7 — 4
(1 gal) 8
9 — 5
10
11 — 6
12 — 7
13
14 — 8
15
(2 gal) 16 — 9
17 — 10

10
20
30 — 100
40
50
60
70 — 200
80
90
100
110 — 300
120
130
140 — 400
150
160
170
180 — 500
190
(1 pt) 200 — 600

10. Miscellaneous Weights and Measures.

Bushel flat	= A basket measuring 21 inches long, 16 inches wide, and 10 inches deep
Imperial bushel	= 1·28 cubic feet. A box with inside measurements 22 inches × 10 inches × 10 inches will hold approximately an Imperial bushel
Litre	= ·22 gallon
Centimetre	= ·3937 inch
Metre	= 39·37 inches
Gross	= 12 doz. (144)

1 gallon of water weighs 10 lb.

1 cubic foot of water contains approximately $6\frac{1}{4}$ gals.

1 lb. of any substance dissolved in 10 gals. of water makes a 1 per cent. solution, 2 lb. a 2 per cent. solution, and so on.

1 teaspoonful of water is approximately $\frac{1}{8}$ fl. oz.

1 dessertspoonful of water is approximately $\frac{1}{4}$ fl. oz.

1 tablespoonful of water is approximately $\frac{1}{2}$ fl. oz.

11. Measuring Superficial Areas.

Measurements are made across the widest and the narrowest parts of the plot, the two figures are added together and then divided by two. Two similar measurements are made across the greatest and least lengths of the plot and treated in the same manner. The average width and average length obtained by this means are multiplied together to give the approximate superficial area – in square feet if the measurements were in feet, in square yards if in yards, or in square metres if the measurements were in metres. Square feet can be reduced to square yards by dividing by nine. Conversely, square yards can be converted into square feet by multiplying by nine (2).

If the plot or bed is rectangular, only two measurements need be made, one for width and the other for length. These are then multiplied together.

To estimate the area of a circle, measure from the centre to the edge, multiply this by itself and the result by $3\frac{1}{7}$.

12. Estimating Bulk. Measurements of capacity or bulk are made in cubic feet, cubic yards, cubic centimetres or cubic metres (3). Three, instead of two, preliminary sets of measurements must be obtained – one for average length, one for average breadth, and one for average depth – but these are made in the manner just described. All three are then multiplied together, the answer being in cubic feet if the original measurements were in feet, cubic yards if in yards, cubic centimetres or cubic metres. Cubic feet can be reduced to cubic yards by dividing by twenty-seven.

13. Estimating Gravel. A ton of gravel contains from 19 to 20 cubic feet (3), but gravel is usually sold not by the ton but by the 'yard' (*i.e.*, cubic yard). A thickness of from 2 to 3 inches of gravel is required for surfacing a path, and at this rate a ton of gravel will cover from 9 to 13 square yards, while a 'yard' of gravel will cover from 12 to 18 square yards.

14. Estimating Paving Slabs. Crazy pavement is proportionately heavier than gravel. A ton contains from 13 to 14 cubic feet (3), and the covering area depends upon the thickness. Usually 'crazy' is sold in two grades, 'thin' varying from $\frac{3}{4}$ to $1\frac{1}{2}$ inch in thickness, and 'thick' from $1\frac{1}{2}$ to $2\frac{1}{2}$ inches thick. The former has a covering capacity of from 14 to 16 square yards and the latter from 8 to 9 square yards per ton (2). Similar remarks apply to rectangular paving. York paving covers 10 to 11 square yards per ton.

14a. Conversion of Fahrenheit into Centigrade. To convert any Fahrenheit reading to Centigrade the formula is $\frac{5}{9}$ $(F - 32) = C$ when $F = $ Fahrenheit and $C = $ Centigrade.

Fahrenheit	0°	10	20	32	40	50	60	70	80	90	100°
Centigrade	-18°	-10	-5	0	5	10	15	20	25	30	35	40°

TABLE OF APPROXIMATE QUANTITIES OF PAVING MATERIAL REQUIRED FOR 10-FEET LENGTH OF PATH

Width of Path	*2 ft.*	*2½ ft.*	*3 ft.*	*4 ft.*	*6 ft.*
Bricks (flat)	71	89	107	143	214
Bricks (on edge)	107	134	160	213	320
Crazy pavement, ¾ to	*cwt.*	*cwt.*	*cwt.*	*cwt.*	*cwt.*
1½ in.	3	3¾	4½	6	9
Crazy pavement, 1½ to					
2½ in.	5¼	6½	8	10½	16
York paving slabs	4	5	6	8	12
Gravel (2 in. thick)	3¼	4	5	7	10
	(1/9 yd.)	(1/7 yd.)	(1/5 yd.)	(¼ yd.)	(⅓ yd.)
Gravel (3 in. thick)	5	6¼	7½	10	15
	(⅙ yd.)	(2/9 yd.)	(¼ yd.)	(⅓ yd.)	(½ yd.)
Concrete (2 in. thick)					
Gravel	3	3¾	4½	6	9
Sand	1	1¼	1½	2	3
Cement	1	1¼	1½	2	3
Concrete (3 in. thick)					
Gravel	4½	5½	6	9	13
Sand	1½	1⅔	2	3	4¼
Cement	1½	1⅔	2	3	4¼

15. Estimating Walling Stone. Walling stone is similar to crazy paving and its covering capacity depends upon its thickness. A usual measurement is 6 inches, and this has a covering capacity of about 3 to 4 square yards per ton (2).

16. Estimating Soil for Filling. Soil for filling up beds, etc., varies in bulk according to its texture and the amount of water that it contains. Sandy soils are the lightest and may reach 26 to 27 cubic feet to the ton (3), while heavy clay barely touches 18 cubic feet for the same weight. The average for good fibrous loam is about 23 to 24 cubic feet. Potting loam can be estimated at the same rate, while potting sand averages 24 cubic feet per ton. Leaf-mould is much lighter, though it will vary considerably according to its age. Often these materials are sold by the load instead of by the ton. The volume of a load is approximately 27 cubic feet (1 cubic yard).

17. Estimating Concrete for Pools. A rough but reasonably accurate method of calculating quantities of gravel, sand, and cement required for preparing base concrete consisting of 3 parts of gravel, 1 part of sand, and 1 part of cement is to provide enough gravel to supply the whole required bulk and then add the sand and cement as extras. Their bulk will be lost in mixing and the shrinkage that takes place as the concrete dries. This method will not serve for finishing concrete made up of equal parts of small gravel, sand, and cement. In this case add together the bulk of all three ingredients, reckoning cement at 18 cubic feet per ton, and subtract one-third of the total for shrinkage.

The bulk of fully dried concrete required for a rectangular pool is obtained as follows: Multiply the length by the breadth and this by the thickness of the concrete. This gives the volume of concrete for the bottom. Add twice the length to twice the width, multiply the figure so obtained by the depth and the result by the thickness of the concrete. This gives the volume of concrete for the sides. Add the sum of the two calculations together to obtain the total volume of concrete.

For a circular pool the volume of concrete for the bottom is obtained by measuring from the centre to the side and multiplying this by itself. Multiply the result by $3\frac{1}{7}$ and this, in turn, by the thickness of the concrete. The volume of concrete for the sides is obtained by doubling the measurement from the centre of the pool to the edge, multiplying this by $3\frac{1}{7}$, the result by the thickness of the concrete, and then by the depth. The sum of the two calculations is added together as before.

The simplest way of dealing with an irregular pool is to measure out a circle or rectangle which approximately covers it and calculate the volume of concrete for the bottom on this basis. The length of the sides can be measured with string.

Do not forget that all measurements must be made in the same units – yards, feet, metres or whatever is suitable.

18. Estimating Volume of Water. The approximate volume of water in a rectangular pool or tank is obtained by multiplying together the length, breadth, and depth, all in feet, and then multiplying the result by $6\frac{1}{4}$. This gives the volume in gallons (7). For a circular pool or tank the measurement from the centre to the side (in feet) is multiplied by itself, and the result is multiplied by $3\frac{1}{7}$. The figure so obtained is multiplied by the depth (in feet), this giving the volume in cubic feet (3). To obtain the volume in gallons multiply by $6\frac{1}{4}$ as before. If the volume is required in litres make all measurements in metres and multiply the result (cubic metres) by 1000.

19. Estimating Fish for Aquarium or Pool. There are two methods of calculating the maximum number of fish that can be accommodated in an aquarium. Method 1 is to allow an inch of body length, excluding tail, per gallon of water. Method 2 is to allow 4 inches of body length per square foot of surface area. This latter system usually results in a considerably lower estimate and is the safer for general purposes. Example: a pool is 6 feet long by 3 feet wide by 1 foot deep. It contains 112 gallons of water (18) and has a surface area of 18 square feet (11). By method 1, fish with a total body length of 112 inches can be accommodated, or, say, eighteen 6-inch fish. By method 2 there would be room for only 72 inches of body length or twelve 6-inch fish.

20. Estimating Plants for Borders. When planning herbaceous borders an average of 4 plants per square yard may be adopted as a rough guide to requirements, though in actual practice the distance of planting will vary from the front to the back of the border, as the smaller marginal plants can be set much more closely than the larger kinds used in the background. As there is likely to be a greater proportion of small plants in a narrow border than in a wide one, it follows that the number of plants per square yard will be greater.

NUMBER OF HERBACEOUS PLANTS REQUIRED FOR
BORDERS OF VARIOUS DIMENSIONS

Width of Border	Length of Border							
	10 *ft.*	20 *ft.*	30 *ft.*	40 *ft.*	50 *ft.*	60 *ft.*	75 *ft.*	100 *ft.*
2 ft.	12	24	36	48	60	72	90	120
3 ft.	15	30	45	60	75	90	112	150
4 ft.	18	36	54	72	90	108	135	180
5 ft.	20	40	60	80	100	120	150	200
6 ft.	22	44	66	88	110	132	165	220
7 ft.	24	48	72	96	120	144	180	240
8 ft.	26	52	78	104	130	156	195	260
9 ft.	27	54	81	108	135	162	202	270
10 ft.	28	56	84	112	140	168	210	280
12 ft.	30	60	90	120	150	180	225	300
15 ft.	33	66	99	132	165	198	246	330
20 ft.	36	72	108	144	180	216	270	360

Note. The number of plants required per square yard becomes progressively smaller as the border increases in width due to the greater proportion of large-growing varieties that can be accommodated. These figures must be taken as very approximate, as much depends upon the type of plant chosen.

21. Estimating Turves for Lawns. Turves are sold at so much per hundred and are almost invariably cut in strips 1 foot wide and 3 feet long. One hundred of these will cover 33⅓ square yards of ground. The best turves for bowling greens, etc., are sometimes cut in foot squares, as there is then less variation in thickness and it is consequently possible to lay them more evenly. Such turves have a covering capacity of approximately 11 square yards per hundred.

22. NUMBER OF FRUIT TREES, ETC., PER ACRE
AND DISTANCES FOR PLANTING

Name of Tree	Distance Apart in Feet	Between Rows in Feet	No. per Acre
Apples, Cordon	2	6	3,630
„ Bush	12	12	302
„ Standard	25–30	25–30	48–70
Cherries, Bush	15	15	193
„ Standard	30	30	48
Cob Nuts, Bush	12	12	302
Currants, Bush	4–5	4–5	1,740–2,720
Gooseberries, Bush	4–5	4–5	1,740–2,720
Pears, Cordon	2	6	3,630
„ Bush	12	12	302
„ Standard	25	25	70
Plums, Bush	15	15	193
„ Standard	25–30	25–30	48–70
Raspberries	2	6	3,630
Strawberries	1	2½–3	14,500–17,425

23. Calculating Cubic Capacity for a Greenhouse. This is a necessary calculation before fumigation can be carried out, as the quantity of fumigant to be employed is determined by the cubic capacity of the house. It is almost invariably estimated in cubic feet (3).

The method is to multiply the length of the house by the breadth and this by the height measured midway between the eaves and the ridge. (See illustration on facing page.)

24. Marking out Right Angles. Stretch a line to mark one side of the angle (lawn edge, bed, or border). At the corner drive in a small peg and attach to it a piece of string 3 feet in length. From the peg measure along the base line 4 feet, drive in a second peg, and attach to it a piece of string 5 feet in length. Draw the two loose ends of string together and at the point at which they meet drive in a third peg. A line stretched

18

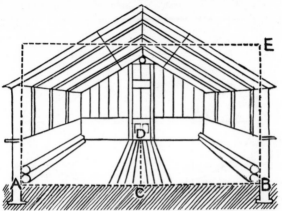

Calculating Greenhouse Volume for Fumigation. In a span-roofed house the breadth (AB), the length (CD) and the height (BE), to halfway up the roof slope are multiplied together. If all these measurements are taken in feet or fractions of feet the result will give the volume of the house in cubic feet.

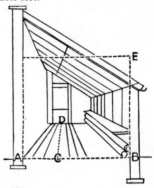

Volume of a Lean-to House. Here again the breadth (AB) is multiplied by the length (CD) and the height (BE) halfway up the slope of the roof.

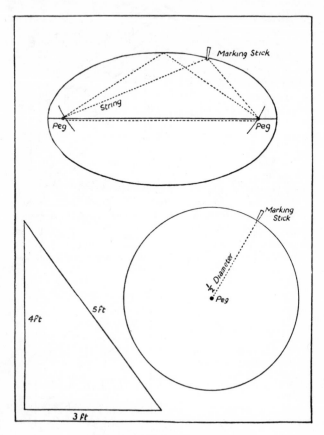

Marking out (See paragraphs 24, 25)

between the first and third peg will make a right angle with the base. (See illustration on facing page.)

25. Marking out Circles and Ovals. A circle is very simple to make. Drive in a peg at the centre, attach to it a piece of string half the diameter of the required circle and draw the end of this around the centre, scratching out a line meanwhile with a pointed stick or indicating it with a trickle of finely powdered lime.

An oval bed is a little more difficult. First peg down two lines bisecting each other at right angles to mark the extreme length and breadth of the bed. Then the two focal points are ascertained by attaching a string half the length of the oval to one of the pegs marking the extreme width and drawing the free end round so that it touches the longer line first on one side and then on the other of the shorter line. Strong pegs are driven in at each of these points. A piece of twine, twice the length of the distance from one of these pegs to the farthest extremity of the bed, is then knotted into a loop, thrown over the two focal pegs and drawn around them with a sharp-pointed stick which is used to scratch the outline of the oval on the soil. (See illustration on facing page.)

26. Marking Irregular Outlines. Present-day tendency is to get away from formality by introducing irregular outlines into the garden. These cannot be drawn geometrically. Instead, mark them out roughly with small sticks and then outline them more definitely with finely powdered lime poured from a bottle or through a narrow-necked funnel. Then, if the curve does not please, it is only a matter of moments to brush the lime away and mark out a different line.

27. Table for Calculating Dilutions

Quantity of Water Required

Quantity of Solution Required	1 pt.	1 qt.	1 gall.	2 galls.	5 galls.	10 galls.	25 galls.	50 galls.	100 galls.	%
	2 fl. oz.	4 fl. oz.	16 fl. oz.	1¾ pts.	4 pts.	8 pts.	2½ galls.	5 galls.	10 galls.	10
	1¾ "	3½ "	14 "	1⅜ "	3½ "	7¼ "	2¼ "	4½ "	9 "	9
	1⅝ "	3 "	13 "	1³⁄₁₀ "	3¼ "	6¼ "	2 "	4 "	8 "	8
	1⁷⁄₁₆ "	2¾ "	11 "	1¹⁄₁₀ "	2¾ "	5½ "	1¾ "	3½ "	7 "	7
	1¼ "	2½ "	10 "	1 "	2¼ "	5 "	1½ "	3 "	6 "	6
	1 "	2 "	8 "	16 fl. oz.	2 "	4 "	1¼ "	2½ "	5 "	5
	6 drs.	1½ "	6 "	13 "	1½ "	3½ "	1 "	2 "	4 "	4
	5 "	1¼ "	5 "	10 "	1¼ "	2¼ "	6 pts.	1½ "	3 "	3
	3 "	6 dr.	3 "	6 "	16 fl. oz.	1½ "	4 "	1 "	2 "	2
	1½ "	3 "	12 dr.	3 "	8 "	16 fl. oz.	2 "	½ "	1 "	1

Note. The above calculations are not mathematically exact but are worked to the nearest unit that would be employed horticulturally.

Examples. (1) Suppose lime sulphur is to be used at the strength of 3 galls. of water (a 3 per cent. dilution), the table shows that to make approximately 2 galls. of wash 10 fl. oz. of concentrated solution should be mixed with 2 galls. of water. (2) Suppose formalin is to be used at 3 fl. oz. per gallon (2 per cent. solution), 1 gall. of formalin mixed with 50 galls. of water will give the same strength. (For appropriate measures see (6) and (7).)

_N.B._ Using metric measures it is very easy to calculate dilutions since 10 cc. of a concentrate made up to 1 litre with water gives a 1 per cent. dilution, 20 cc. a 2 per cent. dilution and so on.

28. Table for Calculating Solutions

Water Required

Weight of Chemical or Other Substance Required — 1 gall. (oz.)	2 galls. lb.	oz.	3 galls. lb.	oz.	4 galls. lb.	oz.	5 galls. lb.	oz.	10 galls. lb.	oz.	20 galls. lb.	oz.	50 galls. lb.	oz.	100 galls. lb.	oz.
¼	0	½	0	¾	0	1	0	1¼	0	2½	0	5	0	12½	1	9
½	0	1	0	1½	0	2	0	2½	0	5	0	10	1	9	3	2
¾	0	1½	0	2¼	0	3	0	3¾	0	7½	0	15	2	5½	4	11
1	0	2	0	3	0	4	0	5	0	10	1	4	3	2	6	4
1½	0	3	0	4½	0	6	0	7½	0	15	1	14	4	11	9	6
2	0	4	0	6	0	8	0	10	1	4	2	8	6	4	12	8
3	0	6	0	9	0	12	0	15	1	14	3	12	9	6	18	12
4	0	8	0	12	1	0	1	4	2	8	5	0	12	8	25	0
5	0	10	0	15	1	4	1	9	3	2	6	4	15	10	31	4
6	0	12	1	2	1	8	1	14	3	12	7	8	18	12	37	8
7	0	14	1	5	1	12	2	3	4	6	8	12	21	14	43	12
8	1	0	1	8	2	0	2	8	5	0	10	0	25	0	50	0

Note. These calculations are not mathematically correct but are worked to the nearest unit that would be used horticulturally.

Example. It is known that a fertilizer is to be dissolved in water at the rate of ¾ oz. per gall. The table shows that 7½ oz. of this fertilizer will be required to make 10 galls. of the liquid.

For appropriate measures see (7) and (8).

29. Table for Calculating Fertilizer Quantities

Amounts Required at Same Rate for Various Areas

Per Sq. Yard	*Per Rod*	*Per Acre*	*Per Acre*	*Per Rod*	*Per Sq. Yard*
½ oz.	1 lb.	150 lb.	1 cwt.	11 oz.	⅓ oz.
1 ,,	2 ,,	300 ,,	2 ,,	22 ,,	⅔ ,,
1½ ,,	3 ,,	450 ,,	3 ,,	2 lb.	1 ,,
2 ,,	3¾ ,,	600 ,,	4 ,,	2¾ ,,	1½ ,,
3 ,,	5¾ ,,	8 cwt.	5 ,,	3½ ,,	2 ,,
4 ,,	7½ ,,	10¾ ,,	6 ,,	4½ ,,	2½ ,,
5 ,,	9½ ,,	13½ ,,	7 ,,	5¼ ,,	2¾ ,,
6 ,,	11¼ ,,	16¼ ,,	8 ,,	5¾ ,,	3 ,,
7 ,,	13¼ ,,	19 ,,	9 ,,	6¼ ,,	3¼ ,,
8 ,,	15 ,,	21½ ,,	10 ,,	7 ,,	3¾ ,,
9 ,,	17 ,,	24½ ,,	15 ,,	10½ ,,	5½ ,,
10 ,,	19 ,,	27 ,,	20 ,,	14 ,,	7½ ,,
11 ,,	21 ,,	30 ,,	25 ,,	17½ ,,	9¼ ,,
12 ,,	22½ ,,	32½ ,,	30 ,,	21 ,,	11 ,,
13 ,,	24½ ,,	35 ,,	35 ,,	24½ ,,	13 ,,
14 ,,	26½ ,,	38 ,,	40 ,,	29 ,,	15 ,,
15 ,,	28½ ,,	40½ ,,	45 ,,	31½ ,,	16¾ ,,
16 ,,	30¼ ,,	43 ,,	50 ,,	35 ,,	18½ ,,

Note. These calculations are not mathematically correct but are worked to the nearest unit that would be used horticulturally.

Examples. (1) It is known that a fertilizer is to be used at 3 oz. per sq. yd. The table shows that 8 cwt. will be needed to dress an acre. (2) It is known that a certain manure is applied at the rate of 1 ton (20 cwt.) per acre. This means that 7½ oz. will be required per square yard, and 14 lb. per rod.

For appropriate measures see (2) and (8).

SECTION TWO

SOIL CULTIVATION, MANURES, AND FERTILIZERS

SOIL CULTIVATION

30. Digging. Technically this means turning soil over to the full depth of an ordinary spade, approximately 10 inches. First a trench should be opened across one end of the plot, 10 inches deep and about the same in width. The soil removed is wheeled to the other end. Then a further narrow strip is turned over into the trench, the process being repeated backwards across the plot until the far end is reached, when the barrowed soil is used to fill in the last trench. Care must be taken to turn each sod right over so that weeds or grass are completely covered.

To save barrowing soil over the length of long plots, these are divided longitudinally into any number of convenient sections of even number. The gardener works down one, back up another, and so on, finishing at the same end as that at which he started.

If grassland is to be dug, the turves should be well chopped as they are turned over, otherwise decay will be slow. A dusting of sulphate of ammonia or Nitro-chalk, 2 ounces per square yard, will hasten decay, as will a dressing of well-rotted dung. If bulky manure is to be incorporated by digging, spread it first on the surface at the required rate and then turn it in in the process of digging.

31. Trenching. This term is used to describe two distinct operations. Full trenching involves digging the soil 3 feet deep and bringing the lowest spit to the top. This is seldom practised, as subsoil is relatively infertile and it is best to keep the richer surface soil on top. This may be done by a special method of trenching as follows: The plot, if large, is divided into strips as for plain digging, but the preliminary trench is at least 2 feet wide. Some gardeners prefer to work with a 3-foot trench, as this gives more room for movement.

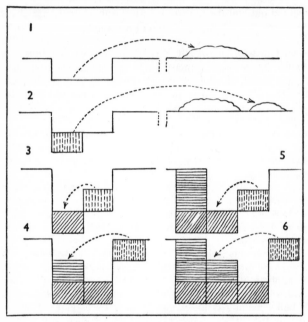

Trenching explained diagrammatically (31)

The soil from this trench is wheeled to the far end of the plot
(Fig. 1 in diagram above). The bottom of the trench is
divided in half and a further depth of 10 inches is dug out of
the front portion and carted back (Fig. 2, above). The subsoil so exposed is broken up with a fork. The step of soil left
at the back of the trench is turned over with a spade on top of
this subsoil (Fig. 3), thus exposing a further strip of subsoil to
be forked. Now another trench, half the width of the first, is

26

marked out and the top soil is turned right over on top of the step formed by the second-spit soil in trench No. 1 (Fig. 4). The second-spit soil in trench No. 2 is turned on top of the subsoil exposed in trench No. 1 (Fig. 5) and the subsoil in trench No. 2 is broken with a fork. Another half-measure trench is marked off and turned over in the same way (Fig. 6). This sequence is continued until the ground is all dug, the last trench being filled with two heaps of soil from the first.

BASTARD OR HALF TRENCHING is midway between trenching and digging and consists in turning over the soil one spade deep and forking the spit immediately below, without actually altering its position.

If manure is to be incorporated with the soil, either by trenching or by bastard trenching, fork it into the second spit as thoroughly as possible and turn a little in with the top spit as described under 'Digging' (30), but do not get any quite close to the surface, where it would impede planting or sowing.

32. Ridging. This is most serviceable in autumn or early winter. The soil is thrown or drawn into steep ridges, the object being to expose a large surface to the beneficial action of wind, rain, frost, and thaw. Two methods are employed. One is to pull the soil into ridges with a draw hoe as described under 'Earthing Up' (39). The other is to mark the plot into 3-foot wide strips, each of which is dug separately lengthwise, i.e. starting at one end and working backwards down the length of the strip with narrow trenches. In digging, the centre spadeful is always turned forward, but the left- and right-hand spadefuls are turned inwards to lie on top of the centre one and so form a ridge as shown in the illustration on the next page.

33. Stripping Turf. If turf on new land is reasonably free from deep-rooting perenial weeds such as convolvulus (bindweed), coltsfoot, dock, perennial thistle, horsetail (equisetum), and ground elder, it may be turned in by digging

27

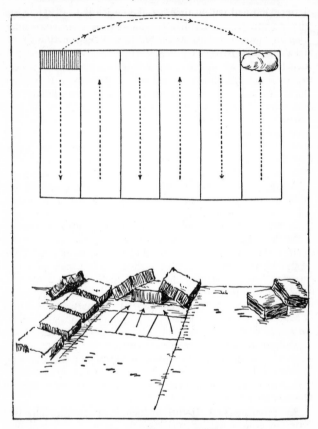

How to ridge ground (32)

or trenching and will in time rot and enrich the soil. Dressing with a nitrogenous fertilizer or manure as described under 'Digging' (30) will hasten the process. Very weedy turf or turf containing pests such as leather-jackets, wireworms, and cockchafer larvae is best stripped and stacked for twelve months to rot. The stack may be of any size but will rot most rapidly if in a sheltered, shady place. Dust alternate layers with sulphate of ammonia or fresh soot and powdered quick-lime or fresh hydrated lime. The sulphate of ammonia or soot should not be mixed with lime in the same layer.

34. Drainage. This may be necessary on heavy or low-lying land if surface water lies for a long time. Land drains are of two types, stone drains and pipe drains.

STONE DRAINS may be prepared with any hard rubble, broken clinker, etc. Trenches are cut about 10 inches wide and 18 inches or more in depth, with a fall of at least 1 foot in 20 feet in one direction. The bottom 9 inches of the trench is filled with the stones, clinkers, or rubble. An inch or so of finer rubble or gravel is placed on top. This is covered with inverted turves and the trench is finally filled with soil. All drains should communicate at their lowest points with a main drain, ditch, or large soakaway.

PIPE DRAINS are laid in trenches cut in the same manner. A little gravel, broken clinker, or small rubble is placed in the bottom of each trench. Special earthenware land-drain pipes are laid end to end but not quite touching on this layer. They are surrounded and just covered with small rubble. Inverted turves are placed on top and the trench is filled with soil. Again, all drains must communicate at their lowest points with a main drain, ditch, or soakaway.

A SOAKAWAY is made by digging a large hole, preferably deep enough to penetrate impervious subsoil such as clay and reach more open or stony soil below. This hole should be filled to within a foot of the surface with clinkers, brick ends, or other hard rubble, the last foot being covered with small rubble, turves, and soil as for land drains.

Drainage can often be improved without making land drains by digging or trenching in plenty of *strawy manure*, *sifted cinders, sharp boiler ashes,* or *coarse sand.* In bad cases *faggots* of bushy wood may be laid in the bottom of each trench as work proceeds. Household ashes are of no use for improving the drainage of soil, as they are too soft and fine in texture. See also 'Lime' (68).

35. Forking. Principally used for breaking down the surface of ground that has already been dug or trenched and mixing fertilizers and manure with the soil. Sometimes a digging fork with broad, flat tines is substituted for a spade for ordinary digging or trenching, especially if ground is heavy or wet. When a fork is used to break surface clods the back is employed with swinging, sideways blows.

36. Hoeing. There are several types of hoe, serviceable according to soil and requirements.

THE DRAW HOE has a blade at right angles to the handle. It is employed with chopping, drawing motions, the operator moving forwards and thus treading on the hoed ground. It is useful for breaking down rough surfaces, hacking off thick growth of weeds, drawing deep drills for large seeds and potatoes, or drawing soil towards plants.

THE CANTERBURY HOE has three broad prongs at right angles to the handle and is used like the draw hoe for breaking down clods.

THE DUTCH HOE has a flat blade approximately in the same plane as the handle and is the best tool for keeping the surface soil loose and cutting off light weed growth and mixing top dressings with the soil. It is employed with sweeping backward and forward movements. The blade passes just beneath the surface and the operator moves backwards so that the hoed soil is not trodden on.

CULTIVATORS AND PATENT HOES of many kinds have been devised and some are serviceable. Particularly useful are the clawed cultivators with three or five tines, used principally instead of a fork for breaking clods and loosening the surface round plants in growth.

WHEELED HOES are made by several firms and are most suitable for working between crops planted in straight lines. The wheels of the tool bear most of the weight and the gardener pushes the hoe forward in successive sharp jerks. Ground can be covered very rapidly, but the operator necessarily treads on soil that has been hoed. Some patterns can be fitted with cultivating tines for breaking rough soil and with a small plough for potato planting and earthing up.

SURFACE CULTIVATION has three main objects – to break the surface into fine particles and thus make it suitable for seeds and small plants; to maintain a loose surface layer or dust mulch of soil, which has a tidy appearance and acts as a kind of blanket over the lower soil; and to destroy weeds.

37. Raking. This is required in final preparation of seed beds and beds intended for small plants, and also for removing moss and creeping weeds from lawns. Raking of soil should be done only when the surface is reasonably dry. Excessive fineness is not an advantage and may cause surface caking. The ideal will depend on the size of the seeds or plants. The smaller these are the more the soil should be raked. For lawns a spring-toothed rake is better for regular use than the ordinary rigid rake, as it is less likely to tear out grass or otherwise damage the surface of the lawn.

38. Seed Sowing. Apart from forking, hoeing, and raking the surface to a fine crumbly condition known as ' *a good tilth*,' seed beds must be trodden to give even firmness throughout. Tread slowly backwards and forwards across the surface, choosing a time when the soil is drying white on top. Boards about 1 foot by 6 inches may be fixed to the boots to hasten

31

treading. Rake the surface level after treading is finished.

DRILLS FOR SEEDS may be drawn with the edge of a dutch hoe, the corner of a draw hoe, or a pointed stick. Small drills may be made by pressing a broom handle into the surface. Wide drills for peas and beans may be made with a spade used flat to scoop out the soil 2 to 3 inches deep. Cover seeds by drawing the displaced soil back with the rake. Finally use the rake vertically with gentle ramming motions to firm the soil over the seeds.

39. Earthing Up. This means drawing the soil towards plants. It is practised for two reasons, first to exclude light and secondly to provide plenty of loose soil in which such plants as potatoes and artichokes may form their tubers. Exclusion of light is principally required with leeks and celery to blanch the stems and make them palatable, but it is also an important object in earthing potatoes, as if the tubers are exposed to light they become green, bitter, and poisonous. A draw hoe is commonly used for this task and the soil is drawn up a little at a time rather than in one operation.

40. Planting. This may be done with dibber, trowel, spade, or special tool according to the type of plant.

THE DIBBER is serviceable for planting seedlings rapidly. Its drawback is a tendency to consolidate the soil unevenly and cramp roots in a narrow hole. Special steel-shod dibbers may be purchased or good dibbers can be made from old spades or fork handles cut to a length of about 18 inches and sharpened to a point. Avoid making holes too deep. When the roots have been dropped into position, push the dibber into the soil again alongside the plant and, with a levering movement towards it, press the soil firmly around the roots.

A TROWEL is the best tool for planting most small and medium-sized plants. Long-handled trowels save stooping but place greater strain on the wrist muscles. Holes made with the trowel should be of ample size to accommodate all roots disposed naturally. Work the soil by hand round these and firm on all sides with the foot or knuckles. Loose planting is a common cause of failure, as loose soil dries rapidly and plants cannot make sturdy growth in it.

A SPADE may be used for planting all large things such as shrubs, fruit trees, and bushes, etc. Holes should be wide and comparatively shallow so that roots may be spread out laterally to their full extent. The uppermost should, as a rule, be covered with from 3 to 6 inches of soil. Break the soil finely, scatter round the roots, a little at a time, and jerk the tree or shrub gently meanwhile so that soil settles between the roots. When all are covered tread firmly, scatter more loose soil on top, and water in if dry.

WATER all newly planted seedlings and plants freely during dry weather until established. QUICK-ACTING FERTILIZERS should not be given to anything freshly planted.

SPECIAL TOOLS are employed for certain purposes. A bulb planter which removes a neat core of turf is serviceable for naturalizing daffodils, etc., in grassland. It has a wide handle, a shaft similar to that of a spade, a crossbar near the bottom and a circular blade. A two-sided hand plough (36) which draws a deep furrow is occasionally employed in large gardens for planting potatoes and similar roots.

41. Mulching. This consists of spreading a layer of manure, leaf-mould, peat, grass clippings, or some similar substance over the surface of the soil. Its object is twofold, first to feed plants and second to act as a blanket to the lower soil in which roots are growing. Mulches are most serviceable in the spring and early summer, particularly round newly planted subjects. Mulching material should be loose. If it becomes beaten down by rain or other causes, it should be shaken up again with a fork. A thick mulch of grass clippings maintained on rose beds from May to August has proved a useful preventive of rose black spot (711).

42. Top Dressing is allied to mulching, but is employed solely to feed plants. Usually some fairly concentrated and readily soluble fertilizer or manure is employed such as sulphate of ammonia, nitrate of soda, superphosphate of lime, sulphate of potash, dried blood, etc. Care must be taken not to give an excessive quantity. Top dressings are most useful for plants in full growth or bearing. They should be spread evenly over the full presumed root spread and must not be heaped around the stems.

43. Plant Foods. Plants require many different chemicals, but three only are likely to be deficient under normal conditions in most parts of this country. These are nitrogen, phosphorus (supplied as phosphoric acid), and potash. Occasionally iron, magnesium, manganese, boron, and a few other chemicals must be added to these, but as wrong use of these may cause damage the advice of an expert should usually be obtained if their application is contemplated. In general, nitrogen tends to promote stem and leaf growth, phosphorus root growth, and potash fruitfulness and ripening, but one tends to interact with another so that, for example, lack of potash may prevent the plant making proper use of the nitrogen available in the soil and so on.

A 'balanced' manure or fertilizer is one that supplies the essential ingredients in approximately the right proportions for the crop in question. Most animal manures are not balanced in this sense though they may contain all necessary foods. Chemicals usually supply one plant food each, though a few, such as nitrate of potash (72) and phosphate of potash (76), supply two. In order to obtain a well-balanced chemical fertilizer several chemicals must be mixed in correct proportions (91) to (108).

By law it is necessary that the nitrogen, phosphoric acid and potash content of mixed commercial fertilizers should be quoted. This is done on the basis of percentage of each of these foods in the complete mixture. The analysis is always given in the order as above and is occasionally abbreviated to figures only. Thus a fertilizer described as 7 : 5 : 4 would contain 7% nitrogen, 5% phosphoric acid and 4% potash.

MANURES

44. Manure from Stable and Byre. Bulky manures of this type contain nitrogen, phosphates, and potash, but not in the right proportions for all plants. Consequently it is necessary to 'balance' these animal manures with appropriate chemicals. Animal manures, by virtue of the humus they produce, improve the texture of the soil, making light soils more retentive and improving the drainage of heavy soils. Cow and horse manure are excellent for general use: the former is most suitable for light and the latter for heavy soil. Pig manure is rich in nitrogen and best for poor, sandy soils. Horse, cow, and pig manures should be stacked in the dry and allowed to rot for some months. When fresh the food they contain is in organic compounds and not available for plants. Bacterial action causes decay and breaks down some parts of the manure into simple, inorganic chemicals. Average dressings are 1 cwt. (a good barrowload) to from 6 to 15 square yards (16 to 40 tons per acre).

Rotted dung may be spread thinly as a mulch or top dressing round plants in full growth or bearing. It may also be used in liquid form (50). Rotted dung may be dug in at any time of the year. If fresh dung must be used, it is best applied to vacant ground in the autumn. Fresh horse manure is required for mushrooms (157) and hotbeds (514). Analyses vary greatly according to the food on which the animals have been fed, bedding used, its age, storage conditions, etc. If stored well, dung tends to become richer, bulk for bulk, with age. Averages for good rotted samples of mixed farm manure are: nitrogen

35

$\frac{1}{2}$–1% (10–20 lb. per ton), phosphoric acid $\frac{1}{4}$–$\frac{1}{2}$% (5–10 lb. per ton), potash $\frac{1}{2}$–1% (10–20 lb. per ton). Urine is, in general, richer in nitrogen and potash.

45. The Compost Heap. This may be built with any vegetable refuse. Old plants, pea and bean haulms, grass clippings, leaves, straw, hay, green manure crops, and even paper and soft hedge clippings may go into it. If the greater part is soft green refuse, no further steps need be taken to ensure decay. Make the heap about 3 feet high, 3 feet through, and of any convenient length, turn it after a month, so far as possible bringing the inner portions out and turning the outside in. When the heap has decayed to a brown, manure-like mass it can be dug in at the same rate as animal manure. If there is much dry or hard rubbish, such as hay, straw, cabbage stumps, hedge clippings, or paper, a rotting agent such as Nitro-chalk, sulphate of ammonia, or one of the special proprietary products should be used. Dust each 6-inch-thick layer lightly with the chemical (with sulphate of ammonia it is advisable to treat alternate layers with hydrated lime instead) and wet thoroughly any part of the material that seems dry. When turning, add more water to dry parts.

46. Indore Process. This is a controlled method of compost making. As far as possible animal and vegetable refuses are mixed in definite proportions with dung and urine. Excessive acidity is counteracted with calcium carbonate (chalk) or potassium carbonate. Occasionally slaked lime is employed. No other chemicals are used, but wood ashes are mixed in if available. Rotting is usually in pits 3 feet deep, not more than 5 yards wide, and any convenient length. Air vents are made with a crowbar every few feet. The heap or pit is turned twice, the first time after a month and again after a further month. Water is used freely if necessary to prevent the compost becoming dry.

47. Green Manures. A quick-growing crop such as mustard, rape, vetches, or annual lupins may be sown and dug in just as it is about to come into flower. This adds organic matter to the soil, improves its texture, and holds up soluble foods which might otherwise be washed out. Where lupins, vetches, and other legumes are grown the nitrogen content of the soil is increased, as these plants harbour bacteria which fix nitrogen from the air. Mustard may be sown as late as August for autumn digging, rape or annual lupins until July, while vetches are best sown in spring. Dust the ground with Nitro-chalk or sulphate of ammonia at 2 oz. per square yard as the green crop is dug in, to hasten decay and prevent temporary nitrogen shortage.

48. Hair. The scrapings from hides treated in tanneries are sometimes available and are a useful source of humus and slowly available nitrogen. May be dug in freely at any time.

49. Hops. Spent hops contain about $\frac{1}{2}\%$ nitrogen, 1–2% phosphoric acid and a very small quantity of potash. They decay slowly and improve soil texture. They can be dug in freely at any time of the year in the same way as such bulky manures as stable manure and cow dung.

HOP MANURE is treated chemically to make it a balanced plant food. There are a number of proprietary brands differing in the manner in which they have been treated and consequently in their rate of application. Usually this is about 4 oz., or a double handful, per square yard, but some makes can be employed more freely. Manufacturers' instructions should be consulted. Hop manure is best applied in late winter or spring and should be mixed with the surface soil or used as a top dressing.

50. Liquid Manures. These may be prepared with animal manures from stable, byre, pigsty, etc., or with soot or chemicals. The advantage of applying manures or fertilizers in liquid form is that they are more rapidly available, but plants cannot make use of organic substances even in solution (44). It is only after such compounds have been split into inorganic chemicals by bacterial action that they are available as plant food. In consequence, it is useless to prepare liquid manure from undecayed animal droppings. Liquid manure of animal origin may be prepared by diluting urine, or by steeping a bag of rotted manure in a tub of water. In either method the liquor must be diluted to the colour of straw. Applications may be given frequently to ornamental plants, fruits, and vegetables in full growth.

51. Night Soil. The contents of earth closets are very valuable as manure, and richer, weight for weight, than farmyard or stable manure. They may be dug in at any time in similar manner to animal manures. The contents of cess pits, septic tanks, and chemical closets may also be dug in as manure, but their value will vary according to the amount of water present and the chemicals used to prevent unpleasant odour.

52. Poultry Droppings. Droppings of all types of poultry may be used as manure. They contain a higher percentage of nitrogen and phosphates than stable and farmyard manure, but less potash, and must be balanced by appropriate chemicals (43). Weight for weight they are about four times as rich as animal manure. One cwt. of moist droppings will dress from 24 to 40 square yards. If dried and powdered, the quantity would have to be even more reduced, and such manure is best employed like a chemical fertilizer at 8–12 oz. per square yard. Poultry manure should be stored under cover. An average analysis of a moist sample is nitrogen $1\frac{1}{2}\%$, phosphoric acid $1\frac{1}{2}\%$, potash $\frac{1}{2}-\frac{3}{4}\%$. If thoroughly dried, this would rise to nitrogen 4%, phosphoric acid 3%, potash $1\frac{1}{2}\%$. Can also be used to make liquid manure in the same way as other animal manures but should be well diluted (50).

53. Sewage Sludge. When good, is a useful substitute for farmyard manure and can be dug in at rates up to 2 cwt. per rod. An analysis should be given, however, as some samples are too poor to be of much value. The analysis should show 2% or more of nitrogen and about 1·5% of phosphoric acid.

54. Seaweed. A valuable subsititute for dung. Compared with this, seaweed is rich in potash and almost lacking in phosphates, so is even more in need of balancing with chemicals (43). Seaweed may either be dug in as gathered at rates of about 1 cwt. to 8 square yards or may be dried and dug in at about 1 cwt. to 24 square yards. The bladder seaweeds and driftweeds with long, broad fronds are the best kinds. Analysis varies according to variety. An average for fresh seaweed is nitrogen $\frac{1}{3}$% (7 lb. per ton), phosphoric acid $\frac{1}{10}$% (2 lb. per ton), potash 1% (20 lb. per ton).

55. Shoddy. Waste from wool factories which decays slowly in the soil and may be used as a substitute for farmyard manure. Pure wool shoddy is more valuable than samples containing cotton. Shoddy is a bulky nitrogenous manure and improves the texture of the soil. Average rate of application 1–2 tons per acre, approximately $\frac{1}{2}$–1 lb. per square yard. Analyses show from 5 to 15% nitrogen.

56. Town Refuse. Selected town refuse, particularly that of organic origin, can be converted into useful manure. Quality will depend upon its origin and treatment, and an analysis should be required as in the case of sewage sludge. These manures are usually slow acting and improve the texture of the soil. Rate of application will depend on analysis but is roughly 1 cwt. (a good barrowload) to from 15 to 45 square yards (5–15 tons per acre). An average analysis is nitrogen $\frac{3}{4}$%, phosphoric acid $\frac{1}{2}$%, potash $\frac{1}{2}$%.

FERTILIZERS

57. Basic Slag. A slow-acting phosphatic fertilizer which also supplies lime. It is a steel-industry by-product and must be ground by machinery; the coarser the grinding the slower its action. Slag may remain in the soil for several years. Quality varies, and analysis may show anything from 8 to 22% phosphoric acid. Also the solubility, and consequently the availability, of the phosphoric acid varies. This is quoted on basis of solubility in citric acid. Over 80% soluble is good; below 40% poor and exceptionally slow acting. Most useful for autumn or winter application at rates from 4 to 8 oz. per square yard.

58. Blood. Contains nitrogen and is a useful manure. Fresh blood may be dug freely into vacant ground but is messy and unpleasant to handle. Usually it is dried. This can be done at home by adding 1 lb. of fresh slaked lime to each gallon of blood, stirring, pouring into a shallow box and covering with a thin layer of lime. Leave until dry, then apply at 4 oz. per square yard. Commercial dried blood is a fine dry powder containing about 7–14% nitrogen. This can be applied at rates up to 2 oz. per square yard or stirred into water (it is not usually fully soluble) at rates to 1 oz. per gallon. Most serviceable for spring and early summer use and for plants in full growth or bearing.

59. Bonemeal. An invaluable source of phosphates. Bonemeal is slow acting but this will depend on the grinding. The finer this is the more rapidly will the fertilizer be available. Analysis shows from 1 to 5% nitrogen (the high figure for raw bones containing gelatine not present in prepared bonemeal or bone flour), phosphoric acid 20 to 25%. Rates of application up to 4 oz. per square yard, or 4 oz. per bushel of potting soil. Most useful for autumn and winter application and in potting composts.

60. Calcium Cyanamide. A quick-acting nitrogenous fertilizer which also supplies lime. It is dusty and rather difficult to apply evenly. Has a caustic effect on roots and leaves and should be kept out of direct touch with them. May be used as a weed-killer and fertilizer combined. Rate of application 1–2 oz. per square yard. Use in late winter or spring. Analysis: 20·6% nitrogen, about 22% free lime. May be used as a rotting agent in compost heaps.

61. Coal Ashes. Of no value as a fertilizer. Sharp boiler ashes may be used to lighten clay soils.

62. Fish Guano. The dried refuse from factories engaged in the smoking or canning of fish. It contains nitrogen, phosphorus and other plant foods and may be used like guano. Average analysis: nitrogen 6–10%, phosphoric acid $4\frac{1}{2}$–9%, potash $\frac{1}{2}$–$\frac{3}{4}$%. Fresh fish refuse may also be dug into the soil and forms a good substitute for farmyard or stable manure. Prepared fish manure usually contains other chemicals to make it a better-balanced food and should be used according to manufacturers' instructions.

63. Flue Dust. Usually of no value, but some samples contain potash. Ask for potash analysis before buying.

64. Guano. Strictly this name belongs only to the excreta of sea birds deposited on the sea coast of Peru and other tropical but almost rainless districts. Such guano is a rich, complete manure, chiefly of use as a powerful stimulant during the growing season. It should be used at the rate of 2 to 3 oz. per square yard or about 1 oz. per gallon of water. Analysis varies greatly from: nitrogen 2–12%, phosphoric acid 10–20%, potash 2–4%. The term 'guano' is now loosely applied to many compound chemical fertilizers.

65. Hoof and Horn Meal. A steady-acting manure which is of great value in the garden and especially with potting composts (105). With these it may be mixed at the rate of $1\frac{1}{2}$ oz. per bushel. Outdoors it may be employed at rates up to 2 oz. per square yard. Average analysis: 12–14% nitrogen, 1–3% phosphoric acid.

66. Kainit. A crude form of potash in which muriate of potash is combined with common salt and other chemicals. Kainit is best applied in autumn or winter at rates up to 3 oz.

per square yard. Average analysis: potash 14%, common salt 50–60%, magnesium sulphate 20%. See also (78).

67. Leather Dust. Contains small quantities of nitrogen, but this becomes available very slowly and leather dust is principally of value for adding bulk to more concentrated fertilizers and thus making it easier to distribute them. Rate of application up to 1 lb. per square yard; at any time.

68. Lime. Strictly speaking, lime is calcium oxide, but the term is loosely applied in gardens to several other compounds of calcium. Though required by plants as food, calcium itself is almost invariably present in the soil in sufficient quantity for this purpose. Calcium oxide, calcium hydroxide, calcium carbonate and (less commonly) calcium sulphate are added as soil sweeteners, to liberate other chemicals and to improve the texture of heavy ground. For these purposes all forms of lime, including chalk, are identical except that some act more rapidly and others have better moisture-holding qualities.

HYDRATED LIME (air-slaked lime) is the quickest-acting form which can be used with safety around plants. A powder for use at rates up to 1 lb. per square yard.

CHALK (calcium carbonate) is slower in action, though this depends very much upon the fineness of grinding. Is especially suitable for light soil, as it holds moisture. Can be used at rates up to 2 lb. per square yard.

GROUND LIMESTONE is another form of calcium carbonate. It is even slower acting, but again much depends on fineness. Can be used in the same way as chalk.

QUICKLIME (calcium oxide) is quick acting but caustic and only suitable for use on vacant land at rates up to 1 lb. per square yard. It kills insects, etc., in the soil.

GYPSUM (calcium sulphate) is commonly used for improving soil structure and particularly for heavy clay soils. On heavy soils a dressing of 8 oz. per square yard can be given.

GAS LIME contains sulphurous impurities which are

poisonous to plants and many insects. Can only be used on vacant land and is then valuable both as a source of lime and as a soil fumigant for destroying such pests as wireworms, slugs, etc.

MAGNESIAN LIMESTONE is a special form of limestone which contains magnesium as well as calcium carbonate. It may be used with advantage on all soils lacking in magnesium.

FERTILIZERS which contain *free lime* and therefore add it to the soil are nitrate of lime, Nitro-chalk, calcium cyanamide, and basic slag.

Superphosphate of lime contains no free lime and cannot be employed in place of lime.

METHOD OF TESTING SOIL FOR LIME. Take a typical sample of soil, break up finely and half fill a tumbler with it. Pour in dilute hydrochloric acid. If there is much effervescence, free lime is present; if there is little or no effervescence, there is little or no free lime. This is a very rough and ready method of testing, however, as 'free lime' is not essential to the health of either plants or soil. What is important is 'available lime,' i.e. lime in a particular physical association with the finest soil particles (colloids). This 'available lime,' is not shown by the acid test. A truer estimate can be obtained by means of a chemical 'soil indicator' giving a pH reading. If this shows pH 7·0 the soil is neutral. If the figure is higher than 7·0 the soil is alkaline, if below this figure it is acid. As a rule lime will be required only when the figure drops below 6·5 and even then not by any means for all plants. Rhododendrons and heathers thrive in soils as acid as pH 5·0.

69. Meat Meal. Pure meat refuse is mainly a nitrogenous manure, but meat meal or meat guano usually contains ground bones as well which increases its phosphatic content. Use in the same way as fish guano or refuse (62).

70. Mineral Phosphates. A source of slowly available phosphoric acid comparable with basic slag as a phosphatic fertilizer. Most useful for permanent crops and pastures. Rate of application 3–4 oz. per square yard. Best used in autumn or winter. Average analysis from 25 to 35% phosphoric acid. The finer the mineral is ground the better.

71. Muriate of Potash.. A relatively pure form of potash which must be used with caution, as it is injurious to some tender roots if brought directly into contact with them. Muriate of potash is frequently used in compound fertilizers and is readily soluble. Rate of application $\frac{1}{2}$–1 oz. per square yard. Tends to make potatoes more waxy in texture. Best applied in autumn or winter. Analysis: potash 40–60%, common salt 13–18%. (Correctly known as potassium chloride.)

72. Nitrate of Potash. This is also known as saltpetre. It contains both nitrogen and potassium in readily assimilable form and is of great value as a liquid manure for pot plants if dissolved in water at the rate of $\frac{1}{2}$ oz. per gallon. Is too expensive for outdoor use. Analysis: nitrogen 12–14%, potash 44–46%. Do not confuse with potash nitrate (77).

73. Nitrate of Soda. A very soluble salt rich in nitrogen. Much used as a top dressing in summer, either alone or in combination with other quick-acting fertilizers. Has a caustic effect upon foliage and may do damage if applied carelessly. Nitrate of soda must not be mixed with superphosphate of lime. It tends to make clay soils more sticky. Rate of application $\frac{1}{2}$–1 oz. per square yard, $\frac{1}{4}$–$\frac{1}{2}$ oz. per gallon. Analysis: 16% nitrogen.

74. Nitrate, of Lime. Like Nitro-chalk, a quick-acting, granular nitrogenous fertilizer for general use in spring and early summer. Rate of application 1 oz. per square yard. May be used as a rotting agent on compost heaps (45). Analysis: nitrogen $15\frac{1}{2}$–16%.

75. Nitro-chalk. A quick-acting proprietary fertilizer in granular form which supplies the soil with nitrogen and lime. Particularly valuable for acid and lime-free soils. Rate of

application 1 oz. per square yard. Most suitable for spring or
early summer application. May be used as a rotting agent on
compost heaps (45). Analysis: nitrogen $15\frac{1}{2}\%$, carbonate of
lime 48%.

76. Phosphate of Potash. Contains both phosphorus and
potassium. Is very soluble and most serviceable as a liquid
stimulant for pot plants in full growth. Use at $\frac{1}{2}$ oz. per gallon.
Too expensive for use outdoors. Analysis of commercial
phosphate of potash is phosphoric acid 51%, potash 35%.

77. Potash Nitrate. Often sold as Chilean potash nitrate and
not to be confused with nitrate of potash, a quite different
chemical. This is a quick-acting fertilizer supplying nitrogen
and potash. Rate of application $\frac{1}{2}$–1 oz. per square yard. Most
suitable for spring or early summer application. Average
analysis: nitrogen 15%, potash 10%, but some samples contain
a higher proportion of potash and are correspondingly more
valuable.

78. Potash Salts. A general name given to various natural
deposits containing muriate of potash in combination with
other salts, such as common salt and magnesium sulphate.
Kainit (66) is a potash salt. Others, not usually specifically
named, contain higher percentages of potash. Should be
bought on potash analysis, e.g. 30% potash salts are worth
half again as much as 20% potash salts. Rate of application
1–2 oz. per square yard. They are best applied in autumn or
winter.

79. Rape Meal. A by-product from oil mills. It contains
nitrogen and also adds humus to the soil. Is valuable as a base
for compound fertilizers containing strong chemicals such as
sulphate of ammonia, superphosphate of lime, and muriate of
potash. It aids the even distribution of the more concentrated
chemicals. Rate of application up to 4 oz. per square yard.
Average analysis: 5–6% nitrogen.

Saltpetre. See Nitrate of Potash (72).

80. Salt (sodium chloride). Used more frequently as a weed-killer than as a fertilizer, but is a source of sodium and helps to liberate potash already in the soil. Rate of application 1 oz. per square yard. Best used in winter or early spring. Is sometimes given to asparagus and seakale beds.

81. Sequestrols. Some necessary elements rapidly become insoluble (and therefore unavailable as plant food) through chemical interaction in the soil. This is likely to occur with iron and manganese on alkaline soils, with copper on acid sandy or peaty soils and with zinc on sandy neutral or alkaline soils. Ordinary salts of these chemicals such as sulphate of iron and sulphate of manganese may then prove ineffective and instead special organic compounds known as sequestrols or chelates must be used. In these the necessary element is held for a considerable time immune from chemical reaction, yet available to plants. Sequestrols or chelates are sold as manufactured products sometimes individually, sometimes combined with other plant foods. Since they vary in formulation label instructions must be followed.

82. Soot. A good sample may contain as much as 6% nitrogen in the form of sulphate of ammonia. Fresh soot is rather caustic and may be used as a soil fumigant to destroy insects and slugs. For use as a fertilizer it is best stored in the dry for three or four months. If exposed to rain or mixed with lime it quickly loses its value, though lime makes it yet more effective as a soil fumigant. Soot also enables soil to absorb sun heat more readily. Rate of application up to 6 oz. per square yard. May be used at any time.

83. Steamed Bone Flour. Virtually identical from the garden standpoint with fine bonemeal (59) except that all gelatine has been extracted so the flour is very dry, and mixed with other fertilizers it prevents them caking.

84. Sulphate of Ammonia. A nitrogenous fertilizer used in a similar manner to nitrate of soda. On the whole a safer

chemical to use, as it is not quite so quick acting or caustic.
Tends to increase the acidity of acid soils. Must not be mixed
with lime but may be mixed with superphosphate of lime,
sulphate of potash, and muriate of potash. Rate of application
$\frac{1}{2}$–1 oz. per square yard. Best used in spring or early summer.
Analysis: 20·6% nitrogen.

85. Sulphate of Iron. If iron is lacking in the soil it may be
applied in this form. Dressings at the rate of up to 1 oz. per
square yard may be made in spring. Is also used as a fungicide
to kill toadstools, etc., on lawns and root-rot fungi at rates
up to 4 oz. per gallon of water. See also Sequestrols (81).

86. Sulphate of Magnesium. If magnesium is lacking, this
is the form in which it is usually supplied. The common salt
as purchased is Epsom salt and contains water of crystallization
which reduces its concentration to 10% magnesium. The rate
of application for this commercial product is 1 oz. per square
yard or $\frac{1}{2}$–1 oz. per gallon of water.

87. Sulphate of Potash. The best form of potash for general
use. It is non-caustic and reasonably quick acting. May be
used at any time of the year. Rate of application $\frac{1}{2}$–1 oz. per
square yard. Analysis: 48% potash. Frequently increases disease
resistance.

88. Superphosphate of Lime. The best form in which to
apply phosphates where a quick result is desired. Contains
no free lime and will not affect acidity. Rate of application
1–3 oz. per square yard. Most suitable for application in spring
or early summer, but is apt to burn delicate foliage or flowers.
Analysis: 18% phosphoric acid.

89. Wood Ashes. A useful but variable source of potash.
The amount present will depend upon the type and age of the
wood burnt and the method of storage. Much potash may be
washed away if wood ashes are left in the open. A good sample
will contain 15% potash, a poor one as little as 4%. Apply up
to 8 oz. per square yard, at any time of the year.

COMPOUND FERTILIZERS

90. General Description. The following formulae supply nitrogen, phosphoric acid, and potash and so fufil the requirements stated under (43) for complete plant foods. There are also many proprietary compound fertilizers specially blended for certain plants.

A useful formula that can be used when preparing mixed fertilizers to give a definite percentage of certain plant foods is as follows:

$$N \left(\frac{100}{N^1} \right) + P \left(\frac{100}{P^1} \right) + K \left(\frac{100}{K^1} \right) + x = 100.$$

Where N, P, and K represent respectively the percentages of nitrogen, phosphoric acid, and potash required in the mixture, while N^1, P^1, and K^1 represent the corresponding percentages in the individual ingredients, x will be the amount of non-active 'filler' (e.g. sand or fine peat) required to give bulk to the mixture. Note that this formula is serviceable only when each ingredient supplies one only of the plant foods required.

91. Potato Fertilizer (for early varieties).

Sulphate of ammonia	5 parts by weight	
Superphosphate of lime	8 ,,	,,
Sulphate or muriate of potash	3 ,,	,,

Mix well and apply before or at planting time at the rate of 4 oz. per square yard.

92. Potato Fertilizer (for late varieties).

Sulphate of ammonia	3 parts by weight	
Superphosphate of lime	4 ,,	,,
Sulphate of potash	2 ,,	,,

Mix well and apply before or at planting time at the rate of 5 oz. per square yard.

93. Root Crop Fertilizer (carrots, parsnips, beetroot, etc.).

Sulphate of ammonia	1 part by weight	
Superphosphate of lime	4 ,,	,,

Sulphate of potash   2 parts by weight

Mix well and use prior to sowing at the rate of 4 oz. per square yard.

94. Cabbage Crop Fertilizer (cabbages, savoys, brussels sprouts, kale, broccoli, etc.).

Sulphate of ammonia   2 parts by weight
Superphosphate of lime   3   ,,   ,,
Sulphate of potash   1   ,,   ,,

Mix and use prior to planting at the rate of 3 oz. per square yard.

95. Pea and Bean Fertilizer.

Sulphate of ammonia   1 part by weight
Superphosphate of lime   3   ,,   ,,
Sulphate of potash   2   ,,   ,,

Mix and use prior to sowing at the rate of 2 oz. per yard of row.

96. Tomato Fertilizer.

Sulphate of ammonia   2 parts by weight
Superphosphate of lime   3   ,,   ,,
Sulphate of potash   2   ,,   ,,

Mix well and use as a top dressing at the rate of one teaspoonful per plant every week or ten days from the time the first fruits begin to swell.

97. Fruit Tree Fertilizer.

Sulphate of ammonia   2 parts by weight
Sulphate of potash   1   ,,   ,,

Apply at the rate of 3 oz. per sq. yd. in March. Every alternate year give, in addition, basic slag, at the rate of 4 oz. per square yard, in October.

98, Vine Fertilizer (for winter use).

Hoof and horn meal   2 parts by weight
Bonemeal   4   ,,   ,,
Sulphate of potash   1   ,,   ,,

Mix well and use at the rate of 6 oz. per square yard.

99. Vine Fertilizer (for summer use).

Dried blood	2 parts by weight	
Superphosphate of lime	2 ,,	,,
Sulphate of potash	1 ,,	,,

Mix well and use at the rate of 4 oz. per square yard.

100. Basic Chrysanthemum Fertilizer.

Hoof and horn meal	2 parts by weight	
Bonemeal	4 ,,	,,
Sulphate of potash	1 ,,	,,
Ground chalk	1 ,,	,,

Mix in potting soil at the rate of 6 oz. per bushel.

101. Chrysanthemum Fertilizer (for summer feeding).

Sulphate of ammonia	2 parts by weight	
Superphosphate of lime	4 ,,	,,
Sulphate of potash	1 ,,	,,

Mix well and use in water at the rate of 1 oz. to 3 gallons once a week from about mid-July till buds start to show colour.

102. Carnation Fertilizer.

Sulphate of ammonia	2 parts by weight	
Superphosphate of lime	3 ,,	,,
Sulphate of potash	1 ,,	,,

Mix well and use ½ teaspoonful per plant every week or ten days while in full growth and forming flower buds.

103. Rose Fertilizer (Tonk's formula).

Nitrate of potash	10 parts by weight	
Superphosphate of lime	12 ,,	,,
Sulphate of magnesium	2 ,,	,,
Sulphate of iron	1 ,,	,,
Sulphate of lime (gypsum)	8 ,,	,,

Crush and mix thoroughly and apply in April at the rate of 4 oz. per square yard.

104. General Garden Fertilizer.

Sulphate of ammonia	5 parts by weight

Superphosphate of lime	7 parts by weight	
Sulphate of potash	2 ,,	,,
Steamed bone flour	1 ,,	,,

Mix well and use as a top dressing, or prior to sowing or planting in spring or summer at rates from 3 to 5 oz. per square yard or in water at 1 to 2 oz. per gallon. This is an exceptionally well-balanced fertilizer.

105. Fertilizer for Mixing with General Potting Composts (John Innes formula). See (505).

106. Fertilizer for Mixing with General Seed Composts (John Innes formula). See (501).

107. Fertilizer for Revitalizing Weak Lawns.

Sulphate of ammonia	1 part by weight	
Dried blood	2 ,,	,,
Sulphate of potash	2 ,,	,,
Sharp sand	20 ,,	,,

Mix well and give two applications during the spring, each at the rate of 6 oz. per square yard.

108. Lawn Sand.

Sulphate of ammonia	3 parts by weight	
Sulphate of iron	1 ,,	,,
Fine silver sand	20 ,,	,,

Mix well and apply as necessary at the rate of 4 oz. per square yard during dry weather in spring and summer. This mixture burns out broad-leaved weeds and moss but stimulates the finer grasses.

MISCELLANEOUS NOTES

109. Mixing by Parts. This system has been adopted in the foregoing recipes of mixed fertilizers because it is the most elastic and easily adjustable to individual needs. Note that all parts are by weight, not by bulk. The individual part can be of any convenient weight so long as the same unit of weight is used throughout the preparation of one mixture. For

51

example, supposing 1 oz. is chosen as the unit and the general fertilizer (104) is to be mixed, then 7 times 1 oz. – namely, 7 oz. – of superphosphate will be required, 5 oz. sulphate of ammonia, 2 oz. sulphate of potash, and 1 oz. steamed bone flour, making 15 oz. of fertilizer altogether, or enough to treat 5 square yards at 3 oz. per square yard. If 1 lb. had been chosen as the unit, all the quantities would have been in pounds, and 15 lb. of fertilizer would have been prepared – i.e. enough for 80 square yards at 3 oz. per square yard. Suppose the total amount of fertilizer required is known. Then the best method is to divide this by the total number of parts in the mixture and use the result as the unit. If 1 rod ($30\frac{1}{4}$ square yards) of ground is to be dressed, this would require a total of $90\frac{3}{4}$ oz. of mixed fertilizer at 3 oz. per square yard. The total number of parts $7+5+2+1=15$, so the unit should be $90\frac{3}{4}$ divided by 15, or approximately 6 oz. Thus the quantities required would be 42 oz. of superphosphate, 30 oz. of sulphate of ammonia, 12 oz. of sulphate of potash, and 6 oz. of steamed bone flour, totalling 90 oz.

110. Fertilizers and Manures which must not be Mixed. Some substances interact chemically with one another and lose their value. Such should never be mixed. The most important are sulphate of ammonia, Nitro-chalk, or soot with chalk or lime or any substance containing free lime, such as basic slag; and lime with dung or poultry droppings. Nitrates must not be mixed with acid substances. Superphosphate of lime can sometimes be acid, and must not be mixed with chalk, lime, or substances containing free lime.

111. Plant Hormones. Strictly, this term applies to certain substances produced by plants which regulate growth but it is also used for some synthetic chemicals producing similar effects. A better term for these is 'growth regulators'. Often these have an effect quite disproportionate to the concentration at which they are used. For example, alpha-indole-acetic acid has been used at dilutions of 1 part in 50,000 to induce rapid root formation on tomato cuttings. Beta-naphthoxyacetic acid used in extremely weak solution as a spray on tomato flowers causes fruits to set irrespective of normal pollination. Root-forming hormones can be purchased in proprietary brands both as liquids and as powders. The former are diluted with water according to manufacturers' instructions. Cuttings are stood erect in this solution for twenty-four hours (longer for hard cuttings). Only the basal part of each cutting is immersed. Powders are mixed with the soil in which the cuttings are to be inserted. The root-forming hormones principally used are alpha-naphthalene-acetic acid, indole-acetic acid and indolebutyric acid, but there are many other effective substances.

Beta-naphthoxyacetic acid also has the property of causing some fruits to swell and mature even though unfertilized. This chemical has been used with excellent effect on tomatoes, the method being to apply as a very fine spray to the open blossoms. The dilution is 50 to 60 parts per million of water, but proprietary brands are already much diluted, so manufacturers' instructions should be followed for these.

A third use for growth regulators has been found in the prevention of pre-harvest drop of apples by spraying with alpha-naphthalene-acetic acid. This is applied at a strength of 10 to 20 parts per million of water in August or early September, five to ten days before the date at which the apples normally start to fall badly. A second application may be given ten days later. By this means the ripening period is extended and much fruit is saved.

Growth regulators in excess are toxic to plants and this has suggested their use as weed-killers. Some are used to kill annual and perennial broad-leaved weeds, without harming grasses and similar plants, and are sprayed on to the plants so that the solution is absorbed through the leaves and stems.

These weed-killers are also absorbed through the roots. Plants sprayed with them curl and become distorted, gradually turn brown and eventually die.

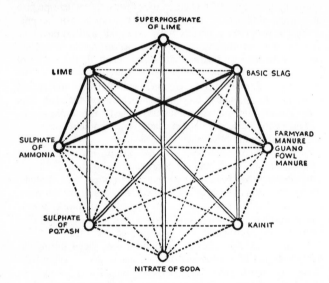

A Fertilizer Mixing Chart. Fertilizers connected by a thick black line should never be mixed, while those joined by double lines must only be mixed when for immediate use. Those connected by dotted lines can be mixed quite safely.

SECTION THREE

THE VEGETABLE GARDEN

MISCELLANEOUS NOTES

112. Rotational Cropping. This idea has been taken over from farmers, who employ a definite rotation of crops from one year to the next with the object of making the very best use of the ground. Root crops may be used to clean newly broken ground prior to the cultivation of cereals, after which the land is allowed to lie fallow for a year or is put down once more to grass. No such clearly defined annual system of rotation is practicable on the allotment or in small gardens, partly because it is necessary to keep much of the ground in constant use, and partly because of the difficulty of devising any rotation which will give an ideal sequence of crops together with a sensible division of the ground according to the requirements of the consumer.

One advantage of rotation is that it conserves the food reserves of the soil and so reduces the need for manuring. Green crops and potatoes make a comparatively high demand on the nitrogen in the soil, and both benefit greatly from applications of well-rotted animal manure. Such manure is harmful to carrots, parsnips, and beetroots, which require abundant potash rather than nitrogen. A fundamental point in any system of garden rotation should be that, so far as possible, green crops and potatoes should be followed by roots.

A type of rotation that can be followed roughly in most gardens is to divide the ground into three approximately equal sections and devote one mainly to green crops, one to potatoes, and one to roots, peas, and beans and other vegeables. Then in the second year everything can be shifted on one place, the greens coming to the potato plot, the potatoes going on to the ground cleared of roots, and the roots occupying the plot cleared of greens. The third year there is a similar shift on, and the fourth year the crops come back to their original plots (113). Onions may well stand outside such a system of rotation and have a more or less permanent bed to themselves.

113. Suggested Three-year Rotation

A
Cabbages, cauliflowers, brussels sprouts, kale, savoys, and other brassicas. Preceded by, or inter-cropped with lettuces, radishes, and other small salads.

Plot dressed with animal manure or compost and limed (not together). Crops fed while in growth with nitrate of soda or sulphate of ammonia.

B
Potatoes. Followed by broccoli, spring cabbage, coleworts, leeks, and late-sown turnip (for tops).

Plot dressed with animal manure or compost, but *not* lime.

Complete artificial fertilizer applied just prior to planting potatoes (92).

C
Carrots, parsnips, turnips, and beetroots.

Peas and beans with summer spinach and lettuces between.

No animal manure or compost except for pea and bean trenches. Wood ashes forked in. Complete fertilizer (low nitrogen ratio) applied just prior to sowing (93).

D
Onions.

Plot dressed with animal manure or compost and wood ashes. Nitrate of soda after thinning.

The scheme is applicable to plots of any size or shape, so no dimensions are necessary. The only essential is that sections A, B, and C should be of approximately the same area. They need not be of the same shape. The second year the order of the crops from top to bottom is C, A, B, D; the third year B, C, A, D; the fourth year the same as the first year. Onions are not included in the rotation because they appear to derive greater benefit from being grown on the same plot for a number of years, If, however, it is preferred to include them they should go to plot C.

114. Intercropping. Some crops take up a good deal of space without anything like occupying all the ground with their roots. Examples are the taller varieties of peas and runner beans. Space is necessary with these to prevent one row from shading the next so heavily that the plants would fall into ill health. But some crops appreciate shade, and it is an obvious deduction to plant these between tall subjects that require a lot of room. That is the simplest form of inter-cropping. Cleverly practised, it can be a great space saver in the garden.

Winter greens or other plants raised in a reserve bed may be ready for planting out before any ground is vacant for them, though a crop is nearing maturity and will shortly be harvested. Under such circumstances it is in order to plant the new crop between the old. Do not intercrop in this way too long in advance of the time of harvesting the preceding crop or the result may be starved and drawn plants.

115. Catch Cropping. Sometimes ground has to be prepared some considerable time before it will be needed, and it may be possible to get a quick-growing crop off if before that for which it was actually intended is ready to go in. This is known as catch cropping, and is a method of economizing both space and time in the vegetable garden. Lettuces, radishes, spring onions (for use in salads), summer spinach, mustard and cress are a few of the best catch crops, and they may be sown in celery trenches or on the ridges on each side of such trenches, on the ground prepared for the later kinds of winter greens or for very late sowings of quick-maturing peas and in other similar places.

116. Successional Sowing. If all the seeds of such things as lettuces, radishes, spinach, early carrots, early turnips, or peas are put in at one time the result will be a glut of these vegetables for a few weeks followed by a complete lack of supplies. The right course is to make a number of small sowings at intervals of a fortnight or three weeks so that as fast as one lot is used up another is just coming to maturity.

There are early, mid-season, and late varieties of many vegetables. One important difference in these is in the time they take to reach maturity. For example, an early pea may be ready for picking twelve weeks after sowing, whereas a mid-season variety sown at the same time will not be ready for a further fortnight, and a late kind may take a full sixteen weeks. By a wise selection of these different kinds it will also be possible to lengthen the season and maintain continuity of supply.

For very late sowings an early variety is often selected. This apparent paradox is explained by the fact that there is such a limited period of good weather left for growth that only a naturally quick-growing variety can mature in the available time. This is particularly noticeable with peas, carrots, and turnips.

117. Approximate Yield of Vegetables.

The following figures can only give a rough guide to average production. Yield varies greatly according to soil, weather, and degree of cultural skill. Figures 50% in excess of those given may be obtained under favourable conditions.

Almost all the weights quoted are for maincrop varieties allowed to mature. Earlies may be harvested at practically any stage of growth, so no reliable weights can be given. Exception is made with early carrots, as figures are taken from the average market yield of shorthorn varieties allowed to develop.

Vegetable	Yield			
	Per Acre	Per Rod	Per Square Yard	Per Foot of Row
Beans, broad	4 tons	. 56 lb.	2 lb.	8 oz.
,, french	3 ,,	42 ,,	1½ ,,	4 ,,
,, runner	10 ,,	140 ,,	5 ,,	4 lb.
,, haricot*	15 cwt.	10–12 lb.	5–6 oz.	—
Beetroot	12 tons	168 lb.	5½ lb.	14 oz.
Broccoli	8 ,,	112 ,,	3¾ ,,	19 ,,
Brussels sprouts	4 ,,	56 ,,	2 ,,	9 ,,
Cabbage (spring)	9 ,,	126 ,,	4 ,,	11 ,,
,, (autumn and winter)	15 ,,	210 ,,	7 ,,	1½ lb.
Cauliflower	6 ,,	84 ,,	3 ,,	1 ,,
Carrots (main crop)	14 ,,	196 ,,	6½ ,,	12 oz.
,, (early)	8 ,,	112 ,,	3¾ ,,	5 ,,
Endive	—	300 heads	10 heads	¾ head
Kale	10 tons	140 lb.	5 lb.	1½ lb.
Leek	10 ,,	140 ,,	5 ,,	13 oz.
Lettuce	—	300–400 heads	10–13 heads	1½–2 heads
Mushrooms	—	—	10 lb.	—
Onions	12 tons	168 lb.	5½ ,,	10 oz.
Parsnips	10 ,,	140 ,,	5 ,,	13 ,,
Peas	3 ,,	42 ,,	1½ ,,	6 ,,
Potatoes (main crop)	10 ,,	140 ,,	5 ,,	1½ lb.
Savoys	15 ,,	210 ,,	7 ,,	1½ ,,
Shallots	—	240 ,,	8 ,,	10 ,,
Spinach (summer)	8 tons	112 ,,	3¾ ,,	5 ,,
Swedes	13 ,,	182 ,,	6 ,,	14 ,,
Turnips (main crop)	13 ,,	182 ,,	6 ,,	14 ,,
Tomatoes (under glass)	30 ,,	420 ,,	15 ,,	6 lb. per plant
(outdoors)	20 ,,	280 ,,	10 ,,	4 lb. per plant

* Seeds only

118. Continuity Chart for Principal Vegetables

Jan. Feb. Mar. Apr. May June July Aug. Sept. Oct. Nov. Dec.

Artichokes

Beet

Beans (broad)

,, (french)

,, (runner)

Broccoli

,, (sprouting)

Brussels sprouts

Cabbages

Carrots

Cauliflowers

Celeriac

Celery

Endive

Kale

60

	Jan.	Feb.	Mar.	Apr.	May	June	July	Aug.	Sept.	Oct.	Nov.	Dec.
Kohl Rabi												
Leeks												
Lettuces												
Onions												
Parsnips												
Peas												
Potatoes												
Savoys												
Shallots												
Spinach												
Spinach beet												
Turnips												
Turnip tops												
Vegetable marrows												

The times at which vegetables are available from the open ground are indicated by continuous lines, while the dotted lines show the additional period during which they may be stored or preserved. With careful management it may be possible to extend the season of some of the crops even further.

119. Vegetable Sowing

SEEDS TO BE SOWN OR

Name of Vegetable	Seeds for 50 ft. of Row	When to Sow	Distance between Rows	Distance to Sow or Thin
Beans, broad	½ pt.	Early Nov. Mar.–Apl.	2 ft.	6 in.
„ french	¼ „	Apl.–May	18 in.	8 „
„ haricot	¼ „	Apl.–May	18 „	8 „
„ runner	½ „	May–June	8 ft.	8 „
Beet	¼ oz.	Apl.–June	12 in. 15 in.	6–8 in.
„ seakale	¼ „	Mar. & Aug.	18 in.	9 in.
Carrot	¼ „	Mar.–June	8 in. 15 in.	2–4 in.
Endive	⅛ „	Apl.–Aug.	1 ft.	9 in.
Kohl Rabi	⅛ „	Apl.–Aug.	18 in.	1 ft.
Lettuce	⅛ „	Mar.–Aug.	9 in. 1 ft.	6–9 in.
Onion	⅙ „	Mar.	1 ft.	6 in.
Parsley	¼ „	Mar.–Aug.	9 in.	5 „
Parsnip	¼ „	Feb.–Mar.	18 „	8 „
Peas	¼ pt.	Mar.–June	2–5 ft.	3 „
Radish	½ oz.	Mar.–Aug.	6 in.	—
Spinach, summer	¼ „	Mar.–July	1 ft.	8 in.
„ winter	¼ „	Aug.	1 ft.	6 „
„ beet	¼ „	Mar.–Aug.	18 in.	9 „
Swede	¼ „	May–June	15 „	8 „
Turnip	¼ „	Mar.–July	12 in. 15 in.	4–8 in.

and Planting Chart

THINNED IN THE ROW

Depth to Sow	When Ready for Use	Remarks
1 in.	June–Aug.	Autumn sowing should only be attempted in fairly sheltered places.
1 ,,	July–Oct.	Gather the beans while still young.
1 ,,	Oct. onwards	Leave beans to ripen in pod, and then shell out and store dry for winter use.
1 ,,	July–Oct.	Plants may be grown as bushes by frequent pinching of runners.
1 ,,	July onwards	Globe varieties are best for early use; cylindrical rooted kinds for storing.
1 ,,	All the year round	The leaves are cut as required, and boiled in the same way as spinach.
$\frac{1}{4}$,,	June onwards	Sow stump-rooted varieties for early use and intermediate kinds for storing.
$\frac{1}{2}$,,	Aug.–Mar.	Specially welcome in winter.
$\frac{1}{2}$,,	July–Nov.	Withstands drought remarkably well.
$\frac{1}{2}$,,	June–Oct.	Winter supplies obtained by placing seedlings in frames in October.
$\frac{1}{2}$,,	Aug. onwards	Lift in September for storing.
$\frac{1}{2}$,,	June–Dec.	Winter supplies obtained by placing seedlings in a frame in October.
1 ,,	Sept. onwards	Roots may be left in the ground all winter, or lifted and stored.
1 ,,	June–Oct.	Make frequent small sowings so that a successional supply is maintained.
$\frac{1}{4}$,,	April–Sept.	Early supplies may be obtained by sowing in February on a hotbed.
1 ,,	May–Sept.	Make small successional sowings.
1 ,,	Oct.–April	A sheltered position should be chosen.
1 ,,	July onwards	Continues to crop for a long time.
1 ,,	Oct. onwards	A wholesale and profitable vegetable.
$\frac{1}{2}$,,	June onwards	For summer supplies it is best to sow in a partially shaded position.

SEEDS TO BE SOWN IN SEEDBED AND

Name of Vegetable	Seeds to Supply 100 Plts.	When to Sow	When to Transplant	Dist. btn. Rows	Dist. btn. Plts.
Borecole (kale)	$\frac{1}{8}$ oz.	Apl.–May	July–Aug.	2½ ft.	18 in.
Broccoli	$\frac{1}{5}$,,	Mar.–May	May–July	2½ ,,	2 ft.
Brussels sprouts	$\frac{1}{8}$,,	Mar.–Apl.	May–June	2½ ,,	2 ,,
Cabbage, summer, autumn, winter	$\frac{1}{8}$,,	Mar.–Apl.	May–July	2 ,,	18 in.
Cabbage, spring	$\frac{1}{8}$,,	July–Aug.	Sept.–Oct., Mar.	18 in.	1 ft.
Cauliflower	$\frac{1}{8}$,,	Feb.–Apl.	May–June	2½ ft.	2 ,,
Celery	$\frac{1}{32}$,,	Feb.–Apl.	June–July	3 ,,	1 ,,
Cucumber (ridge)	100 seeds	Apl.–May	June	4 ,,	3 ,,
Leek	$\frac{1}{16}$ oz.	Mar.	June	18 in.	9 in.
Onion (for transplanting)	$\frac{1}{16}$,,	Aug.–Jan. (in frame)	Mid-Apl.	1 ft.	6 in.
Savoy	$\frac{1}{7}$,,	Apl.–May	June–Aug.	2 ,,	18 ,,
Tomato	$\frac{1}{4}$,,	Mar. (under glass)	June	3 ,,	18 ,,
Vegetable marrow	100 seeds	Apl.–May	June	4 ,,	3 ft.

TRANSPLANTED TO WHERE THEY ARE TO BE GROWN

Depth to Sow	When Ready for Use	Remarks
$\frac{1}{2}$ in.	Nov.–May	There are numerous varieties, including the well-known curled kales.
$\frac{1}{2}$,,	Oct.–June	Varieties can be obtained to give a succession from autumn until late spring.
$\frac{1}{2}$,,	Sept.–Feb.	Plant very firmly in soil that has not been over-manured.
$\frac{1}{2}$,,	July–Feb.	Varieties should be chosen to give the required succession.
$\frac{1}{2}$,,	Mar.–June	Not all kinds are suitable for summer sowing. Consult catalogue on this point.
$\frac{1}{2}$,,	Aug.–Dec.	More delicate in flavour than the broccoli, and also more tender.
$\frac{1}{4}$,,	Sept.–Mar.	Raise the seedlings in a greenhouse or frame.
1 ,,	July–Sept.	Pinch out tips of main runners, to encourage formation of side growths.
$\frac{1}{4}$,,	Sept.–May	Earlier supplies can be obtained by sowing in a warm greenhouse in January and transplanting outdoors in April.
$\frac{1}{4}$,,	June onwards	White Lisbon onions can be sown more thickly in late summer for use as salading in the spring.
$\frac{1}{2}$,,	Oct.–Mar.	A hardy and profitable vegetable.
$\frac{1}{4}$,,	Aug.–Oct.	Earlier plants for cultivation throughout in the greenhouse can be raised from seed sown in January or February.
1 ,,	July–Oct.	Pinch main runners of trailing varieties to induce formation of side growths.

ROOTS AND TUBERS

Name of Vegetable	Roots for 50 ft. of Row	When to Plant	Distance between Rows	Distance between Plants
Artichoke, globe	16	April	3 ft.	3 ft.
Artichoke, Jerusalem	7 lb.	Feb.	2½ ft.	15 in.
Asparagus	40	April	15 in.	15 ,,
Onion sets	½ lb.	March	1 ft.	6 ,,
Potatoes, early	8 lb.	March	2½ ,,	1 ft.
,, mid-season and late	7 lb.	April	3 ,,	15 in.
Rhubarb	16	March	3 ,,	3 ft.
Shallots	2–3 lb.	Feb.–Mar.	12 in.	6 in.

120. Germinating Period of Vegetable Seeds. The following table of germination times is necessarily only approximate. Actual times will vary greatly according to soil, warmth and weather. Given a sufficiently low temperature or dry soil, seeds will remain dormant indefinitely. The times below are for normal conditions at the usual sowing times.

Name	Time (days)	Name	Time (days)
Beans, broad	8–12	Broccoli	7–12
,, french	10–14	Brussels sprouts	7–12
,, runner	10–14	Cabbage	7–12
Beet	18–24	Carrot	17–24
,, seakale	18–24	Cauliflower	7–12
Borecole	7–12	Celery	18–28

FOR PLANTING

Depth to Plant	When Ready for Use	Remarks
—	July–Oct.	The flower heads are cut before they begin to expand.
6 in.	Nov.–March	May be used as a windbreak.
2–3 in.	May–June	Do not cut asparagus for at least two years and never after June.
Half-covered	July onwards	A good method for those who cannot practise autumn sowing.
4–5 in.	June–July	It is an advantage to sprout the tubers in a light frost-proof place before planting.
4–5 in.	Aug. onwards	Dig when the skins are firm.
—	March–July	Earlier supplies can be obtained by covering the roots with barrels in January.
Half-covered	July onwards	First class for pickling.

Germinating Period of Vegetable Seeds – *continued*

Name	Time (days)	Name	Time (days)
Cress	5– 8	Parsnip	21–28
Cucumber	5–15	Pea	7–12
Endive	14–21	Radish	6–10
Kale	7–12	Savoy	7–12
Kohl Rabi	7–12	Spinach, summer	10–15
Leek	21–24	,, winter	10–15
Lettuce	10–15	,, beet	18–24
Mustard	4– 8	Swede	7–12
Onion, spring-sown	21–25	Tomato	7–14
,, August-sown	12–18	Turnip	7–12
Parsley	28–42	Vegetable Marrow	6–10

CULTIVATION OF VEGETABLES
ALPHABETICALLY ARRANGED

The following notes are based on kitchen and not exhibition requirements. Vegetables required for show must, in general, be given considerably more space and a higher rate of feeding.

121. Artichokes, Jerusalem. Much like a perennial sunflower, and belongs to the same family. One important difference is that it has tuberous edible roots not unlike those of the potato. Soil is not a matter of first importance. Heaviest crops are obtained by thorough autumn or winter digging and application of manure or vegetable compost at 1 cwt. to 12 sq. yd. Position in sun or partial shade. Plant in February with spade or trowel, 15 in. apart in rows $2\frac{1}{2}$ ft. apart. Holes should be 6 in. deep. No subsequent cultivation required except periodic hoeing. Draw a little soil towards the stems when hoeing. Tubers are ready between November and March and may be dug as required or lifted at once and stored in sacks or clamp like potatoes. A proportion of the tubers may be set aside for replanting, but no sprouting is required.

122. Artichokes, Globe. Highly ornamental plants grown for their flower heads, which are eaten before they open, when the fleshy scales are regarded as a delicacy. Plants can be raised from seed sown in a frame in March or outdoors in April, but this is not recommended. The best method is to detach offsets early in April, selecting from the best plants. These are replanted in well dug, fairly rich soil and open position. Space 3 ft. apart each way. Mulch with manure in May. Cut off all flower stems the first season. Cropping is most profitable in the second and third years, after which beds should be remade. Remove dead leaves in October and cover crowns with bracken or straw until March. Cut heads regularly as soon as they are plump and the scales fleshy.

THE VEGETABLE GARDEN

123. Asparagus. Plants can be raised from seed sown in a greenhouse or frame in March or outdoors in May, but it is better to purchase two-year-old roots early in April. These will start to crop two years after planting. Plant 15 in. apart in rows 15 in. apart. Common practice is to make beds 4 ft. wide containing three rows each raised above ground level to improve winter drainage, or plants may be grown on the flat 15 in. apart in rows $3\frac{1}{2}$ ft. apart and after two years soil is drawn over the plants as when earthing up potatoes. Either way, soil must be deeply dug and liberally manured. Top dress each March with short, well-rotted manure or hop manure. Do not cut after the middle of June but allow plants to make foliage, which should be cut off above soil level at the end of October.

124. Aubergine (Egg Plant). These are grown for their fleshy fruits. Seeds are sown in pans or boxes in a warm greenhouse during January or February. Seedlings are pricked off and later potted singly into small pots from which they are worked on into 6- or 7-in. pots for fruiting. Soils and treatment throughout this period are the same as for tomatoes (177) except that side shoots are not removed; the points of growth are pinched out when seedlings are 6 in. high and each plant is restricted to about six fruits. Water freely.

125. Beans, Broad. Three types are grown – the Mazagon, Longpod, and the Windsor. The first is the hardiest, but inferior in other respects; the second is sufficiently hardy for autumn sowing in many districts; while the third is best for bottling or freezing.

For spring sowing, manure or compost may be applied at 1 cwt. to 15 sq. yd. It is an excellent plan to follow the crop after brassicas or potatoes, for which the ground has already been manured. Prior to autumn sowing, dust the ground with basic slag, 3 oz., and sulphate of potash, 1 oz. per square yard. These fertilizers may also be used prior to spring sowing,

69

plus sulphate of ammonia, at the rate of 1 oz. per square yard, if no manure is available.

Sow 6 in. apart in drills 1 in. deep and 2 ft. apart. Autumn sowings should be made in late October or early November, spring sowings during March and April. An early crop can be obtained by sowing seeds 2 in. apart each way in boxes in early February and germinating in a warm greenhouse, or a month later in a frame set on a hotbed. Seedlings are planted outdoors about the middle of April, spaced as seeds outdoors.

Pinch out the growing points as soon as the plants have set two or three clusters of pods each. Gather beans frequently as they attain suitable size. Good varieties are Aquadulce Claudia for autumn sowing and Unrivalled Green Windsor and Exhibition Longpod for spring sowing. The Sutton is a fine dwarf variety.

Black fly and chocolate spot are common foes (711).

126. Beans, Haricot. These are really french beans (127), but are grown for their ripened seeds, which are stored and used during the winter. Preparation of ground and cultivation are the same as for french beans, and it is only in the harvesting that there is any difference of treatment. Pods should be allowed to hang until they turn brown, when the whole plants are pulled up, tied in small bundles, and hung head downwards in a shed or room to dry off. Then the seeds can be shelled out and stored in dry bins for the winter. Reliable varieties are Brown Dutch (brown seeded) and Comtesse de Chambord (white seeded).

Mosaic and anthracnose are the commonest diseases (711).

127. Beans, French. There are two main types, the dwarf and the climbing. The former are of more use to the amateur, as they require no staking. Soil should be prepared as for broad beans (125), and the same fertilizers used. Sow in late April or in early May outdoors. Earlier crops can be obtained by sowing seeds 2 in. apart each way in boxes in mid-

April and germinating in a greenhouse or frame. The seedlings should be planted outdoors early in June. Seeds sown outdoors should be spaced 8 in. apart in drills 1 in. deep and 18 in. apart. These are also correct spacings for seedlings. Gather beans frequently while still quite tender. Water freely during dry weather. Surplus beans may be frozen, stored in salt, or allowed to dry, the seeds being used as haricots.

Reliable varieties are Canadian Wonder, Masterpiece, and The Prince.

Foes as for haricot beans (126).

128. Beans, Runner. Soil should be prepared as for broad beans (125). Manure or compost, though not essential, is useful. An economical method is to prepare a trench 18 in. wide and deep for each row and mix manure thoroughly with the soil in this. Fertilizers as for broad beans.

Sow outdoors about the middle of May. The plants are even more tender than french beans. Alternatively, plants may be raised in boxes as described for french beans (127) and be planted out about the first week in June. Seeds or plants should be spaced outdoors 8 in. apart in a double line 10 in. apart. If more than one such double line is required, a space of at least 8 ft. must be left between each. Stakes at least 8 ft. in length must be placed in position, one to each plant, before the beans commence to climb.

An alternative method of cultivation is to sow or plant 2 ft. apart in rows 3 ft. apart and pinch out the tips of young shoots repeatedly from June until August. This makes the plants become bushy, and no stakes are required.

Good varieties are Twenty One, Streamline and Prizewinner. Hammond's Dwarf is bushy, short and needs no staking.

Flower dropping is the commonest trouble. It is usually caused by cold nights, but may be aggravated by dry soil.

129. Beetroot. There are three distinct types of beetroot,

grown for their roots – the globe, or round-rooted, the intermediate, or cylindrical-rooted, and the long. The first is valuable
for early crops, but the others are capable of giving
heavier crops and should, in consequence, be planted for the
maincrop. Spinach and seakale beetroots are grown for their
stems and leaves and not for their roots, and are separately
dealt with (171), (174). Dig the soil thoroughly, work in
manure or compost at the rate of 1 cwt. to 20 sq. yd., if none
has been applied for a previous crop, and, just prior to sowing,
rake in a dressing of the following mixture at 3 to 4 oz. per
square yard: 1 part of sulphate of ammonia, 1 part of sulphate
of potash, 5 parts of superphosphate of lime.

Seed for an early crop may be sown at the end of April,
and for the main crop from the beginning to the middle of
May. Draw drills 1 in. deep and 12–15 in. apart, and sow
seeds in small groups 6 in. apart for round and 8 in. for
intermediate and long-rooted varieties. Reduce seedlings to one
at each cluster. After thinning, dust sulphate of ammonia or
nitrate of soda between the rows at the rate of 1 oz. to every
12 ft. Germination of beetroot seed is usually rather poor.

Lift early kinds from the end of June onwards, as required.
Maincrop beetroot should be lifted in September and stored
in sand or peat in a dry, frost-proof place. Twist off the tops.

Good kinds are Crimson Globe, Detroit, Cylindra, and
Cheltenham Greentop.

Foes seldom give much trouble, but cutworms may damage
the roots while leaves are occasionally attacked by leaf
miners (711).

130. Broccoli, Heading. Closely allied to cauliflower, and
from the culinary point of view identical except that flavour
is less delicate. It is also hardier and has a much longer season.
Where possible, follow broccoli after early potatoes or some
other crop that has already had manure, and give chemicals
only. It will then only be necessary to clear off weeds and other

rubbish, dust the surface with the fertilizers, fork in, and tread firmly. Recommended chemicals are hydrated lime at 8 oz. per square yard; basic slag at 3 oz. per square yard; and either sulphate of potash or muriate of potash 1 oz. per square yard. If ground manured for a previous crop is not available, work in a moderate dressing of dung or compost, about 1 cwt. to 18 sq yd.; then give the chemicals described above as a top dressing.

Seed should be sown outdoors in April and May. For early supplies it is an advantage to sow a few seeds in a frame in March. In all methods sow thinly in drills $\frac{1}{2}$ in. deep and 6 in. apart.

Plant from May to late July with a trowel and press soil firmly around the roots. Water freely if the weather is dry, but when possible plant during showery weather. Space 2 ft. apart in rows $2\frac{1}{2}$ ft. apart.

As the plants approach maturity, bend inner leaves inwards over the curds for protection.

Varieties may be grouped as early, mid-season, and late. The first are ready from October to Christmas, the second from that date until April, and the third carry on the supply until June. Standard kinds are: *early*, Veitch's Self-Protecting; *mid-season*, Leamington, Snow's Winter White, Roscoff Nos. 1 and 2; *late*, Late Queen, St. George, Roscoff Nos. 3 and 4, May Blossom.

Club root, cabbage caterpillars, flea beetle, and cabbage root fly are the commonest foes (711).

131. Broccoli, Sprouting. Grown for the flowering shoots, which are cut off when 6 to 9 in. in length. Sprouting broccoli are hardier than heading kinds, and the sprouts are produced successively for a long time. Soil should be well dug and moderately enriched with manure (about 1 cwt. to 12 sq. yd.), unless plants follow a crop for which manure has been applied, when give soot at 8 oz. per square yard, or the fertilizer mixture as recommended for heading broccoli (130).

Seed should be sown in April in the same manner as for heading broccoli. Plant seedlings from June to Sept. 18 in. apart in rows 2½ ft. apart. Sprouts should be cut as they become available.

Good varieties are Calabrese, Christmas Purple Sprouting, and early and late purple and white sprouting.

Club root, cabbage caterpillars, flea beetle, and cabbage root fly are the commonest foes (711).

132. Brussels Sprouts. Soil preparation should be thorough. Work in animal manure or compost at the rate of 1 cwt. to from 12 to 20 sq. yd., or, better still, choose a plot that has been manured for some previous crop, such as potatoes. Then chemicals only will be required. Sulphate of ammonia may be applied in spring at ½ oz. per sq. yd.; supplement with sulphate of potash, ½ oz. per sq. yd., and superphosphate of lime, 2 oz. per sq. yd. Six or eight weeks after planting, give another dressing of sulphate of ammonia, Nitro-chalk, or nitrate of soda at ½ oz. per yard run. Do not apply fertilizers after mid-August.

Seed should be sown in a frame or greenhouse in March or outdoors in early April as described for heading broccoli (130) and young plants treated in a similar manner. Plant out very firmly early in May, or, if the sprouts are to follow some other crop, as soon as this can be cleared. Set plants 2 ft. apart in rows 2½ ft. apart.

Picking may begin as soon as the most forward buttons attain usable size. Do not strip the plants, but leave smaller sprouts to gain size. The tops can be cut and used as 'greens' in Sept.–Oct. and this will help sprouts to swell.

Cambridge Nos. 1 and 5, Rous Lench, Fillbasket, Cambridge Special, Irish Elegance and Jade Cross are good varieties.

Club root, caterpillars, root fly, flea beetle, aphis and white fly are the pests most to be feared. Gall weevils, often present, do little harm (711).

133. Cabbage. By judicious selection of varieties and by successional sowing it is possible to maintain a supply of cabbage throughout the year. Soil should be well prepared. Manure or compost at the rate of 1 cwt. to 10 or 12 sq. yd. will be well repaid, but may be omitted for late-summer-planted cabbages following a crop such as potatoes or peas, for which manure has already been given. If the manure is omitted, a top dressing of soot at 4 oz. per square yard or sulphate of ammonia at 1 oz. per square yard will be sufficient.

Usually two sowings are enough, one made outdoors in April and the other between the middle of July and the middle of August. If a mid-summer supply is required, a third sowing should be made in a frame or greenhouse in late February or early March. Sometimes a fourth sowing is made outdoors in May or early June to give cabbages after Christmas. Details of sowing are the same as for heading broccoli (130), and planting is carried out in the same manner except that it will be sufficient to allow 1 ft. between the plants and 18 in. between the rows for spring cabbage – that is to say, those that are planted out in autumn and harvested the following spring – and 18 in. between plants and 2 ft. between rows for autumn and winter cabbage.

Reliable kinds are as follows: *For spring sowing,* Golden Acre, Primo, Greyhound, Winnigstadt, January King, and Christmas Drumhead; *for summer sowing,* April, Flower of Spring, Harbinger, Early Offenham, and Ellam's Early Dwarf; *for February sowing,* May Express, Golden Acre.

Club root, caterpillars, cabbage root fly, cabbage aphid, flea beetle and white fly are the worst foes (711).

134. Cardoons. Ornamental plants grown for their blanched stems, which are used, both cooked and raw, in salads. Plants may be raised from seed sown in a warm greenhouse or in a frame in April, two or three seeds in each 3-in. pot. Reduce seedlings to one per pot and harden off for planting out at the end of May. The plants should be 18 in. apart in rows 3 ft. apart. Situation should be open and the soil well dug and manured. Blanching starts in September, when plants are well grown, and is done as for celery (138), or by tying corrugated brown paper or clean straw around the stems. Usually about eight weeks are required to obtain well-blanched stems.

135. Carrots. These may be divided according to the length of their roots, viz. long, intermediate or short, and also according to shape, viz. tapering or stump rooted (cylindrical). The short, stump-rooted varieties are used for early crops; longer stump-rooted varieties are the most popular for general use, long tapered carrots being grown primarily for exhibition.

Soil for intermediate and long types must be dug deeply, but stump-rooted varieties will thrive with shallower cultivation. Dung and compost should not be applied, though it is an advantage if ground can be chosen that has been manured for some previous crop. Prior to sowing give sulphate or muriate of potash at 1 oz. per square yard, superphosphate at 2 oz. per square yard, and sulphate of ammonia at ½ oz. per square yard.

Sow the seed of a stump-rooted variety for the earliest crop in a sheltered position outdoors in early March. Even earlier sowings can be made in a frame or under handlights. Sow thinly in drills ¼ in. deep and 8 in. apart. No thinning will be required until the most forward are ready for use; the remainder will be left to grow on. Make further small sowings of a stump-rooted variety every three weeks or so until the middle of June to give a successional supply of young roots for summer and early autumn use. Sow maincrop carrots for storing about the middle of April. Drills should be ½ in. deep and 12–15 in. apart, and the seedlings must be thinned to about 4 in. apart. Maincrop carrots should be dug in mid-September before the roots get too tough and start to crack. Store in sand or ashes.

Reliable varieties are Early Scarlet Horn, Chantenay, Early Nantes, James's Intermediate, St Valery, and Autumn King.

Carrot fly is the commonest pest (711).

136. Cauliflower. Not so generally useful as broccoli, as the season is shorter and the plants less hardy. The flavour is very delicate. It is almost impossible to give too much manure or compost. The situation should be sunny, but reasonably sheltered. Seed may be sown in boxes in a warm greenhouse in February or direct in a frame in March. Outdoor sowing cannot be attempted till early April, and then plants are usually too late to be of much use. Another plan is to sow outdoors in early September and transfer seedlings to a frame or cloche at the end of October, spacing them 3 in. apart each way. They are transplanted to the open ground the following April to crop in late summer.

Plants from late winter and early spring sowings should be hardened off in readiness for planting out in May or early June. Set them 2 ft. apart in rows 2½ ft. apart. A week or so later give a sprinkling of nitrate of soda or Nitro-chalk at 1 oz. per square yard.

Reliable varieties are Pioneer, All the Year Round, Novo, Early White London, Snowball, Veitch's Autumn Giant, and Walcheren.

Club root, cabbage caterpillars, cabbage root fly and flea beetle are the commonest foes (711).

137. Celeriac. A useful substitute for celery for cooking and one that will grow in poorer and drier soil. Seeds should be sown in a cool greenhouse or frame during March or early April and seedlings hardened off for planting out in May.

Choose an open site and dig the soil well, enriching with manure if possible. Plant 1 ft. apart in rows 18 in. apart. No earthing up is required. Roots can be lifted in October and stored in sand or ashes in a shed. Giant Prague is a good variety.

138. Celery. Soil must be deeply dug and well manured. The usual practice is to prepare trenches either 15 or 18 in. wide, the former for single, the latter for double rows. If there is more than one such trench they must be at least 3 ft. apart. All soil is removed to a depth of 18 in. The bottom is broken up with a fork and manure or compost worked in. A layer 9 in. thick of good top-spit soil and manure in about equal parts is placed on top and then a further 6 in. of soil only.

Seed is sown in shallow boxes in February for an early crop or in March or early April for a later supply. First sowing should be made in a warm greenhouse, later ones in a frame. The seedlings are picked off as soon as they can be handled, and are spaced 2 in. apart each way. Plant out in June or July 1 ft. apart, down the middle of the trench in the narrow trenches or one row on each side in the wide ones. Water in very freely. Subsequently water liberally in dry weather, and give one or two light dressings of nitrate of soda at 1 oz. to 12 ft. of trench. Earthing up will be necessary with most varieties, but self-blanching celeries can be obtained. Work must not be started till plants are fully grown. This will be between early September and the end of October. Remove offshoots round the base, tie stems together, and draw soil round them in a steep ridge. Celery is fit for use about six weeks after earthing up. It can be left in the open all the winter, and be dug as required, but it is advisable to protect the plants by placing two boards on edge along each ridge.

Varieties are Solid White and Standard Bearer.

The best of the self-blanching varieties is Golden Self

Blanching. This is particulary valuable for early use. Raise as ordinary celery but plant out on the flat, not in trenches. Ground should be rich and well dug. Space 9 in. apart each way and make a number of short rows rather than a few long ones. When well grown, place boards on edge round the bed to help blanch the outside plants.

Celery leaf miner and celery leaf spot are the worst foes. There is also a heart rot disease (711).

139. Chicory. The blanched leaves and stems make a useful addition to autumn and winter salad. Seeds should be sown outdoors from April to June in drills 1 ft. apart. Soil should be well dug and prepared as for lettuce (155). Thin seedlings to 9 in. apart. The roots are lifted in November and heeled in in a sheltered place in sand or ashes. They are forced as required in complete darkness, the whole process being identical to that applied to seakale (170).

140. Chives. These are used as a substitute for onions for flavouring and also for salads, and are appreciated on account of their mild flavour. Chives will grow in almost any soil and situation. Plants should be obtained early in March and, after being divided into small tufts, planted 6 in. apart in rows 8 to 9 in. apart. When chives are required for the table, cut off some of the shoots close to soil level. When the beds become overgrown, the plants can be lifted and divided.

141. Coleworts. Really small, quick-growing cabbages, taken as a catch crop from the spring-cabbage bed. They take up little room, and are often cut and used as greens before they have formed hearts. There are two kinds, the Rosette and the Hardy Green. The latter is the more useful, as it can be sown in July and used immediately after Christmas when autumn cabbages are over and before the spring crop has attained sufficient size. Culture is exactly as for cabbage (133), and the plants are put out in their final quarters in

October. A convenient method is to have a row of coleworts between each two rows of spring cabbage, spacing the plants 9 in. apart in the rows.

Foes are the same as for cabbage.

142. Corn Salad. A useful and easily grown addition to summer salads. Seed may be sown thinly either broadcast or in drills 4 to 5 in. apart at frequent intervals from March until July. Plants will thrive in any open or partially shaded position and reasonably rich soil. Leaves should be cut when the plants are a few inches high and before they run to flower.

143. Couve Tronchuda. A relative of the cabbage, more grown on the Continent than in British gardens. Cultivation is exactly the same as for autumn cabbage (133). Seed should be sown in March or April and plants put out on well-manured soil in June. Allow them at least 2 ft. each way and water well in dry weather. Gather the mid-ribs of the outer leaves first and the hearts last.

Cress. See Mustard and Cress (158).

144. Cucumbers, Ridge. Beds should be prepared in the open in the same manner as for vegetable marrows (179), except that it is an advantage to build the soil and manure into a low mound or ridge so that the plants are as fully exposed to the sun as possible. Seed is sown singly in small pots in a frame or greenhouse as advised for marrows. The plants, after hardening off, are planted on their mounds in early June. Plant 3–4 ft. apart, and pinch out the tips of each runner when it has made about six leaves. Later, train the side shoots evenly to cover the surface of the bed, fixing them in position with wooden or galvanized-wire pegs. Water freely and feed once a week with weak liquid manure as soon as the first fruits start to swell. Fertilize female flowers (distinguishable by the embryo cucumbers immediately behind them) with pollen from the male blooms. Cutting should begin as soon as the most forward cucumbers are of usable size and should continue regularly throughout the season.

Varieties are Stockwood Ridge and Perfection.

145. Cucumbers, Frame. These may be grown in either greenhouses or frames. Amateurs will be well advised not to sow before the end of February in a heated greenhouse, or mid-April in an unheated one. In a frame on a hotbed (514) sowing may start early in April. The seeds are best sown singly in small pots in the same manner as vegetable marrows (179), and the early treatment is similar.

Planting should be done when the seedlings have two rough leaves each. Prepare the bed either on the ground or on the greenhouse staging. Slates or sheets of corrugated iron make a good base. On this spread some old clinkers or straw and then a 6-in. layer of rough turfy loam mixed with about one-third its own bulk of well-rotted stable manure and a good sprinkling of bonemeal and wood ashes. At intervals of 3 ft. make low mounds (or one mound to each 4 ft. by 3 ft. light in a frame), each consisting of $\frac{1}{2}$ bushel of the same compost, and plant one cucumber on the summit of each. Place a stake to each plant and make it secure.

Train the main stem towards the apex of the house, pinching out its tip when it reaches this, and tie in side growths to horizontal wires 15 in. apart and 9 in. below the glass. Pinch out tip of each side growth two leaves beyond the first fruit. In frames pinch out tip of each plant when it is about 6 inches high. Spread out the side shoots that result evenly around each plant and peg to the soil. They are, in turn, stopped when they have formed about six leaves. It is the tertiary side shoots from these that will produce fruits. Male flowers should be removed, as, unlike ridge cucumbers, it is undesirable that the female flowers should be fertilized.

Water freely and syringe twice daily with tepid water to keep the atmosphere moist. Little air will be needed at first, but open the top ventilators when the temperature reaches

75°. As soon as surface roots appear, a top dressing of the same compost as that used to form the mounds should be given. This may be repeated whenever more surface roots appear. Liquid manure is not required until plants are fruiting freely, when weekly or bi-weekly doses will be appreciated. Shade is necessary from late May.

Telegraph, Butchers' Disease Resister, and Conqueror are reliable free-cropping varieties. The last-named is particularly good for unheated greenhouses or frames. Feminex has nearly all female flowers.

Red spider and white fly are the commonest pests. Gummosis, foot rot, wilt, and mildew are the worst diseases (711).

146. Endive. One of the virtues of this is its hardiness, which makes it possible to secure supplies in winter at a time when lettuces are difficult to produce. Soil should be rich in order to ensure quick growth and tender leaves. Dung at the rate of 1 cwt. to 8 sq. yd. may be supplemented by a top dressing of superphosphate at 1 oz. per square yard just prior to sowing. During the summer one or two top dressings of nitrate of soda, Nitro-chalk, or sulphate of ammonia may be given between the rows at the rate of 1 oz. to 12 ft., but should be discontinued after August.

Seed may be sown in small quantities at intervals between April and mid-August, but it is the later sowings that are most useful. Sow thinly in drills $\frac{1}{2}$ in. deep and 1 ft. apart, and thin seedlings to 9 in. apart. The thinnings can be transplanted elsewhere, and in October it is a good plan to place some in a frame or cloche to maintain supply if the weather is severe. Blanching must be done when the plants have attained sufficient size for use. The simplest method is to cover the centre of each plant with an inverted plate or saucer and leave this undisturbed until the leaves have become white, which usually takes about six weeks.

Varieties are Moss Curled, Green Curled, and Batavian.

147. Garlic. Useful as a flavouring. The cultivation of garlic is similar to that of shallots (172). Old cloves or clusters of bulbs are split up in February or early March and replanted 6 in. apart in rows 1 ft. apart. Just cover the bulbs with soil. Lift in July when the foliage turns yellow and lay in a sunny place for a few days to dry off. Then store in a dry, cool, but frost-proof place.

148. Good King Henry. Used as a substitute for spinach and a valuable plant as it is perennial, very hardy, and will grow almost anywhere. Seed can be sown outdoors in March or April, or plants can be purchased and established at the same time. Seedlings or plants should be spaced 1 ft. apart in rows 18 in. apart. Choose a sunny position and reasonably rich soil. A plantation will continue to crop for many years, and young leaves can be gathered throughout the spring and early summer as required.

149. Gourds and Pumpkins. These are used for jam making and also for pies. Cultivation is identical with that of marrows (179), with the exception that the fruits are allowed to grow fully and become ripe before they are cut. They may be stored in a cool, dry place for many months.

150. Horseradish. Obtain good roots in March, and plant in holes made with a long dibber. These holes should be 1 ft. apart each way and deep enough to allow the roots to be dropped in and covered with 4 in. of soil. No further cultivation, beyond occasional weeding and hoeing, will be necessary. Instead of leaving the bed from year to year to become over-crowded, all roots should be lifted in November and the thickest and straightest laid in sand, ashes, or dry soil in any shed or outhouse for use, the remainder being trimmed up, tied in small bundles, and placed in sand or ashes outdoors, ready for re-planting the following March. The only preparation needed for the soil is thorough digging and the application of a little manure or compost.

151. Indian Corn (Maize). A favourite vegetable in America and now more widely grown in this country. It is the seed heads or cobs which are eaten, and these are cut while the seeds themselves are still milky if opened up. Seed is sown singly in small pots in late April and germinated in a frame or, alternatively, seeds are sown in early May outdoors where the plants are to grow. If the latter procedure is adopted, the seeds should be sown in twos or threes 18 in. apart in rows 3 ft. apart. This is also the correct spacing for planting seedlings raised in pots. Seedlings are planted outdoors at the end of May after proper hardening off. Fairly rich soil is required and a sunny, preferably sheltered position. Water freely or mulch with grass clippings as the cobs commence to form. At this period go over plants occasionally and shake the plumes of male flowers to scatter pollen over the female 'tassels' which protrude from the ends of the cobs. Examine cobs for gathering when tassels wither, and remove as soon as the seeds become milky. Only sweetcorn varieties are used for cooking, others for ornament and stock feeding.

Reliable varieties are Earliking, First of All, Golden Bantam, Kelvedon Glory and John Innes Hybrid.

152. Kale (Borecole). This name covers a group of vegetables rather than one kind. They are of great importance on account of their hardiness, ease of culture, and heavy-cropping qualities. Culture is in all details the same as for sprouting broccoli (131). Plants are put out in July and August, often on the ground cleared of early and mid-season peas and potatoes, and are in use from November to May.

Varieties grown for their leaves cooked as greens are Curled Scotch, of which there are dwarf and tall forms, and Victoria. Varieties grown for their young shoots are Asparagus Kale, Cottager's Kale, Thousand-headed Kale, Russian Kale and Hungry Gap.

Foes as for cabbages (133).

153. Kohl Rabi. This is grown for its swollen stems, which are cooked and eaten like turnips. Good crops can be obtained during summers which are too hot and dry for turnips. Soil preparation is exactly as for turnips (178), and the same fertilizers should be employed. Seed is sown thinly in drills $\frac{1}{2}$ in. deep and 18 in. apart, and the seedlings are thinned to 1 ft. apart. If this is done a little at a time, some of the later thinnings will have grown sufficiently to be of use for the pot.

Successional sowings, from early April until early August, are necessary to even out the supply.

154. Leeks. These make heavy demands on the land. Farmyard or stable manure or good vegetable compost should be dug in during autumn or winter at the rate of 1 cwt. to 10 sq. yd. Just prior to planting out, a dressing should be given of a mixture of 3 parts of superphosphate, 1 part of sulphate of ammonia, and 1 part of sulphate of potash, used at the rate of 2 oz. per square yard. Seed is sown thinly in drills $\frac{1}{4}$ in. deep and 9 in. apart between the middle and end of March. For an early crop and exhibition, seed is sown in a warm greenhouse in January or February.

Planting is done with a stout, steel-shod dibber. With this, holes are prepared 9 in. deep and 9 in. apart in rows 18 in. apart, and one plant dropped well down into each. Do not make any attempt to refill the holes with soil, but simply water the plants in thoroughly. This deep planting will blanch the stems without need for much further earthing up. For exhibition, leeks are planted with a trowel in shallow trenches prepared as advised for celery (138), and the soil is gradually drawn around the stems as they lengthen. This method results in very large, well-blanched stems. Nitrate of soda, Nitro-chalk, or sulphate of ammonia may be used at 1 oz. to 10 ft. of row, or soot at 1 oz. to 4 ft. when plants are well established. Lifting and storing are unnecessary. Leeks are quite hardy and may be left in the ground all the winter, being lifted as the occasion arises when required for use.

Varieties of merit are Musselburgh and The Lyon.

Principal foes are as for onions (159).

155. Lettuce. There are three types, the cabbage, cos and loose leaf. Choice may be determined by personal taste, some people liking the crispness of the cos, while others prefer the softness of the cabbage and loose-leaf types. Soil must be rich and well prepared to encourage quick growth. Manure or compost should be worked in prior to planting at the rate of 1 cwt. to 10 sq. yd. Just prior to seed sowing, the soil should be dressed with a mixture of 5 parts of superphosphate, 2 parts of sulphate of ammonia, and 2 parts of sulphate of potash at the rate of 3 oz. per square yard.

Seed should be sown thinly in drills $\frac{1}{2}$ in. deep and 1 ft. apart for the bigger varieties or 9 in. for small kinds such as Tom Thumb. Small successional sowings should be made about once every three weeks from the end of March to the middle of August. Earlier supplies can be obtained by sowing in February in a greenhouse or in a frame or cloche on a hot-bed (514). Sow broadcast in shallow boxes; prick seedlings out 2 in. apart each way into similar boxes as soon as they can be handled. Then the plants can be gradually accustomed to outdoor conditions in readiness for planting out in mid-April. Winter supplies can be obtained by sowing in a frame during the first week in October and transplanting the seedlings to another frame or greenhouse when they can be handled. It is very important with all lettuces grown under glass to plant shallowly. The lowest leaves must be above soil level or damping off may occur.

Thinning out of seedlings raised in the open should be done as soon as they have two or three true leaves each. Leave the plants standing 6–9 in. apart in the rows. The thinnings can be replanted in another bed.

An occasional dusting of soot (1 oz. to 4 ft.) or of nitrate of soda, Nitro-chalk, or sulphate of ammonia (1 oz. to 12 ft.) may be given between the rows. Discontinue application of fertilizers as hearts form.

Reliable kinds are – *Cabbage type:* Continuity, All the Year Round, Trocadero, Webb's Wonderful, and Tom Thumb; *Cos type:* Little Gem and Paris White. For autumn and winter use, Arctic King and Imperial (cabbage) and Winter Density (cos) are reliable. For frame or greenhouse culture the cabbage varieties May Queen, Delta and Cheshunt Early Giant are recommended. Salad Bowl is a good loose-leaf (heartless) variety. Buttercrunch is intermediate and semi-hearted.

Aphids on leaf and root, cutworms, and slugs are the pests most to be feared. Grey mould, mildew and damping off, the worst fungal diseases (711).

156. Mint. Choose an open position and one where the plants can spread some distance without becoming a nuisance. Roots should be obtained in March and be strewn thinly all over the selected site, then covered with $1\frac{1}{2}$ in. of finely broken soil. Almost any ground will grow mint, but it is an advantage if a little manure or compost can be dug in first. If a winter supply is required, some roots should be lifted in October or November, placed in shallow boxes and lightly covered with soil. Then place them in a warm greenhouse, where they will soon produce fresh green shoots.

Mint rust is the only important disease (711).

157. Mushrooms. These can be grown in sheds, outhouses, cellars, mine workings, frames and greenhouses if darkened, and outdoors. Outdoor beds are unreliable, as an even temperature and cool, damp atmosphere are essential for success. Fresh horse manure or straw or chaff treated with special proprietary preparations are necessary for making the compost. If manure is used it should be strawy and free from shavings and must be obtained from horses that are in good health. Remove twigs or other refuse and make into a stack 3 ft. high Cover with 1 in. of soil. After a week shake and mix thoroughly; water any parts that appear dry and stack again but without soil. Continue in this manner every four or five days for about three weeks. By this time the manure and straw should have rotted to an even texture and dark brown colour and should smell sweet, without trace of ammonia. Place in boxes 9–12 in. deep or build into beds 8–10 in. deep, 2–3 ft. wide, and any convenient length. For outdoor cultivation, ridge beds 3 ft. wide and 2½ ft. in height are to be preferred. In either method the manure should be trodden down firmly little by little as the bed is filled. Place a thermometer in the bed and wait till the temperature falls to between 70° and 75°F. Then break up purchased spawn into pieces the size of a walnut and place one every 9 in., 1 in. beneath the surface. Cover with a layer of straw 6 in. thick under cover, 1 ft. outdoors. Ten days to a fortnight later examine the bed to discover whether the spawn is running i.e. producing white filaments of mycelium. If so, remove the straw and case the bed with peat or good soil to a thickness of 1½ in. for ridge beds, 1 in. for flat beds. Re-cover outdoor beds with straw or matting. Under cover, if temperature can be controlled, maintain at about 65° until mushrooms appear, when it may fall to 55°–60°. Maintain a damp atmosphere throughout. Water if beds become dry, but avoid watering overmuch. Indoor beds can be made at any time; outdoor beds are best made in July.

If proprietary preparations are used to convert straw or chaff into mushroom compost, obtain manufacturers' directions for use and follow these closely.

Maggots are the principal foes (711).

158. Mustard and Cress. Two of the most easily and rapidly grown salad vegetables. Sowing may commence under glass in January in a temperature of 60° to 65°. Outdoors it is not wise to start sowing until mid-April or to continue after August. Shallow boxes are used for greenhouse cultivation, and these may be filled with any fine soil. Sow evenly and fairly thickly, press into the surface with a smooth flat piece of wood and do not cover with any soil. Place a slate or board over each box, but tilt this as soon as seedlings appear and remove a day later. Water when necessary with lukewarm water. Outdoors seeds can be broadcast on the surface of finely broken soil and pressed in as described, and then covered with a sack or mat until germination takes place. Cut with a pair of scissors just above soil level when seedlings are 2–3 in. in height. Cress takes twelve to eighteen days to reach cutting stage; mustard eight to twelve days.

Damping off is the only serious disease (711).

159. Onions. Dung or compost should be dug in as long as possible in advance of seed sowing at 1 cwt. to 12 sq. yd. Bonfire ashes can also be worked in at $\frac{1}{2}$ lb. per square yard. Alternatively, give sulphate or muriate of potash just before sowing at 1 oz. per square yard. In any case apply either basic slag or bonemeal at 4 oz. per square yard, with the dung, or superphosphate of lime, 2 oz. per square yard, before sowing. Seed for the main crop should be sown as early in March as the state of the ground will permit. Sow thinly in drills $\frac{1}{2}$ in. deep and 9 in. apart. Later, thin seedlings to 6 in. apart. This can be done gradually, the thinnings being used for salads.

For an early supply, seed may be sown in the same way at the end of August. The seedlings will then stand the winter without thinning, and in the spring some can be used for salad and some be planted 6 in. apart in rows 1 ft. apart in a well-prepared bed. Bulbs can be used direct from the ground from June to September, while from the spring sowing bulbs will be lifted in early September and stored for autumn and winter. An alternative method is to sow thinly in boxes in a warm greenhouse in January and harden off (515) for planting out in April.

Give one or two top dressings of nitrate of soda, 1 oz. to 12 ft. of row, during May and June, to encourage growth. In mid-August the leaves should be bent over at the neck to check further growth and encourage ripening of the bulbs. Lifting should be done with a fork in September. Leave the bulbs on the ground or place them in a greenhouse, frame, or shed to dry out for a few days and then store in a cool, dry place. Bulbs with thick soft necks do not keep well. Another method of growing onions is by sets or small bulbs. These are planted in April 6 in. apart in rows 12 in. apart. The sets should be pressed firmly into the soil to a third of their depth.

Varieties for spring sowing are Ailsa Craig, James's Keeping, Bedfordshire Champion, and Rousham Park Hero. For autumn sowing, Giant Rocca and Solidity are recommended. White Lisbon is useful for salads. Stuttgarter Reisen is a good variety for sets.

Mildew, neck rot, white rot, eelworms, and onion fly are the worst foes (711).

160. Parsley. In order to ensure an all-year supply, three sowings should be made, the first towards the end of March or early in April, the second in June, and the third early in August. The first two can be made in any open position, but the last should be made in as sheltered a position as possible. Even so, it is advisable to transplant some of the seedlings to a frame, or alternatively cover them with cloches, in October. Ground should be moderately rich, and the seed should be sown as thinly as possible, in drills $\frac{1}{4}$ in. deep and 6 or 8 in. apart. Thin out seedlings to 5 in. apart.

161. Parsnips. Soil should be dug deeply to encourage the production of long, unforked roots. Manure is not desirable before sowing, but choose, if possible, a plot that had manure or compost for some previous crop. In any case apply prior to sowing a mixture of 4 parts of superphosphate, 1 part of sulphate of ammonia, and 1 part of sulphate or muriate of potash at the rate of 3 oz. per square yard. Lime is necessary on acid soils and should be applied as hydrated lime, 8 oz. per square yard, during the autumn or winter. Sow seed as early in March as the weather will permit. Drills should be 1 in. deep and 18 in. apart, and later, seedlings must be thinned out to 8 in. apart. Give one top dressing of nitrate of soda, Nitro-chalk, or sulphate of ammonia at the rate of 1 oz. to 12 ft. of row after thinning. Roots may be left in the ground all the winter if desired, and be dug as required. It is usually convenient, however, to lift a proportion in November and store in sand or ashes in a shed or other place.

For exhibition roots, deep holes are made 1 ft. apart in rows 2 ft. apart with a crowbar and filled with fine soil. Two seeds are sown in the top of each hole in early March and seedlings are thinned later to one per hole. The roots follow the line of least resistance and so are perfectly straight.

Reliable varieties are Avonresister (resistant to carrot fly), Tender and True, The Student, and Hollow Crown.

Carrot fly, which causes a rusty condition of the roots often erroneously called 'canker,' is the commonest pest.

162. Peas. Digging should be done thoroughly as early in the autumn as possible. Dung or compost should be applied at the same time at the rate of 1 cwt. to 15 sq. yd. unless the peas are to be grown on ground that has been well manured for a preceding crop. Chemical fertilizers should be used just before seed sowing, whether manure is given or not. Use a mixture prepared with 3 parts of superphosphate, 2 parts of sulphate of potash, and 1 part of sulphate of ammonia, and scatter at 2 oz. per yard or row for a width of 1 ft. on each side of the drill.

A first sowing of a hardy early pea may be made in a sheltered place outdoors late in February. The seeds may first be damped with a very little paraffin and then rolled in red lead as a protection against mice. Scoop out a trench the width of a spade and just over an inch in depth and sow a double line of peas in this, one at each side, the peas themselves being about 3 in. apart in the lines. Then cover with soil. A second sowing of an early variety should be made in mid-March and a third in early April. At about the latter date the first maincrop peas should be sown. Another sowing of maincrops may follow at the end of the month, a final sowing being made at the end of May with, if desired, a few rows of a first early variety sown about midsummer to give the chance of young peas in October if the season is favourable. Successive rows should be at least as far apart as the eventual height of the peas. It is an advantage if the taller peas can be sown in rows running north and south.

Sticking will be necessary for all peas over 18 in. in height and is an advantage even with dwarf peas. Water freely during dry weather. If water is scarce, spread a mulch of strawy manure or grass clippings 2 or 3 in. thick for a width of 1 ft. on each side of the row.

Reliable kinds are as follows: *Earlies* – Little Marvel, Peter Pan, Kelvedon Wonder, Kelvedon Triumph, Foremost, Gradus, and Thomas Laxton. *Maincrop* – Alderman, Autocrat, Stratagem, Onward, Admiral Beatty, Giant Stride, Lord Chancellor, and Gladstone.

The principal foes are mildew and thrips (711).

163. Potatoes. These are first rate for cleaning newly broken grassland, as their heavy growth smothers weeds and their big root systems break up the clods of soil, leaving the land in good condition for succeeding crops. Soil should be dug at least 10 in. deep as early in the autumn as possible and left rough for the winter. Manure or compost may be applied at 1 cwt. to 15 sq. yd. Lime should not be used unless the ground is known to be sour, when application should be restricted to about 6 oz. per square yard of hydrated lime. This may be given as a top dressing six or eight weeks after digging in the manure. Chemical fertilizers should be employed, whether or not dung is available. See (91), (92).

The best planting sets come from districts in Scotland and Ireland in which virus diseases are almost unknown. Home-saved planting sets may be used for one year, provided there has been no virus disease, but new stock should be imported from virus-free districts at least every second year. Sets should be obtained as early as possible. Immediately on arrival, stand them with their eyed ends uppermost in shallow boxes and place these in a light but frost-proof place.

Early potatoes may be planted outdoors in a sheltered position in early March. Maincrop varieties are planted during April. Spacing for earlies should be 1 ft. apart in rows $2\frac{1}{2}$ ft. apart; for maincrop kinds 15 in. apart in rows 3 ft. apart Methods of planting vary greatly. One of the simplest is to take out with a spade a V-shaped trench about 5 in. in depth. The tubers are spaced in this, care being taken to keep the shoots uppermost and not to break any, and the soil removed is drawn back with a rake or draw hoe. Large tubers may be cut so that each section has at least two sprouts.

Earthing up must begin as soon as the shoots appear through the soil. This is particularly important in the case of the earliest-planted potatoes, as the sprouts may be killed by May frosts. Pull soil over them with a draw hoe and continue to earth up week by week until the ground is all drawn up in flat-topped ridges about 9 in. in height. Digging of earlies can start as soon as the tubers are of usable size. For late varieties digging should be delayed until the skins of the tubers are mature and will not rub off readily. Exception to this rule may be necessary if disease is severe, when it may be desirable to lift the crop without delay to save what there is. If some tubers are to be saved for planting the following year, good plants should be marked for the purpose and dug before their tubers are quite ripe. The tubers should then be left on the surface for a few days to green. Potatoes for eating must not be allowed to green.

Store all in sacks in a dark, dry shed, outhouse, etc., temperature 40–45° F., or in clamps in the open. These are ridge-shaped mounds of tubers, 4–6 ft. through at the base, covered with 6 in. of clean straw and 9 in. of beaten soil, Clamps must be made in a well-drained place. It is an advantage to place straw beneath the potatoes. A handful of straw should be drawn through the soil every 3 ft. along the ridge for ventilation.

Varieties are numerous. A few of the best are as follows— *Earlies:* Ulster Chieftain, *Home Guard, *Arran Pilot, Sharpe's Express, Duke of York, *Ulster Chieftain, Ulster Premier, Ulster Prince and Epicure. *Second Early and Maincrop:* *Arran Banner, *Arran Peak, King Edward, *Catriona, *Dunbar Standard, *Great Scot, *Pentland Dell, *Majestic, *Dr McIntosh and *Craig's Royal. Those varieties marked with an asterisk are immune to wart disease.

The principal diseases are potato blight, virus, scab, wart disease, and blackleg. Slugs, eelworms, and wireworms are pests which do much damage (711).

164. Radishes. Soil can scarcely be too rich, and liberal dressings of dung or compost may be given. There is no better place for the earlier sowings than the beds prepared for winter greens. Radishes sown there in March or April will be used before most of the greens are ready for planting out. Seed should be sown in small batches every fortnight from the end of March until August. Even earlier supplies can be obtained by sowing in a frame or cloche in February. Sow seed thinly all over the bed and cover lightly by sifting a little dry soil over it. Growth will be rapid, and no further attention should be necessary until the roots are large

94

enough for pulling. Use the most forward first. Winter radishes can be obtained by sowing suitable varieties in July or August in rows 9 in. apart and thinning to 4 in.

French Breakfast and Wood's Frame are good varieties for spring and summer use; Black Spanish and China Rose for winter use.

165. Rhubarb. Soil should be rather .rich, and plenty of dung or compost can be dug in if available. Dust the surface with basic slag at the rate of 6 oz. per square yard. Strong roots should be obtained in early March and planted with a spade 3 ft. apart each way. The crowns should just appear on the surface of the ground when all the soil has been returned. Plant firmly, treading the soil around the roots. The young stems are pulled away from the crowns as they attain sufficient size. It is a mistake to take too many from one plant as this weakens it, and for the same reason it is not wise to continue pulling after July. Outdoors, without any forcing, supplies will be available from about mid - April onwards, but earlier sticks can be obtained by covering roots with barrels, drainpipes, boxes, or special forcing pots in early January and heaping manure or leaves over these. All light must be excluded.

If rhubarb is required earlier in the year, it will be necessary to force in a heated greenhouse or shed. Roots should be dug as required from early November onwards, and be exposed for a day or so to frost. Then they are packed into boxes with light soil around them and are placed under the staging in the greenhouse or in any other convenient place from which light can be excluded, and in which a temperature of from 60° to 75° can be maintained. Water moderately at first, but freely as growth begins.

Rhubarb can also be raised from seed sown thinly in a frame in March. Thin seedlings to at least 6 in. and transplant to permanent quarters the following spring.

Champagne, The Sutton, and Victoria are reliable varieties and give sticks of fine red colour. Glaskin's Perpetual is a particularly good variety to raise from seed.

166. Sage. Plants should be obtained in the spring and planted at least 18 in. apart in any sunny and ordinary, though preferably well-drained, soil. If at any time it is desired to work up a further stock, cuttings can be rooted during August or September. Prepare these from firm young growths 3 or 4 in. in length. Sever each immediately below a joint, remove the lower leaves and insert in sandy soil in a frame or under a cloche, keeping shaded and well watered until rooted.

167. Salsify. Grown for its roots, which look much like those of parsnip (161) and are cooked in the same way. Cultivation is also similar to that of parsnip, and the soil is prepared in the same way. Sow seed in April in drills $\frac{1}{2}$ in. deep and 1 ft. apart; thin seedlings to 6 or 8 in. apart. Lift roots in November and store in sand or ashes until required.

168. Savoy. This is a type of cabbage with crinkled leaves. Savoys are very hardy and of great value during the winter months. Cultivation is identical with that of winter cabbage (133) and seed should be sown during April and early May. Plants should be put out during June, July, and August, the later ones following early potatoes and peas. Varieties are numerous and should be chosen for succession. Good kinds are Best of All, Christmas Drumhead, Ormskirk Early, Medium and Late, Rearguard, Autumn Green, and Omega.

Foes as for cabbage (133).

169. Scorzonera. A root vegetable very little grown in this country. Cultivation is similar to that of parsnip (161), and soil is prepared in the same way. Seed should be sown in early May and roots lifted towards the end of September for storing in sand or ashes in a frost-proof frame. The roots are boiled in the same way as those of parsnip (161) or salsify (167).

170. Seakale. Grown for blanching both outdoors and under glass. Plants may be raised from seed sown outdoors in April, but two years must elapse before seedlings are strong enough for forcing. A better method is to purchase crowns and maintain a stock by root cuttings. These are prepared from thongy roots about 6 in. in length. Plant either crowns or root cuttings in March 1 ft. aprt in rows 18 in. apart, dropping them into dibber holes and just covering with soil. Take care that root cuttings are planted the right way up. By November they will have developed into strong crowns, some of which may be lifted for forcing. Trim off side roots from which further cuttings can be prepared, tie in bundles, and lay in sand or ashes until March. Stack the crowns right way up beneath a wall facing north and surround with sand or ashes. Pot up a few crowns at a time, three or four in a 7-in. pot, and bring into a heated greenhouse, placing beneath the staging and keeping quite dark. Cut growth at soil level when 6–9 in. in length. The shoots should be perfectly white. In January, crowns left outdoors can be covered with boxes or inverted flower pots, or soil or ashes may be piled over them to effect blanching.

171. Seakale Beet. This closely resembles spinach beet and cultivation is identical. The only point of difference is that the mid-rib of each leaf is very large and fleshy and can be used as a substitute for seakale, the green portion of the leaves being stripped off and boiled as spinach. For other details see spinach beet (174).

172. Shallots. Soil should be well cultivated, but need not be so rich as for onions. It is an advantage if a plot can be chosen that has been manured for the preceding crop. In any case, apply a mixture of 3 parts of superphosphate, 2 parts of sulphate or muriate of potash and 1 part of sulphate of ammonia, at 3 oz. per square yard, prior to planting. This is done as early in February as the weather will allow. Good bulbs saved from the previous crop are pushed firmly two-thirds their depth into the soil. They should be spaced 6 in. apart in rows 9 in. apart. The bulbs should be ripe and ready for harvesting at the end of June. A week or so before this, draw the soil away from the clusters of bulbs so that they are exposed to the light and can swell readily. After lifting with a fork, lay the clusters on the surface or in a frame for a few days to dry off. Then separate the bulbs and store them in a in a dry, cool place. Hâtive de Niort is the most shapely variety but Giant Red and Giant Yellow crop more heavily.

Foes are as for onions, but virus disease is also sometimes very troublesome (711).

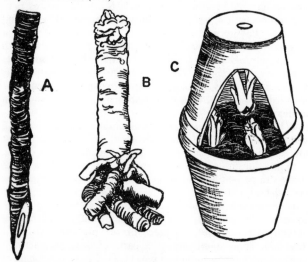

Culture of Seakale. (A) Suitable thong or root cutting for planting out; (B) a sturdy crown lifted for forcing; (C) forcing crowns potted up and covered to ensure proper blanching.

173. Spinach. Soil for summer spinach should be rich and rather moist. Dung or compost may be used at 1 cwt. to 10 sq. yd. It is often possible to take a catch crop (115) of spinach off ground already prepared for some other vegetable, but which will not actually be required for a month or so. For summer supplies it is an advantage to sow in partial shade, and in dry places spinach may be grown in furrows about 3 in. deep and 10 in. wide as these can be easily flooded with water.

For winter spinach a sheltered but sunny position should be chosen, and the soil must not be quite so rich. Sulphate of potash, $\frac{1}{2}$ oz. per square yard, should be applied prior to sowing.

Sowing of summer spinach should start in early March and continue at intervals of three or four weeks until mid-July. Then in mid-August a sowing of winter spinach may be made. The seed should always be sown very thinly in drills 1 in. deep and about 1 ft. apart. Thin out the seedlings to 4 in. apart as soon as they can be handled and a little later to 8 in. Give a light top dressing of nitrate of soda, Nitro-chalk, or sulphate of ammonia at 1 oz. to 12 ft. between the rows, after thinning summer spinach, and in March for the winter kind. The outer leaves should be cut as soon as they attain sufficient size.

174. Spinach Beet. A form of beetroot, grown solely for its leaves. These are cut as they become large enough, and are used as a substitute for spinach. The plants continue to crop for months and are very hardy. Soil is prepared as for summer spinach (173), but there is no need to choose a partially shady position for either summer or winter supplies. Seed should be sown twice to ensure an all-year supply, the first time in late March or early April, and the second in mid-August. Sow the seeds in pairs about 9 in. apart in rows 18 in. apart and, if all germinate, single them out later.

175. Swedes. These are grown in exactly the same way as turnips (178) and are especially servicable for storing for winter use. For this purpose seed should be sown during May or June in drills $\frac{1}{2}$ in. deep and 15 in. apart. Thin to 8 in. apart and lift for use as required or store a few like parsnips (161). Purple Top, Bronze Top, and Green Top are the varieties principally grown.

Foes as turnips (178).

Sweet Corn, *see* **Indian Corn (151).**

176. Thyme. Plants will succeed in any sunny position and ordinary soil, but prefer one that is rather light and of a well-drained nature. It is best to start with young plants purchased in the spring and planted 8 or 9 in. apart each way. Alternatively, seeds may be sown thinly in April, either in a frame or in a sheltered border outdoors and covered with $\frac{1}{4}$ in. of soil. Seedlings should be transferred to a sunny bed of finely broken soil in May or early June, and planted 2–3 in. apart each way to develop into sturdy young plants for removal to their final quarters the following spring.

177. Tomatoes. For an early crop under glass, seed should be sown in a warm greenhouse during January or February. In unheated houses it is not wise to start until early April. For outdoor planting, seed is best sown in a warm greenhouse in mid-March. In all methods the seeds should be sown very thinly in well-drained pots or boxes filled with a good seed compost (501). Cover with a light sprinkling of fine soil and place a pane of glass and a sheet of paper over each receptacle until germination takes place. Then give as much light as possible. Prick off into similar trays and compost when the seedlings have formed two rough leaves each, spacing them 2 in. apart each way. When they are about 4 in. in height, pot singly in 3-in. pots, and when these are full of roots remove to 4- or 5-in. pots. For these later pottings use a rougher compost (505). This same compost, with the loam in lumps about the size of a small hen's egg, will also do for the final potting or planting. The plants can be fruited singly in 9-in. pots; in boxes about 1 ft. cube; in 10-in. diameter bottomless rings standing on a 6-in. thick layer of washed boiler ashes or small gravel; or they may be planted 18 in. apart in rows 2½ ft. apart direct in a bed of soil prepared on the floor or staging of the house.

Remove all side growths, and keep each plant to a single stem. Water freely and, when flowers appear, syringe the plants each morning to assist pollination. Top dress the soil with finely broken cow or horse manure when roots appear on the surface, and from the time the first fruits start to swell feed once a week with tomato fertilizer (96).

Temperature throughout should range from 60°–70°. It will not matter if it runs up to 80° at times so long as ample water and ventilation are given. When in full crop the plants may easily require a gallon or more of water each daily. Top ventilation should be given whenever outdoor conditions allow, and side ventilators and doors left open in hot weather.

Outdoors, tomatoes may be planted in early June. Set them 18 in. apart, and if there is more than one row, let these be at least 3 ft. apart and run north and south. Remove all side shoots and pinch out the top of each plant when it has formed four trusses of flowers. Stake each plant securely, and in addition tie up each truss of fruit so that it gets as much sun as possible. In September it may be advisable to remove some of the lower leaves. Tomatoes can also be grown by the ring culture method (733).

Bush tomatoes are grown in the same manner except that they are not restricted to a single stem but are allowed to bush out and each stem is tied to a stake or horizontal wire.

Some reliable varieties are Eurocross A, Ailsa Craig, Potentate, Plumpton King, Market King, E.S.I, Stonor's Exhibition, Moneymaker, Kondine Red, Stonor's M.P.,

Hertford Cross, Ware Cross, and Sunrise. Golden Sunrise has yellow fruits. For outdoor planting, Harbinger and Outdoor Girl are recommended. A good bush variety is The Amateur.

Foes most to be feared are leaf mould, potato blight, virus, streak, wilt (sleepy disease), collar rot, and white fly (711).

178. Turnips. Dung or compost must not be used, but it is an advantage if a plot can be chosen that has been manured for a previous crop. Then it will be sufficient to dig thoroughly in autumn or winter and dust the surface with superphosphate (3 oz. per square yard) and sulphate of potash ($\frac{1}{2}$ oz. per square yard) prior to sowing. If such ground is not available, it will be advisable in addition to give a dressing of soot (8 oz. per square yard) or sulphate of ammonia ($\frac{1}{2}$ oz. per square yard) at the same time. Small successional sowings should be made every three or four weeks from early March until mid-July to supply young roots to be pulled as required. For winter storing, a sowing may be made during the latter half of July. Turnip tops for use as greens in the spring are produced by sowing seed in drills 18 in. apart in early September and leaving the plants unthinned to stand the winter. Seed for the successional sowings may be sown in drills $\frac{1}{2}$ in. deep and 12 in. apart, but for the winter crop the distance between the rows should be increased to 15 in. Similarly, it will be sufficient to thin the summer crops to 4 in. apart, but the winter turnips must have twice this room. Winter turnips should be lifted for storing in October or early November. They are pulled out, the tops are cut off, and the roots are stored in a shed or cellar. Varieties are Golden Ball, Early White Milan, and Early Snowball for summer supplies, Greentop Stone for winter and supplying turnip tops.

Club root, cabbage gall weevil, and flea beetle are the principal foes (711).

179. Vegetable Marrow. The old practice of growing marrows on heaps is not good, as it is difficult to keep them supplied with sufficient moisture. A better plan is to dig out a trench 2 ft. wide and as much in depth and to fill this with a mixture of soil, dung, compost, old leaves, etc. Then, if a little extra soil is built in a low ridge around the bed, it will be a simple matter to flood the whole with water in dry weather. Seed should be sown in mid-April, singly in small pots filled with any good compost, and germination effected in a frame or greenhouse. Outdoors it is not safe to sow until the middle of May. Planting should not be done until early June. Plant bush varieties 3 ft. apart, trailing 4 ft. apart.

The runners of trailing varieties should be pinched out when they have extended 3 ft. This will force the plants to make side growths, which usually bear female flowers, and

Fertilizing a female marrow flower. The female flower has an embryo marrow behind it. The male flower bearing the pollen should be brought into close contact with the sticky stigma of the female flower.

consequently fruits, more freely than the main growths. Fertilize the female flowers, which can be recognized by the embryo fruits just beneath them, by inverting male blooms over them. Cutting should start as soon as the first marrows are of usable size. Only towards the end of the season should a few be allowed to remain to ripen. These, if cut without injury, may be stored for winter use in a cool, dry place.

Good trailing varieties are Long Green Trailing, Long White Trailing and Table Dainty. Good bush varieties are White Custard, Green Bush and White Bush. Courgette is a very prolific trailing variety grown to be cut when the fruits are about 6 in. long.

180. Watercress. One of the most valuable salad vegetables from the point of view of vitamins. May be grown without running water by digging a trench 2 ft. wide and 1 ft. deep, in a sunny position, placing 6 in. of rotten manure in the bottom, covering with 3 in. of soil and sowing seed thinly in April and again in August, or planting cuttings. The trench should be flooded with water fairly frequently while the plants are in growth. Permanent beds are usually made of concrete and are about 4 ft. wide and 6–10 in. in depth. The flow of water should be controlled by suitable sluices or valves. Three inches of good soil should be placed in the bottom of the bed and a little clean gravel or sand on top. Cuttings from selected plants are dibbled into this bed 6 in. apart each way. Usually two plantings are made, one in May or June and the other in October. Restrict water to a depth of $1\frac{1}{2}$ in. at first, but increase slowly according to the growth of the plants. Three to four inches is sufficient under ordinary conditions.

The principal disease is mildew (711).

SECTION FOUR

THE FRUIT GARDEN

MISCELLANEOUS NOTES

181. Arrangement of Trees. There are several ways of arranging the trees in an orchard. The principal are as follows: Square, all trees at equal distances in rows at right angles to one another. Quincunx, as the last with one tree in the middle of each square. Triangular, trees at the points of an equal-sided triangle, this being repeated right through the plantation. Cordons and trained trees are almost always planted in straight, parallel rows or against walls and fences.

In large orchards it is a frequent practice to plant permanent, slow-maturing varieties at the full distance apart with quick-maturing trees or small fruits (e.g. currants, gooseberries, etc.) in between. These latter are known as fillers and are removed after from ten to fifteen years, by which time the permanent trees are beginning to require all the space. A drawback to mixed plantations is the difficulty of carrying out spraying and feeding programmes suitable to all the trees.

182. Cultivation of Orchards. Growth is always slower when the ground beneath trees is grassed than when it is cultivated, but trees tend to be more fruitful and bear fruit of better colour and quality when grassed under. In consequence young trees are usually grown on cultivated ground; but this may be grassed down after eight to ten years. Another scheme with much the same object is to keep ground cultivated until fruit is well formed and then allow the growth of summer weeds for a few weeks, digging or ploughing these in later. The weeds must not be allowed to seed.

On no account must deep cultivation be carried out near established fruit trees, or surface roots will be destroyed. Near large fruits, e.g. apples, pears, plums, cherries, etc., it is not safe to dig more than 4 in. deep. For bush fruits, e.g.

105

currants and gooseberries, 2–3 in. should be regarded as the maximum; strawberries, raspberries, etc., 1–2 in.

183. Unfruitfulness. This may be due to one or other of several causes. Most fruits are only formed if the flowers are fertilized with pollen. In some varieties, e.g. Apple Bramley's Seedling, and Pear Pitmaston Duchess, the flowers carry little or no pollen and fertilization can take place only if another variety of the same kind of fruit which bears pollen liberally is grown near by. In other instances, e.g. most sweet cherries and, to a lesser extent, apples, pears, and plums, pollen is borne freely but is partially or wholly ineffective on flowers of its own variety and sometimes also with flowers of certain other varieties. Varieties which will not produce fruit with their own pollen are said to be 'self-sterile'; those which will bear some fruit with their own pollen but more when cross-pollinated, are described as 'partially self-fertile,' while those with pollen which is wholly effective on their own flowers are 'self-fertile.' Where the pollen of one variety will not fertilize the flowers of another, 'incompatibility' is said to exist between the two.

In planting an orchard it is important that varieties should be assorted in such a manner that the pollen of one fertilizes the flowers of another. Note that flowers can be fertilized only with pollen of the same kind, apples with apples, pears with pears, etc.

Even when the right kind of pollen is available in sufficient quantity it must be carried from flower to flower. This is largely the work of bees and other insects. Lack of these may cause unfruitfulness. This can be overcome by introducing bees or by hand fertilizing the flowers by carrying pollen to them on a camel-hair brush.

Cold, damp weather at blossom time may keep insects away, while frost may kill the blossom outright. This is a particular danger with early-flowering fruits such as peaches, nectarines, cherries, and plums. Under-nourishment of trees may also prevent effective fertilization. This can be remedied by proper feeding.

Young trees that are growing very freely often fail to produce any blossom at all. Their excessive vigour can be checked by opening a trench round them in October and severing the coarser roots (root pruning), or by removing a ring of bark ¼ in. wide from around the main trunk or the base of each main bough in early May (bark ringing). This latter method should not be practised with stone fruits (e.g. plums, cherries, etc.), as it is liable to cause gumming (711).

184. Lorette Pruning. In addition to the methods described under particular fruits a system of pruning has been devised by a Frenchman, M. Lorette, and bears his name. It is particularly applicable to trained apples and pears and, though primarily designed for the French climate, has proved very successful in some places in this country. The object is to force the stipulary buds, at the base of each side growth, to form fruit buds and so, in time, very compact spurs. Normally, these buds remain dormant and are all so small that they can scarcely be seen.

Briefly the system is as follows: At the end of April shorten leaders by about one-third their length. In mid-June prune side growths produced from the remaining portion of each leader if they have attained the thickness of a lead pencil at the base. Only ¼ in. of each is retained. The terminal growth may be retained as a leader. In mid-July any further side growths that were not thick enough to be pruned in June are dealt with in a similar manner. In mid-August the process is repeated on still later side growths, and also any which may have grown from old fruit spurs or other parts of the tree. Any which are still weak should be bent down and tied in that position. No winter pruning is practised.

185. Starting Dormant Buds. Sometimes numerous buds

remain dormant, with the result that whole lengths of branch are bare and profitless. This can be overcome by *knife-edge ringing*, i.e. drawing the edge of a knife right round the stem above the bare portion so that the bark is severed to the wood beneath, or *notching*, i.e. removing a triangular section of bark immediately above each dormant bud. Either operation should be done in early May.

186. Suckers. All fruit trees and bushes are liable to produce suckers. These are not necessarily harmful. That depends partly upon whether the trees are grafted or on their own roots. Most apples, pears, plums, damsons, cherries, peaches, nectarines, and apricots are grafted, or budded, which is simply a form of grafting. The roots are provided by a stock which is of different character from the tree growing upon it. Any suckers, i.e. growths from the root, will therefore be part of the stock. They will, in consequence, produce crab apples, quinces, etc., according to their nature, not good garden apples, pears, etc. Such suckers must be removed right to the root from which they grow. If any stumps are left, these will soon throw out further shoots. Such suckers if retained will tend to crowd the tree with useless growth and sap its strength. If desired, these suckers may be detached in autumn, with a portion of root, and be replanted elsewhere to be grafted or budded in due season.

Most of the smaller bush fruits, i.e. gooseberries, currants, raspberries, etc., are grown from cuttings, layers or suckers and are, consequently, on their own roots. Suckers from these partake of the characteristics of the parent and are not harmful unless they are overcrowding the plant with growth or preventing easy access to it. See (225), (253), (255), (263), (283), (371).

187. Fruit Tree Bands. Bands of grease-proof paper covered with a tacky substance are placed around the trunks or main boughs of apples and also, to a lesser extent, pears, plums, and cherries in mid-September to trap various insects which crawl up or down the trunks during the winter and spring. These bands should be 3 ft. above ground level and at least 4 in. wide. Special banding compound should be purchased to smear on these and must be renewed occasionally during the winter if it loses its tackiness. The bands must be kept in position until April. Alternatively special vegetable greases can be purchased to be smeared directly on the bark. Principal among the foes caught are the wingless females of the winter moths.

Bands of hay or old sacking are tied around the trees in early June to provide a comfortable harbourage for the cocoons of the codling moth (711) and the apple blossom weevil (711). If the bands are removed in October, many of these pests will be found and can be destroyed.

188. Fruits for Special Localities. DAMP PLACES. Black-currants, quinces.

NORTH AND EAST WALLS. Morello cherries, currants, goose-berries and such plums as Czar, Belgian Purple, Oullin's Golden Gage, Rivers' Early Prolific, and Victoria.

SOUTH AND SOUTH-WEST WALLS. Apricots, peaches, nectarines, figs, grapes, and choice dessert plums, pears, and apples.

APPLES

189. Soil and Situation. Apples succeed on a wide variety of soils and in most parts of the country. Fertilization is usually uncertain at altitudes above 700 ft. In such places late-flowering varieties such as Crawley Beauty, Edward VII, Court Pendu Plat, Royal Jubilee, and Orleans Reinette usually give best results. Devonshire Quarrendon, Keswick Codlin, and Margil also succeed. Nitrogen and potash are the two most essential foods; phosphates do not show much result and need be supplied only occasionally. Soil must be dug thoroughly. Manure or compost may be incorporated prior to planting at 1 cwt. to 15 sq. yd. Lime is not essential.

190. Planting. This may be done at any time from late October till mid-March; early November is the best time if soil is in good condition. Roots should be spread out in wide holes sufficiently deep to allow the uppermost roots to be covered with 3–4 in. of soil. Make thoroughly firm and stake securely. The union between stock and scion must not be buried. Distance for planting will depend on type of tree. (See Table (22).) Plant horizontal-trained trees 12–15 ft. apart, in rows at least 6 ft. apart; dwarf pyramids 4 ft. apart, in rows at least 8 ft. apart.

191. Forms of Training. Apples are commonly grown as cordons, either single stemmed or double stemmed, dwarf pyramids, horizontal trained, bush, half-standards, and standards. Cordon trees and dwarf pyramids are suitable for confined places or where fruits of very high quality are required. Horizontal-trained trees are suitable for walls and espaliers and give fruit of excellent quality. Bushes may be used in large fruit gardens and orchards; usually ground is cultivated beneath them. Half-standards and standards are for orchard planting or use as specimens. They are frequently grassed under (182).

192. Pollination. A few varieties of apples are self-sterile, i.e. they will not produce fruit with their own pollen, while all set better crops when cross-pollinated. In consequence, it is unwise to plant apples singly. They should be in company with other varieties of apple blooming at approximately the same time.

193. Pruning. Trained trees and small bushes should be pruned in summer and winter. Large bushes, half-standards and standards are usually pruned in winter only, as summer pruning involves too much labour. SUMMER PRUNING is

POLLINATION TABLE FOR APPLES

Early Flowering	Mid-season Flowering	Late Flowering
Adam's Pearmain	Arthur Turner	Allington Pippin
Astrachan Red	*Blenheim Orange	American Mother
Baumann's Reinette	Bowden's Seedling	Annie Elizabeth
Beauty of Bath	*Bramley's Seedling	Cellini
*Belle de Boskoop	Charles Ross	Court Pendu Plat
Bismarck	Cox's Orange Pippin	Cox's Pomona
Brownlee's Russet	*Crimson Bramley	Crawley Beauty
Duchess of Oldenburg	Devonshire Quarrendon	(very late)
Egremont Russet	Duchess Favourite	Delicious
Golden Spire	Early Victoria	Edward VII
*Gravenstein	Encore	Ellison's Orange
Irish Peach	Epicure	Gascoyne's Scarlet
Keswick Codlin	Exquisite	Heusgen's Golden
Lord Lambourne	Fortune	Reinette
Manx Codlin	George Carpenter	Lady Sudeley
Margil	Golden Noble	Lane's Prince Albert
Norfolk Beauty	Grenadier	Laxton's Pearmain
Rev. W. Wilkes	Howgate Wonder	Lord Derby
*Ribston Pippin	James Grieve	Monarch
St. Edmund's Pippin	John Standish	Newton Wonder
Wagener	King of the Pippins	Northern Greening
Warner's King	*King of Tompkins	Orleans Reinette
Washington	County	*Reinette du Canada
White Transparent	King's Acre Pippin	Royal Jubilee
	Laxton's Superb	Winston
	Lord Grosvenor	Worcester Pearmain
	Merton Prolific	
	Merton Worcester	
	Peasgood's Nonsuch	
	Rival	
	St. Cecilia	
	St. Everard	* Varieties marked with
	Stirling Castle	an asterisk produce little
	Sturmer Pippin	pollen. Pollinator should
	Sunset	be chosen from varieties
	Tydeman's Early	in the same group so
	Tydeman's Orange	that their flowering times
	Wealthy	may coincide.

done during July and August, when side growths are
nearly as thick as lead pencils and starting to get woody at
the base. Each is shortened to five well-developed leaves.
Leading growths (those extending branches) are not pruned
in summer. In November laterals are further cut back to two
buds, and leaders are shortened by a quarter or one-third
their length. The object of this double pruning is to overcome
individual peculiarities of growth and make all trees conform
to one type with fruit-bearing spurs closely clustered along
the main branches. See also Lorette pruning (184).

Where WINTER PRUNING only is carried out, individual
peculiarities must be considered. Some varieties tend to
produce fruit buds all along the stems or mainly at the tips.
Examples are Allington Pippin, Irish Peace, Cornish Gilli-
flower, Gladstone, Lady Sudeley, St Everard, and Worcester
Pearmain. These must be pruned lightly. Tip leaders, remove
badly placed or crossing branches and those growing inwards
but, where possible, retain laterals at full length. Other
varieties produce fruit on long spurs. Examples are Bismarck,
Blenheim Orange, Bramley's Seedling, Encore, and Newton
Wonder. Treat as above, but shorten laterals by one-third.
Most other varieties form short spurs readily. These may have
leaders shortened by one-third and laterals cut to fruit buds
wherever these have formed. Other laterals, unprovided with
fruit buds, may be left unpruned for a further year, if there
is room for them, or be cut back to three or four growth buds
if they are overcrowded. All this work may be done at any time
between late October and early February.

In the illustration on the facing page the following buds are
shown:

1. *a.* Fruit bud on tip of young growth. *b.* Growth bud.
2. *a.* Fruit buds in various positions. *b.* Growth buds. *c.* Sti-
pular buds (Lorette Pruning. (184)).
3. Old spur in need of reduction.

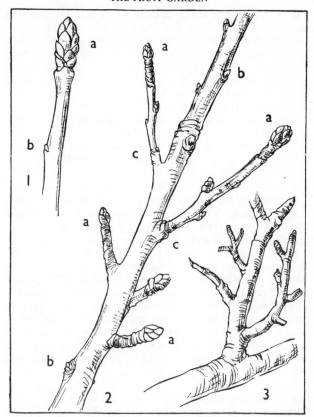

194. Pruning Young Trees. For the first few years growth is more important than fruiting, and pruning must be designed to encourage this. Prune laterals in winter to one or two buds

and shorten leaders to the point at which it is desirable they
should fork. With bush and standard trees this means that
they should be shortened to points at which they are 12–18 in.
apart, considered laterally, or 2–3 ft. apart, considered vertically, these being the correct average spacings for the main
branches. Be particularly careful to remove inward-pointing
shoots in bushes and standards and always to cut leaders to
strong outward-pointing buds.

195. Forming Espaliers. Leading growths of side arms are
shortened by only a few inches. The central vertical growth
is cut back to within about 15 in. of the uppermost pair of
arms. In the spring one shoot from this pruned central stem
is trained vertically and two more are tied down to left and
right to form a new pair of arms. When sufficient arms have
been obtained, the vertical shoot is cut right out and prevented
from re-forming. The same treatment is given to the leading
shoots of arms when these have extended far enough.

196. Forming Cordons. The leading growth is not pruned at
all until the tree has grown to the maximum desired height.
It is then cut out and prevented from re-forming. Laterals are
summer and winter pruned from the outset (193). Cordons
are frequently planted at an angle of 45°, mainly to enable a
greater length of stem to be obtained within reach from the
ground, but also to check the spring uprush of sap and so
obtain more even production of side growths throughout the
length of the tree. The pruning of dwarf pyramids is very
similar except that side shoots are given more liberty and may
eventually be permitted to grow out to a length of a foot
or two.

197. Thinning Fruits. This is necessary if the set is heavy.
Thinning should start in June but not be completed until
July, as there is often a natural drop towards the end of June.
Large cooking varieties require more drastic thinning than
small dessert kinds. In general, not more than one fruit should

remain per spur after final thinning, but frequently this may be exceeded with dessert varieties. Large cookers should be spaced 8 in. apart after final thinning, but this may be deferred until the fruits are large enough to be of service. Always retain the most perfect fruits. Watch carefully for any holed by maggots. Thinning may be done by hand or with pointed vine scissors.

198. Picking. This should start as soon as fruits part readily from the branches. Test by lifting and gently pulling a typical fruit. If it breaks away easily, continue to gather; if it can only be dragged or torn away by force, leave the remainder longer. All fruits should be gathered by the third week in October.

199. Storing. Only the later varieties are suitable for storing. Early varieties shrivel rapidly and must be used within a few weeks of gathering. The apple store should be cool, moderately ventilated, but with a slightly damp atmosphere. An earthen floor and thatched roof are ideal. Fruits keep best if wrapped singly in waxed paper and placed in three or four layers in boxes. Cooking varieties may be laid out thinly on slatted shelves. Too much ventilation and too dry an atmosphere encourage early shrivelling.

200. Routine Feeding. Each spring, spread well-rotted dung or compost round trees at the rate of 1 cwt. to 15 sq. yd. for full presumed root spread. Each autumn, give sulphate or muriate of potash at the rate of $\frac{3}{4}$–$1\frac{1}{2}$ oz. per sq. yd. over same area. Every second autumn give, in addition, basic slag, at 4 oz. per sq. yd. If growth is poor and fruits undersized, give sulphate of ammonia, nitrate of soda, or Nitrochalk in April at 1 oz. per sq. yd. Alternatively, use fruit tree fertilizer (97).

201. Routine Pest Control. Apart from steps taken against pests or diseases which actually occur, it is wise to undertake certain routine measures. In January all trees are sprayed

115

with tar-oil or DNOC winter wash (669) to destroy eggs, hibernating insects, etc. In late March and April trees are sprayed with lime sulphur (675), full winter strength, or captan (649) against scab. Two applications are given, the first while the flower buds are still green and tight clustered, the second when they first loosen out and become pink. With this second dose derris (662) is mixed to kill caterpillars. Lime sulphur (675) at summer strength is applied about ten days after petal fall, or captan may be used every fortnight until August. In mid-September grease bands (187) are placed round the trunks of the trees to prevent female winter moths, etc., from ascending to lay their eggs. The bands must be kept sticky until they are finally removed in April.

202. Lime-sulphur and Bordeaux Scorching. Certain varieties of apples may be scorched by lime sulphur, especially if applied after blossom fall. The principal kinds are Beauty of Bath, Belle de Boskoop, Cox's Orange Pippin, Lane's Prince Albert, Lord Derby, Newton Wonder, Rival, and Stirling Castle. Beauty of Bath, Cox's Orange Pippin, Lane's Prince Albert and Lord Derby are also damaged by copper fungicides. These varieties should be sprayed with captan which harms none of them.

203. Propagation. By grafting in March and early April or by budding from mid-July until mid-September. Many methods of grafting are employed, but three, whip grafting (205), rind grafting (206) and framework grafting (207), are of most use. New varieties are raised from seed sown outdoors or in frames in March.

204. Stocks. These are used for grafting and budding and they have a marked effect upon growth and bearing. Stocks are of two main types: crabs, raised from seed and in consequence very variable in character, and Paradise stocks, raised from layers and constant to type. Paradise stocks are classified under numbers prefixed by M (for Malling) or MM (for Malling-Merton). M.IX and M.26 are very dwarfing and encourage very early fruiting. They are excellent for cordons, especially on rich soils or for fairly vigorous varieties. M.VII and MM.106 are semi-dwarfing and suitable for espaliers, dwarf pyramids and small bushes. M.I, M.II, MM.104, MM.111 are more vigorous and suitable for large bushes. M.XVI and M.24 are still more vigorous and are suitable stock for standard trees. Vigorous stocks must not be used for trained trees.

205. Whip Grafting. This is employed where stock and scion are not far removed in thickness. On both a long, sloping cut is made, with a second, smaller, incision in the opposite direction, forming a tongue. All cuts should be of the same length and width. Scion and stock are fitted together by means of the tongues and are bound firmly. The whole wounded area is sealed with grafting wax. This method is shown in Fig. 2, on page 118.

206. Rind or Crown Grafting. This is used where the stock is much thicker than the scion. A vertical incision is made through the bark at the head of the stock. The bark is lifted with a scalpel. The scion is cut in the form of a long, thin wedge and slipped beneath the raised bark. It is bound in position and waxed. If desired, several scions may be inserted round the head of each stock. This method is shown in Fig. 1, on page 118. Top buds of the scions should point outwards.

207. Framework, or Stub, Grafting is employed to re-work unprofitable trees and get them back into bearing rapidly. Every side growth that is as thick as, or a little thicker than, a lead pencil is grafted separately and the whole main framework of the tree is retained. Several methods are employed, the simplest being to make a downward incision near the base of each side shoot and on its upper side, bend the shoot down so as to open this cut and then insert in it a

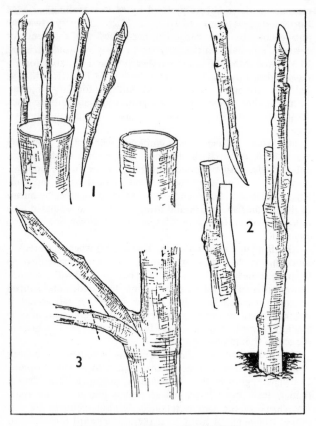

Three types of grafting (205, 206, 207)

scion previously prepared with a short double wedge cut at the base. The shoot is then released so that it springs back and grips the scion in position. Finally the shoot is cut off just beyond the scion and the wounded area covered with wax. No tying is required. This method is shown in Fig. 3, opposite. Several hundred scions may be inserted on one tree.

208. Heading Back. Old trees that are to be rind grafted should be headed back in January. Young stocks are headed back at grafting time.

209. Scions. These can be collected when pruning. Any one-year growths about the thickness of a pencil or slightly less are suitable. Label and heel in under a north wall or fence to retard growth.

210. Budding. This is a quicker operation than grafting, but is suitable only for young stocks in which the bark is still thin and pliable. A T-shaped incision is made in this and the flaps lifted with a scalpel. A dormant growth bud on ripe, young wood is cut with a shield-shaped portion of bark. Any wood contained within this is stripped out. The bud is slipped beneath the flaps of bark and bound in position. No waxing is necessary. Stocks are not headed back till the following November. The illustration on page 120 shows:

1. A suitable shoot from which buds can be cut, also point at which leaves should be severed.

2. The method of cutting out the bud with a shield-shaped portion of bark.

3. The bud ready for insertion.

4. Flap of bark formed by 'T' incision being raised by a scalpel.

5. The finished job with the bud bound in position.

211. Height for Buds and Grafts. Insert all buds and grafts on young stocks 9–15 in. above soil level. Grafts on old stocks can be inserted at any convenient height.

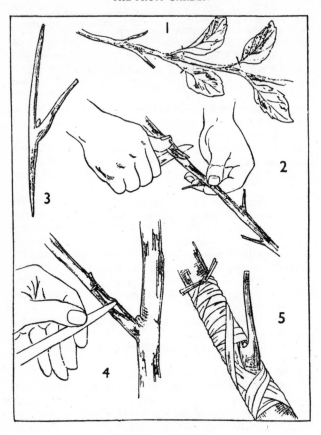

How to bud a stock (210)

212. Varieties of Apple. Adam's Pearmain (D), Dec.–Mar.; Advance (D), Aug.; Allen's Everlasting (D), Apr.–June; Allington Pippin (D), Oct.–Dec.; American Mother (D), Oct.–Nov.; Annie Elizabeth (C), Dec.–June; Arthur Turner (C), Sept.–Oct.; Ashmead's Kernel (D), Dec.–Mar.; Astrachan Red (D), Aug.

Barnack Beauty (D), Dec.–Apr.; Barnack Orange (D), Nov.–Dec.; Baumann's Red Winter Reinette (D), Dec.–Jan.; Beauty of Bath (D), Aug.; Beauty of Kent (C), Nov.–Mar.; Beauty of Stoke (CD), Jan.–Mar.; Belle de Boskoop (CD), Dec.–Apr.; Bismarck (C), Nov.–Jan.; Blenheim Orange (D), Nov.–Jan.; Bowden's Seedling (D), Nov.–Mar.; Bramley's Seedling (C), Nov.–Apr.; Brownlee Russet (D), Jan.–Apr.

Cellini (D), Oct.–Nov.; Charles Ross (CD), Oct.–Nov.; Christmas Pearmain (D), Dec.–Jan.; Claygate Pearmain (D), Dec.–Feb.; Cornish Aromatic (D), Dec.–Feb.; Cornish Gillyflower (D), Dec.–May; Court Pendu Plat (D), Dec.–Apr.; Cortland (D), Nov.–Jan.; Cox's Orange Pippin (D), Nov.–Feb.; Cox's Pomona (CD), Oct.–Nov.; Crawley Beauty (C), Dec.–Apr.; Cutler Grieve (D), Nov.–Jan.

D'Arcy Spice (D), Dec.–Apr.; Delicious (D), Nov.–Feb.; Devonshire Quarrendon (D), Aug.–Sept.; Duchess's Favourite (D), Oct.–Nov.; Duke of Devonshire (D), Feb.–Apr.; Dumelow's Seedling (C), Nov.–Mar.

Early Crimson (D), July; Early Victoria (or Emneth Early) (C), July–Aug.; Early Peach (D), Aug.; Easter Orange (D), Mar.–Apr.; Ecklinville Seedling (C), Aug.–Oct.; Edward VII (C), Jan.–Apr.; Egremont Russet (D), Oct.–Dec.; Ellison's Orange (D), Sept.–Oct.; Emperor Alexander (CD), Oct.–Nov.; Encore (C), Dec.–June; Epicure (D), Sept.; Exquisite (D), Sept.

Fortune (D), Sept.; Gascoyne's Scarlet (D), Sept.–Jan.;

George Carpenter (D), Oct.–Feb.; George Cave (D), Aug.–Sept.; George Neal (C), July–Sept.; Golden Delicious (D), Dec.–Feb.; Golden Noble (C), Oct.–Dec.; Golden Spire (C), Sept.–Oct.; Granny Smith (D), Dec.–Apr.; Gravenstein (CD), Oct.–Dec.; Grenadier (C), Aug.–Sept.

Herring's Pippin (CD), Oct.–Nov.; Heusgen's Golden Reinette (CD), Dec.–Apr.; Holstein (D), Nov.–Dec.; Howgate Wonder (C), Oct.–Jan.

Imperial (D), Nov.–Jan.; Irish Peach (D), Aug.

James Grieve (D), Sept.–Oct.; John Standish (D), Jan.–Mar.; Joy Bells (D), Nov.–Dec.

Keswick Codlin (C), Aug.–Sept.; King George V (D), Feb.–Mar.; King of the Pippins (D), Oct.–Nov.; King of Tompkins County (D), Dec.–Apr.; King's Acre Pippin (D), Jan.–Mar.

Lady Sudeley (D), Aug.–Oct.; Lane's Prince Albert (C), Nov.–Mar.; Langley Pippin (D), Aug.–Sept.; Lord Burghley (D), Feb.–Apr.; Lord Derby (C), Nov.–Dec.; Lord Grosvenor (C), Aug.–Sept.; Lord Hindlip (D), Jan.–Apr.; Lord Lambourne (D), Oct.–Dec.; Lord Suffield (C), Aug.–Sept.

Margil (D), Nov.–Jan.; May Queen (D), Jan.–May; McIntosh Red (CD), Oct.–Jan.; Melba (D), Aug.; Merton Charm (D), Sept.–Oct.; Merton Russet (D), Dec.–Feb.; Merton Worcester (D), Sept.–Oct.; Miller's Seedling (D), Sept.–Oct.; Monarch (C), Dec.–Apr.; Mr Gladstone (D), July–Aug.; Mutsu (D), Dec.–Feb.

Newton Wonder (C), Dec.–May; Norfolk Royal (D), Nov.–Mar.

Ontario (CD), Dec.–May, Orleans Reinette (D), Dec.–Feb.

Peasgood's Nonsuch (CD), Sept.–Nov.; Pioneer (D), Oct.–Nov.; Queen (C), Oct.–Nov.

Reinette du Canada (D), Jan.–Feb.; Rev. W. Wilkes (C), Oct.–Nov.; Ribston Pippin (D), Nov.–Jan.; Rival (CD),

Oct.–Dec.; Rosemary Russet (D), Dec.–Feb.; Roundway Magnum Bonum (CD), Nov.–Mar.; Royal Jubilee (C), Oct.–Dec.; Royal Russet (C), Nov.–Apr.

Saltcote Pippin (D), Oct.–Dec.; Sandringham (C), Dec.–Feb.; Scarlet Pimpernel (D), July–Aug.; St Cecilia (D), Jan.–Mar.; St Edmunds Russet (D), Sept.–Oct.; St Everard (D), Sept.; Stark (D), Apr.–June; Stark Earlies (D), July–Aug.; Stirling Castle (C), Sept.–Oct.; Sturmer Pippin (D), Mar.–June; Sunset (D), Nov.–Dec.; Superb (D), Dec.–Mar.

Thos. Rivers (C), Sept.–Dec.; Triumph (D), Nov.–Jan.; Tydeman's Early (D), Sept.; Tydeman's Late Orange (D), Dec.–Mar.

Wagener (C), Jan.–May; Warner's King (C), Oct.–Dec.; Wealthy (D), Oct.–Nov.; Wellington (C), Nov.–Mar.; White Transparent (CD), July–Aug.; William Crump (D), Dec.–Feb.; Winston (D), Dec.–May; Worcester Pearmain (D), Sept.–Oct.; Wyken Pippin (D), Dec.–Mar.

(*Note.* – C *denotes cooking and* D *dessert varieties;* CD *dual-purpose apples. The months are those in which the variety is at its prime.*)

APRICOTS

213. Soil and Situation. Apricots require a sheltered, sunny position and rather rich, well-drained soil. Extra drainage, with rubble buried 2 ft. beneath surface, may be necessary. They are usually grown against south or south-west walls or in sunny greenhouses. Borders are specially prepared. If the natural soil is very heavy or sandy, it is removed and replaced with good loam. In any case, plenty of old mortar rubble or ground chalk is added and a little well-rotted manure.

214. Planting. This may be done at any time from late October until mid-March. Early November is usually the best time. Trees to be grown in greenhouses should always be planted then. Holes should be wide and rather shallow. Uppermost roots should be covered with 3 in. of soil. All must be made thoroughly firm. Wall trees are spaced 15 ft. apart.

215. Forms of Training. Apricots are almost always grown as fan-trained trees. Details of training and early formation are exactly the same as for fan-trained plums (353).

216. Pruning. Most of the work should be done in summer, when all badly placed or unwanted growths are rubbed out early. Other side growths should be shortened to the sixth good leaf reckoning from the base when about as thick as a pencil and commencing to get woody at the base (usually from about the middle of July outdoors). In winter, leaders are shortened by one-third, or as much as is necessary to confine the tree within bounds. Side growths may be tied in without further pruning if there is room for them. Otherwise they are further shortened to three buds.

217. Routine Feeding. As for plums (356). A spring mulch of decayed manure is especially beneficial to trees grown under glass. Such must also be watered freely while in growth.

218. Routine Pest Control. As for plums (357).

219. Propagation. By budding in July and August as for plums (358). The plum stocks are also used, especially Black Damas, Mussel, Brompton, and St Julien.

220. Varieties of Apricot. UNDER GLASS. Breda, Aug.–Sept.; Early Moorpark, July; Frogmore Early, July; Grosse Pêche, Aug.–Sept.; Hemskerke, Aug.–Sept.; Kaisha, Aug.; Luizet, July–Aug.; Moorpark, Aug.-Sept.; New Large Early, July; Oullin's Early Peach, Aug.; Précoce de Boulbon, July; Royal, Aug.; Shipley or Blenheim, Aug.

OUTDOORS. Breda, Sept.; Hemskerke, Sept.

BLACKBERRIES, LOGANBERRIES, ETC.

221. Soil and Situation. All succeed in most ordinary

garden soils except those of a very dry, poor nature. They will grow in sunny or partially shaded positions. Soil should be prepared exactly as for raspberries (368).

222. Planting. Canes should be spaced 8 ft. apart, and if there is more than one row 8 ft. should be allowed between rows. Very vigorous varieties such as Himalaya Berry should be spaced 12 ft. apart each way. Planting may be done at any time from mid-October to March as for raspberries (369).

223. Training. Common practice is to grow loganberries, blackberries, and allied fruits against walls or fences. Alternatively they may be grown in the open tied to wires strained between posts as for raspberries (370). The uppermost wire should be 7 ft. above ground level.

224. Pollination. Most varieties are self-fertile, i.e. they will produce fruit when pollinated with their own pollen. A few varieties of hybrid berry are self-sterile or produce no pollen and, in consequence, should be planted with other kinds.

225. Pruning. After planting, cut all canes back to within 12 in. of ground level. Young canes should not be allowed to bear fruit the first year. In subsequent years, prune as soon as possible after the crop has been gathered. Cut out to ground level all old fruiting canes and train young canes in their place. With very vigorous varieties such as Himalayan Giant, two or three old canes per plant may be kept for a second season. Do not retain more than ten new canes per plant. Select the sturdiest and cut out the remainder early in the summer. It does not matter if those retained are suckers, i.e. growing direct from the root.

226. Routine Cultivation. As for raspberries (372).

227. Routine Pest Control. Usually unnecessary, as foes are dealt with as noted. If cane spot (711) is troublesome, cut out and burn all affected canes and spray about the middle of March with lime-sulphur wash (675) at twice the normal winter strength.

228. Propagation. May be effected by division of old plants in autumn or winter, but the best method is to tip-root young canes. This is done by bending such canes down in July or August and pegging the tips to the soil. If kept moist, roots will be formed rapidly and by the autumn the canes can be severed from the parents. A few weeks later they may be lifted and transplanted to a nursery bed.

229. Varieties of Blackberry. Bedford Giant, early; Himalaya Giant, mid-season; John Innes, late; Merton Thornless, mid-season; Oregon Thornless, mid-season; Parsley-leaved, mid-season.

230. Varieties of Hybrid Berry. Boysenberry, Loganberry, Thornless Loganberry, Veitchberry, Wineberry. Newberry and Phenomenal Berry resemble the Loganberry and Youngberry the Boysenberry.

CHERRIES

231. Soil and Situation. Well-drained, loamy soils or loam over chalk are most suitable. Cherries do not thrive on badly drained soils, heavy clays, nor on light sands. They bloom early and are subject to frost damage. In consequence, very exposed positions or damp valleys liable to catch frost are unsuitable. Soil preparation is the same as for apples (189), except that manure or compost may be used at 1 cwt. to 10 or 12 sq. yd., according to the nature of the soil.

232. Planting. Season and method are the same as for apples (190). For distances see (22). Fan-trained trees should be spaced 15 ft. apart.

233. Forms of Trees. As a rule these are fan trained, bush, half-standard, and standard. Occasionally cherries are grown as single or double-stemmed cordons, but they are not very suitable for this method of training. Fan-trained trees are planted against walls or fences; bushes, half-standards, and standards in the open, the last two often grassed under.

234. Pruning. For this purpose, cherries fall into two distinct groups. Sweet cherries and the Duke cherries form spurs like apples. The sour cherries such as Morello and Amarelles do not form spurs so freely but fruit also on the previous year's growth. Hard pruning is not desirable with any cherries, as it is inclined to encourage gummosis (711). Standards, half-standards, and bushes can be pruned lightly. Only badly placed or crossing branches and shoots need be removed together with damaged or diseased wood. This is best done in March, just before the trees come into flower.

Trained trees must be kept in hand. SWEET AND DUKE CHERRIES should be summer and winter pruned in a similar manner to trained apples (193), except that wherever there is room young laterals should be trained in at full length. The summer work should start in June and be completed by August. Winter pruning is best deferred till March.

With SOUR CHERRIES a process known as 'disbudding' is carried out throughout the summer. Most young side growths are rubbed out at an early stage, but at least two are retained for each fruiting growth, one as near its base as possible, the other at its tip. In the autumn the old fruiting growth is cut out and the young shoot, retained near its base, is trained in to take its place.

235. Pruning Young Trees. In the early stages rather harder pruning is necessary to form the tree. Leaders may be shortened by a half or two-thirds. All cuts should be made to outward-pointing buds. Fan-trained trees should be prevented from forming a central stem. Cut this back to 18 in. from soil level and so force branching from near the base. Branches should be spread like the ribs of a fan. Training wires or bamboos must be used for this purpose (353).

236. Pollination. Most sweet cherries are self-sterile, i.e. they will not bear fruit if pollinated with their own pollen. In addition, some varieties are inter-sterile, i.e. their pollen is ineffective when

POLLINATION TABLE FOR SWEET CHERRIES

1	2	3	4
Bedford Prolific (e)	Schrecken Bigarreau (e)	Napoleon Bigarreau (m)	Kentish Bigarreau (m)
Early Rivers (e)	Frogmore Early (m)	Emperor Francis (m)	Merton Premier (m)
Knight's Early Black (e)	Merton Bigarreau (m)	Monstreuse de Mezel (e)	
Roundel Heart (m)	Waterloo (e)		
	Black Elton (l)		

5	6	7	8
Late Black Bigarreau (l)	Elton Heart (m)	Géante d'Hedelfingen (l)	Peggy Rivers (m)
Turkey Black Heart (e)	Governor Wood (m)	Bigarreau de Mezel (m)	
	Merton Heart (e)		

9	10	11	12
Red Turk (e)	Bigarreau Jaboulay (e)	Guigne d'Annonay (e)	Noble (l)

Varieties within any one square are not inter-fertile. All can be successfully cross-pollinated by varieties from any of the other squares. Letters in brackets mean: (e) early flowering, (m) mid-season flowering, (l) late flowering.

The following varieties will pollinate one another and members of all other groups: Bigarreau Gaucher (l), Black Tartarian E (e), Florence (l), Merton Glory (m), Noir de Guben (e), Smoky Heart (l).

transferred from one to the other. The only varieties which are fully self-fertile are Morello and Amarelles. The Duke cherries, i.e. May Duke, Late Duke, Archduke, etc., are partially self-fertile, but set much better crops when interplanted with other sour cherries. Other varieties may be classified in groups. The varieties within any group are infertile one with the other. Any kind may be planted with a variety from any other group. See table opposite.

237. Picking. This should start as soon as fruits part readily from the branches. Fruits usually ripen unevenly and on any one tree several pickings should be made. Cherries cannot be stored and should be used as gathered, but they bottle well.

238. Routine Pest Control. Apart from dealing with pests or diseases as noted it is customary to spray cherries with tar-oil wash (703) early in January and fix grease bands (187) around the trees in mid-September. If red spider (711) is troublesome, spray with lime sulphur (675) summer strength immediately before and after flowering.

239. Propagation. By budding during July and August on to a suitable stock. The process is the same as for apples (210). Gean is the best stock for all forms. In different parts of the country it is known as Mazzard and Gaskin. It can be increased vegetatively and, in this way, superior types can be kept true. Malling F.12/1 is such a selection.

240. Varieties of Cherry. Archduke (C), July; Bedford Prolific (D), July; Bigarreau de Mezel (D), July–Aug.; Bigarreau de Schrecken (D), June; Bigarreau Jaboulay (D), June; *Black Tartarian (D), July; Early Rivers (D), June; Elton Heart (D), July; Emperor Francis Bigarreau (D), Aug.; Flemish Red (C), July; Florence (D), Aug.; Frogmore Early (D), July; Géante d'Hedelfingen (D), Aug.; Governor Wood (D), July; Guigne D'Annonay (D), June; Kentish Bigarreau (D), July; Kentish Red (C), July; Knight's Early Black (D),

June; Ludwig's Bigarreau (D), July; May Duke (CD), June; Merton Bigarreau (D), July; Merton Heart (D), July; Merton Premier (D), July; Morello (C), Aug.; Napoleon Bigarreau (D), Aug.; Noble (Tradescant's Heart), (D), July; Noir de Guben (D), July; Peggy Rivers (D), July; Roundel Heart (D), July; Royal Duke (CD), July; Turkey Heart (D), Sept.; Ursula Rivers (D), July; Waterloo (D), June; White Heart (D), July.

*There are several distinct forms bearing this name and now distinguished by the letters A, B, C, D or E after the name. There are also three distinct varieties of Bigarreau de Mezel but these have not been given distinguishing letters.

(*Note. – The months are those in which the fruits normally ripen.* C *indicates cooking,* D *dessert.*)

COBNUTS AND FILBERTS

241. Soil and Situation. Will succeed in a wide variety of positions from full sun to shade and are not particular as regards soil, though they do not crop well on heavy, wet clays. Preparation should be as thorough as possible and a little well-rotted manure may be worked in.

242. Planting. From late October to mid-March as for apples (190). Other details are also the same.

243. Pollination. Incompatibility does not exist, but some varieties produce little pollen and so are bad pollinators. These should be interplanted with varieties that produce pollen freely (250).

244. Form of Training. Trees are almost invariably grown as open-centred bushes. In the early stages of growth, winter pruning should be directed towards forming the main framework of these. Inward-pointing branches are cut right out. Leading shoots are shortened by about a half and always cut to an outward-pointing bud to keep the centre of the bush open.

245. Pruning. Established bushes are pruned in late February and March, while in flower and immediately afterwards. All ingrowing shoots are cut out, also weak or damaged growths. Suckers are removed from the roots by a sharp twist and pull. Side growths are cut back to the first catkin reckoning from the tip, or, if there are no catkins, to the first female (red) flower. Shoots that have catkins only should be left unpruned till these fade, when they are cut back to two buds from the main stem. All strong side growths are broken to half length in August. This is known as brutting.

246. Picking and Storing. Cobnuts and filberts are picked towards the end of September. The yellowing of the husks is the signal for this work to start. Nuts may be stored in earthenware jars or crocks between layers of salt.

247. Routine Feeding. Well-rotted manure or shoddy may be spread around the trees at 1 cwt. to 15 sq. yd. each spring. Basic slag at 6 oz. per sq. yd., and sulphate of potash at 1 oz. per sq. yd., should be given each October.

248. Routine Pest Control. If nuts are damaged by weevils which bore holes in them, spray each year at the end of May with derris (662). Gather up and burn all damaged nuts.

249. Propagation. By suckers, which may be detached at any time during the planting season. Also by layering in autumn, i.e. bending whippy branches down to soil level, pegging them firmly to the ground and heaping a little soil over them. Layers should be well rooted by the following autumn, when they may be detached and planted on their own.

Nuts are also raised from seeds sown outdoors in March, but seedlings are very variable.

250. Varieties. *Cosford, Duke of Edinburgh, Kentish Cob, *Pearson's Prolific, Prolific Filbert, Red Filbert, and White Filbert.

Cobs have short husks, filberts long husks. Kentish Cob is, in fact, a filbert.

Good pollinators.

CURRANTS (BLACK)

251. Soil and Situation. Black currants succeed on a wide variety of soils and do not dislike moist conditions, provided their roots do not stand in stagnant water during winter. Flowers are produced early and are liable to be damaged by frost, so hollows which are likely to be frost traps should be avoided. Soil must be dug thoroughly; manure or compost may be incorporated at 1 cwt. to 8 sq. yd., as black currants like rather rich conditions. Lime is not essential.

252. Planting. This may be done at any time from late October until mid-March, provided soil is working freely. Roots are fine and fibrous, and soil must be carefully worked round and between them. The uppermost should be just covered. Make thoroughly firm. Growth is vigorous and at least 5 ft. should be allowed between the bushes (22).

253. Forms of Training. Black currants are almost invariably grown as bushes. It is no disadvantage if these are legless, i.e. without main stems and with many shoots coming through the soil, direct from the roots. Very occasionally the plants are trained in fan formation against fences or espaliers.

254. Pollination. All black currants are fully self-fertile and also inter-fertile. It is therefore possible to plant one variety only or any combination of varieties and obtain good crops. Poor fertilization is common, but is due to frost or lack of insects to secure pollination, not to sterility. The trouble is known as 'running off,' as it is usually the end flowers of each truss that fail to set. More bees or hand fertilization with a camel-hair brush and a more sheltered position are the remedies.

255. Pruning. All work can be done in winter, between

October and February, or, if preferred, as soon as the crop has been gathered. The object is to eliminate as much as possible of the growth that has just carried fruits without sacrificing strong young shoots on which the following year's crops will be borne. It does not matter if these come right from the roots (253). After planting, all growth should be cut back to within 2 or 3 in. of soil level.

256. Picking. Where fruits are required for home use only, it often pays to pick individual berries, as those nearest to the stem ripen before those at the tips of the truss. For exhibition, fruits must be shown on the truss, and so these are picked whole when all berries are black, but before the biggest start to split. Storing is impracticable, but black currants bottle excellently.

257. Routine Feeding. Mulch each March with well-rotted dung or compost at 1 cwt. to 8–12 sq. yd. Give sulphate of potash at $\frac{3}{4}$ oz. per sq. yd. each October. If dung is not available, substitute nitrate of soda, Nitro-chalk, or sulphate of ammonia at 2 oz. per sq. yd., and follow with a mulch of grass clippings.

258. Routine Pest Control. Usually unnecessary, as foes are dealt with as noted. If big-bud mite (711) is troublesome, spray in March with lime sulphur (675) at twice normal winter strength. The ideal time for application is when the most forward leaves are an inch across. Examine bushes each July for reversion (637) and burn any affected.

259. Propagation. By cuttings taken during October and November. Cuttings are from 8 to 15 in. in length and prepared from well-ripened growths of the current year's formation. Trim each immediately below a joint and insert firmly 4 in. deep in any well-drained soil and reasonably sheltered position. Cuttings should be 6 in. apart in rows 18 in. apart. Transplant to permanent positions after one year's growth.

260. Varieties of Black Currant. Amos Black, Aug.; Baldwin, Aug.–Sept.; Blacksmith (Tinker), Aug.; Boskoop Giant, June–July; Daniel's September, Aug.; Davison's Eight, Aug.; Goliath (Victoria, Edina), Aug.; Laxtons Giant, July; Mendip Cross, July; Seabrook's Black, Aug.; Wellington XXX, Aug.; Westwick Choice, July–Aug.; Worcesterberry is an American hybrid and is grown like a gooseberry.

(*The months are those in which the variety normally ripens.*)

CURRANTS (RED AND WHITE)

261. Soil and Situation. As for black currants (251).

262. Planting. As for black currants (252), except that slightly less room may be allowed between the bushes, say 4 to 5 ft. (22). After planting, cut back to 8 or 9 in. of soil level.

263. Forms of Training. Red and white currants are almost invariably grown as bushes, but with a short leg or main trunk, not with sucker growths as for black currants (253).

264. Pruning. Both summer and winter pruning should be carried out.

SUMMER PRUNING is done in June and July, when all side growths (laterals) should be cut back a few at a time to five well-developed leaves each. Deal with the strongest growths first.

WINTER PRUNING is done at any time from late October until early February. Side growths are further cut back to two or three dormant buds each and leaders are shortened by about one-third their length. Some varieties produce numerous shoots with dead or poorly developed buds. Such should be cut hard back, to strong buds. If necessary, this can be done in the spring, when growth starts, if they are not noted before. Suckers are removed (263).

265. Routine Feeding. The same as for black currants (257).

266. Routine Pest Control. Usually unnecessary, but if caterpillars (711) or aphids (711) are troublesome, apply tar-oil wash (703) at ordinary strength early each January.

267. Propagation. By cuttings prepared and inserted in a similar manner to those of black currants (259), except that all buds on the lower half of each cutting should be nicked out with the point of a knife. This is to prevent sucker growth.

268. Varieties of Red Currant. Cherry, July; Earliest of Fourlands, July; Fay's Prolific, July–Aug.; Jonkheer van Tets, July; Laxton's No. 1, July–Aug.; Laxton's Perfection, July–Aug.; Raby Castle, Aug.; Radboud, Aug.; Red Lake, July–Aug.; Rivers's Late Red, Aug.; Wilson's Long Bunch, Aug.

269. Varieties of White Currant. Transparent, July–Aug.; White Dutch (White Grape), July–Aug.; White Versailles, July–Aug.

(*The months are those in which the fruits normally ripen.*)

FIGS

270. Soil and Situation. Figs require a sheltered, sunny position and well-drained, not over-rich soil. They are more usually grown under glass than outdoors, but will succeed in the open in the south and south-west. Manure should be used sparingly when preparing the ground. A little ground chalk or mortar rubble may be worked in.

271. Planting. This may be done at any time during the dormant period, but is best early. See Apricots (214).

272. Forms of Training. Wall trees and those grown under glass are generally trained as fans. Trees in the open are allowed to form large bushes or even make half-standards.

273. Pruning. Figs bear on one- and two-year-old stems. In spring and early summer rub off badly placed shoots and in June pinch those well placed for tying in. These will produce side growths which will carry the next year's crop.

Thin overcrowded growth in July and cut out weak shoots the following March. In July and August sturdy side growths are shortened to five or six well-developed leaves each. If trees make excessive growth and are unfruitful they are root pruned in October or early November.

274. Thinning Fruits. This is very necessary as the trees are liable to overcrop. Under glass two or, occasionally, even three successive crops, on year-old and new growth, may be produced in the year. Outdoors only one is obtained, in summer on well-ripened side growths produced the previous year. Thin out the smaller fruits towards the ends of these shoots and preserve those of larger size towards the base. In autumn remove all fruits above the size of peas as these will not overwinter outdoors. Under glass they crop early.

275. Routine Feeding. Apply a light mulch of well-rotted manure each spring, supplemented by basic slag at 6 oz. per sq. yd., and sulphate of potash at $1\frac{1}{2}$ oz. per sq. yd., in October. Every second autumn give ground chalk at 8 oz. per sq. yd.

276. Management under Glass. Early figs from which it is desired to obtain three crops of fruit are started in December or early January by closing ventilators, watering borders, and raising the temperature to 65°. Usually, only two crops are attempted, and the house is closed in February. In any case the temperature is gradually allowed to increase to a maximum of 80° as the figs ripen. Paths and walls should be damped and leaves syringed liberally while in growth, except when the fruits are ripening, when a drier atmosphere must be maintained. After the first crop has been gathered, the year-old laterals are thinned out liberally to expose the second-crop fruits to the light, and the borders are well soaked with water or weak liquid manure.

277. Routine Pest Control. Usually unnecessary.

278. Propagation. By cuttings of well-ripened one-year-old growths taken in the autumn and inserted singly in pots filled with a gritty compost. Cuttings are rooted in a frame or cool greenhouse.

279. Varieties. Brown Turkey is the best all-round fig for cultivation in this country. Others are Bourgarotte Grise, Brunswick, *Negro Largo, *St John's, *White Ischia and White Marseilles.

Greenhouse only.

GOOSEBERRIES

280. Soil and Situation. Gooseberries succeed on most soils that are reasonably rich and well drained. They flower early and are susceptible to spring frost. Nitrogen and potash are the two most essential foods. Preparation of soil should be the same as for apples (189). Lime is not essential.

281. Planting. The same as for black currants (252), except that rather less space is required by some of the weaker-growing varieties. Average 4–5 ft. between bushes (22). Cordons should be planted in rows 4 ft. apart. In the rows single-stemmed cordons are spaced 1 ft., double-stemmed 2 ft., and triple-stemmed 3 ft. apart.

282. Forms of Training. Gooseberries are usually grown as bushes on a short leg like red and white currants (263). Occasionally single, double or even triple cordons are grown, especially where fruits of extra quality for exhibition are required.

283. Pruning. This should be done in summer and winter, and in the main is the same as for red currants (264). It is important to keep the centres of bushes fairly clear or picking becomes difficult. For the same reasons sucker growths must be cut right out. Some varieties have weak or arching leaders. These should be cut back each autumn to a strong, upward-pointing bud near the summit of the arch. A few varieties grow very erect. Leaders of these should be cut to strong outward-pointing buds to keep the centre of the bush open.

284. Picking. This should start as soon as the most forward fruits are of useable size; generally about the beginning of June. Do not strip the bushes at first, but thin the fruits, leaving the remainder 1 in. or so apart, to continue swelling and ripening. Storing is impracticable, but all varieties are excellent for bottling.

285. Routine Feeding. Potash is of particular importance. Its lack is indicated by leaf scorching. To prevent this give sulphate of potash at $1\frac{1}{2}$ oz. per sq. yd., each October. Apply well-rotted dung or compost each March at the rate of 1 cwt. to 15 sq. yd. or, failing this, nitrate of soda, Nitro-chalk, or sulphate of ammonia at $\frac{3}{4}$ oz. per sq. yd., followed by a mulch of grass clippings.

286. Routine Pest Control. Usually unnecessary, as foes are dealt with as noted. If greenfly (711), caterpillars (711), or scale insects (711) are troublesome, spray each January with tar-oil wash (703). If mildew (711), either American or English, is prevalent, use lime sulphur (675), washing soda (709) or dinocap (668) just before flowers open, and after flowering if necessary.

287. Propagation. By cuttings prepared and inserted in exactly the same way as those of black currants (259), except that all buds on the lower half of each cutting should be nicked out with a sharp knife. This is to prevent sucker formation.

288. Varieties of Gooseberry. Bedford Yellow (yellow) D, July; Broom Girl (yellow) D, July; Careless (white) C, July; Cousen's Seedling (yellow) D, Aug.; Crown Bob (red) CD, July–Aug.; Dan's Mistake (red) D, July–Aug.; Early Sulphur (yellow) D, July; Golden Drop (yellow) D, July; Green Gem (green) CD, July–Aug.; Gunner (yellow) D, July–Aug.; Keepsake (green) CD, July; Lancashire Lad (red) C, July–Aug.; Lancer (green) CD, Aug.; Langley Gage (white) D,

July–Aug.; Leveller (yellow) CD, July–Aug.; May Duke (red) CD, July; Warrington (red) CD, Aug.; Whinham's Industry (red) CD, July–Aug.; White Lion (white) CD, Aug.; White-smith (white) CD, July–Aug.

(*Note.—The months are those in which the varieties normally ripen. Colour of ripe fruits in brackets. C, culinary. D, dessert. CD, dual purpose.*)

GRAPE VINES

289. Soil and Situation. Grapes can be grown in a wide variety of soils if well prepared. Heavy loams require adequate drainage. Only sandy soils, wet clays, and solid chalks are unsuitable.

When grown in a glasshouse it is usual to prepare a special border. This may be surrounded by brick or concrete to prevent roots penetrating to unprepared soil. Such borders may be inside the house, when they usually occupy its whole length and width with the exception of the path, or outside, when they are the length of the house and 10–12 ft. in width. All should be 3 ft. in depth with a slight slope to the front. Holes are left near soil level in the wall of the vinery if the border is outside. The main stems are taken into the house through these.

Place a layer of rubble in the bottom for drainage. Over this place a layer of turves grass side downwards. Fill the remainder of the border with a mixture of eight parts of chopped turf (preferably medium yellow loam), one part of old mortar rubble, half a part of wood ashes, and a quarter part of charcoal broken to the size of peas. Add $\frac{1}{2}$ lb. of bonemeal to each bushel of mixture.

Vines can be grown indoors or out. For the latter purpose only hardy, early varieties should be chosen (302). The position must be warm and sheltered, such as against a wall facing south or west.

VINERIES may be of any shape and size, but must have ample provision for ventilation at the ridge, along the sides and in the walls near soil level. Lean-to and three-quarter-span houses (491) should face south or south-west. Span-roofed houses should run from north to south. Vines can be planted on both sides of span-roofed houses.

290. Planting. November is the best month for purchasing vines. Obtain strong specimens in pots and prune back so that the top eye is level with the bottom panes of glass in the vinery. Do not plant till buds begin to break in late February or early March. Tease out roots with a pointed stick and spread them widely in a shallow hole. Cover the topmost with 2 in. of soil. Make thoroughly firm. Water in freely. Vines to be grown on the single-stem system (291) are planted 5 to 6 ft. apart. If to be grown on the multiple-stem system (291), any multiple of 4 ft. may be allowed between the vines.

291. System of Training. Each vine may be restricted to a single main stem or 'rod,' which is trained direct from the floor to the ridge of the house. Alternatively, the main stem can be trained horizontally at the top of the front or side wall and at every 4 ft. a branch stem can be trained from it to the ridge of the house. This is known as the multiple-stem system. Almost any number of branch stems may be grown, depending upon the vigour of the vine. Examples are known in which one vine fills the whole of a large house, as at Hampton Court. The single-stem system is the better for the amateur. In all methods, training wires should be provided, stretched horizontally 9 in. beneath the glass and about 15 in. apart.

292. Pruning. Vines are thinned and stopped periodically during the spring and summer and hard pruned in winter.

Thinning and stopping start as soon as the vine starts into growth. In an established vine there are spurs every 15–18 in. on each side of every main rod. Only one new shoot is required from each spur. If more form, the weakest should be rubbed out. That retained is allowed to grow until it produces a flower truss or is 2–3 ft. in length. Its point is then pinched out. One leaf must be left beyond the flower truss. If secondary shoots are produced, these should be pinched beyond the first leaf. All young growths are tied down to the training wires. Foliage must not touch the glass. Tying down must be done gradually, as the young shoots are brittle.

In November or early December, when all leaves have fallen, each lateral (side growth) is cut back to within one dormant bud of the spur on the main rod.

293. Pruning and Training Young Vines. When shoots have made six leaves, remove points from all except the leading one which is to form the rod. Stop all secondary laterals above the first leaf. Tie in young growths gradually to avoid breakage. When the leading growth is 6 ft. long, pinch out the tip, also any side growths it is producing above the first leaf, except the top one, which may be allowed to grow unchecked. Leave all further shoots on the leading growth until mid-September, when they should be pinched. Any later growths that form should be pinched out at once. If vines have grown well, they should have filled available space. In November, when all leaves have fallen, cut back all side growths to the main rod and shorten the leading growth to within 3 or 4 ft. of ground level, according to its strength.

The second year, rub out superfluous side growths on the main stem as they form. Retain one strong growth every 15–18 in. on each side of the main stem to lay the basis of future spurs. Subsequent treatment of these side growths is as for established vines (292). The leading growth is allowed to grow 7 ft., or until it reaches the ridge of the house, when it is stopped. Side growths on this portion are treated as those on the young vine the first year.

294. Starting Vines. Vines may be started at any time from January to March, according to the date at which fruits are required. This is done by closing the ventilators, raising the temperature to a minimum of 50° at night, rising to 60° by day, watering the border, mulching with 3 in. of rotted manure and maintaining a moister atmosphere by syringing with tepid water in the morning, and filling troughs over hot-water pipes with water. Vines are lowered from training wires to check uprush of sap and ensure even growth from bottom to top. Later, when growth starts, they are retied.

295. Vines in Flower. When vines come into flower, syringing should be discontinued and temperature raised by 5°. Soak the border occasionally with very weak liquid manure. Tap the rods daily or dust flowers lightly with a camel-hair brush to assist pollination.

296. Thinning the Fruits. The bunches must be thinned a little at a time from about a fortnight after berries first start to form. Use a pair of pointed grape scissors. Begin thinning at the bottom of the bunch. Leave the extreme point of the bunch, but remove all berries within $\frac{3}{4}$ in. of it. Berries at the top of the bunch can be left almost twice as thick. Those between should be given intermediate spacing. Do not touch berries by hand. Use a small pointed stick to turn them if necessary.

297. General Management. Ventilation throughout should be as free as possible consistent with maintenance of necessary temperatures. Keep water trays filled or damp paths and walls every morning until berries start to colour. Then empty trays or discontinue damping and allow temperature to rise slightly. Water when soil appears dry on surface. Give sufficient to soak border thoroughly. Feed in winter and spring with vine fertilizers (98), (99).

298. Picking and Storing. Early grapes should be gathered as soon as they are well coloured or have a full, sweet flavour. No attempt should be made to keep them for any length of time. They are cut with a short length of lateral to serve as a handle for the bunch. Later varieties may be allowed to hang on the vine for a considerable time if the house is well ventilated and there is plenty of foliage to shade the berries. Later, when the foliage has fallen, each bunch may be cut with about 1 ft. of lateral. The lower end of this is slipped into a bottle nearly filled with water, and this is stood, at an angle of 45°, in a cool, dark, but dry room.

299. Outdoor Culture. This follows the same general lines as for vines under glass, except that growth is allowed to start naturally in the spring, no syringing is practised and a rather freer growth is permitted. Outdoor vines are generally permitted to form several main rods. Overcrowding must be prevented or berries may be shaded excessively by foliage.

300. Routine Pest Control. Each winter, when vines are dormant, loose bark is rubbed off and the rods are sprayed with tar-oil winter wash. If red spider (711) or mildew (711) appears in summer, give increased top ventilation and avoid cold draughts, also dust foliage and berries with powdered green sulphur or dinocap (668) but not after thinning. Scalding of foliage and berries is caused by too hot and dry an atmosphere. Shanking, i.e. withering of the footstalk of the berry with consequent collapse of the berry itself, is an indication of impoverished soil or lack of water.

301. Propagation. May be effected by eyes, cuttings, layers, grafting, inarching and seed. The first named is the best for the amateur. Eyes (dormant growth buds) are secured in autumn or winter from sturdy, well-ripened laterals. They are either scooped out with a shield-shaped portion of bark and wood or else are cut complete with a short section (about $\frac{3}{4}$ in.) of stem. They are inserted singly in small pots filled with a light compost and are started into growth in a propagating box or frame, placed over the hot-water pipes in the greenhouse. The buds should be just level with the surface of the soil.

302. Varieties of Grape. UNDER GLASS. Alicante, Oct.–Feb.; Appley Towers, Nov.; Black Hamburgh, Aug.–Oct.; Black Prince, Sept.; Buckland Sweetwater, July–Aug.; Canon Hall Muscat, Nov.–Jan.; Gros Colmar, Oct.–Jan.; Gros Guillaume, Nov.–Mar.; Lady Downe's Seedling, Nov.–Mar.; Lady Hastings, Oct.–Dec.; Lady Hutt, Nov.–Dec.; Madresfield Court, Aug.–Sept.; Muscat Hamburgh, Oct.; Mrs Pearson, Nov.–Mar.; Mrs Pince, Nov.–May; Muscat of Alexandria, Nov.–Mar.; Prince of Wales, Nov.–May.

OUTDOORS. Brandt, Sept.–Oct.; Buckland Sweetwater, Sept.; Chasselas Rose, Sept.; Foster's Seedling, Sept.; Muscat Hamburgh, Sept.; Perle de Czaba, Sept.; Reine Olga, Sept.; Royal Muscadine, Sept.–Oct.

Loganberry. See Blackberry (221).

MEDLARS

303. Soil and Situation. Succeed in sunny places and rather rich soils, such as those that suit plums (348).

304. Planting. From the end of October to mid-March as for apples (190). Other details are also the same. Trees should be spaced at least 20 ft. apart.

305. Form of Training. Usually grown as a standard but occasionally seen as a bush.

306. Pruning. Early treatment is the same as for apples (194). Established trees that are in bearing do not as a rule require much pruning.

307. Picking. This should be done at the end of October. The fruits are placed in single layers, eyes downwards, on a shelf in a dry store or room, until they turn dark and become soft, a condition known as bletted. Bletting may take several weeks.

308. Routine Feeding. As for apples (200).

309. Routine Pest Control. Unnecessary.

310. Propagation. By budding in July–August, or grafting in March–April, on to pear stocks (346).

311. Varieties. Dutch, Nottingham, Royal.

MELONS

312. Raising and Planting. From the cultural standpoint melons closely resemble cucumbers (145). They must be grown in greenhouses or frames and are not sufficiently hardy for outdoor culture. Seed should be sown and germinated exactly as for cucumbers. For an early crop, seed may be sown in a heated greenhouse (65°–70°) in January, but most amateurs will prefer to wait until March or even early April. The preparation of the bed is as for cucumbers and the plants are put in their fruiting quarters in the same way when they have made three or four rough leaves each. Water freely and maintain a damp atmosphere by frequent syringing and wetting of the path and walls. During the summer, shading may be required to prevent scorching, but should be as light as possible, as sun is necessary for ripening the fruits.

313. Training and Fertilizing. The main stem is allowed to grow unstopped till it is 6 ft. long, when the tip is pinched out. Flowers are produced on the side growths and female flowers may be recognized by the embryo fruits immediately beneath them. They must be fertilized by shaking male flowers with ripe, dry pollen over them. Four fruits are sufficient for one strong plant, and four female flowers to produce these should be fertilized at the same time; all other flowers must then be removed. Side growths should be stopped as soon as they start to interfere with those of other neighbouring plants. Fruits are weighty and must be supported by nets slung from the training wires. From the time fruits set, the plants should be fed liberally with weak liquid manure. Top dress with well-broken rotted manure when white rootlets appear on the surface.

314. Cultivation in Frames. This is similar, except that the plants are pinched as soon as they have made four leaves. The three or four growths produced as a result of this pinching are trained around the plant and stopped again when they reach the confines of the frame. They are pegged to the surface of the soil. As the fruits ripen they are propped above the leaves on inverted flower pots to catch the sun.

315. Varieties of Melon. Hero of Lockinge, King George, Superlative. For frames, Cantaloupe varieties such as Charantais, Dutch Net and Tiger.

MULBERRIES

316. Soil and Situation. Succeed best in rich, rather moist, but not waterlogged soil. Should be given a sunny position.

317. Planting. From late October to mid-March as for apples (190). Trees should be spaced at least 30 ft. apart.

318. Form of Training. Almost always grown as a standard.

319. Pruning. In the early stages of growth the trees are shaped in the same way as young apples (194). Later, when mature, little or no pruning is required.

320. Routine Feeding. Usually unnecessary.

321. Routine Pest Control. Unnecessary.

322. Propagation. By seeds sown under glass in March or outdoors in May. Also by cuttings, partly of current and partly of two-year-old wood inserted half their depth in sandy soil in autumn. By layering (481) whippy branches in autumn and by grafting on to seedlings in March.

323. Varieties. The Black Mulberry is the variety usually planted for fruiting.

PEACHES AND NECTARINES

324. Soil and Situation. Both fruits require a warm, sunny position and good, well-drained soil. In these respects they resemble apricots, and the same general treatment should be observed (213). They are equally suitable for sunny greenhouses or walls and fences.

325. Planting. This may be done at any time during the dormant period as for apricots. The same particulars apply (214).

326. Training. Outdoors sometimes as bushes; against walls and under glass in fan formation. The details of training and early pruning are the same as for plums (353).

327. Pollination. So far as is known, all varieties will set fruit with their own pollen. To ensure pollination it is advisable to dust pollen from flower to flower when these are fully open and the atmosphere is dry. This is especially necessary under glass. An alternative is to rap the tree smartly every day while in flower.

328. Pruning. This is the same as for Morello cherries (234), as the fruit is borne on year-old side growths.

329. Thinning Fruits. This should begin as soon as the fruits are as large as marbles but must not be completed until the stones are formed. This can be ascertained by cutting a typical fruit in half. At first the fruits should be reduced to one per cluster. Later they may be further spaced out 9 in. to 1 ft. apart for peaches, a little closer for nectarines. Select healthy, well-formed fruits that are placed where they will get the maximum amount of sunshine. Later, a few leaves that are shading fruits may be removed and the latter propped forward to catch the sun.

330. Routine Feeding and Watering. Mulch with strawy, well-rotted manure each March. This is especially necessary with greenhouse trees. Give Nitro-chalk, nitrate of soda, or sulphate of ammonia in March and again in early May, 1 oz. per square yard at each application. Give sulphate of potash, 1 oz. per square yard each October, with basic slag, 6 oz. per square yard, one year, hydrated lime, 8 oz. per square yard, the following year. Borders against walls and fences must be soaked thoroughly with water at frequent intervals while the fruits are swelling.

331. Routine Pest Control. Spray with tar-oil wash, 5% strength (703), in December. At the end of February spray with Bordeaux mixture (646) or captan (649) to check leaf curl (711). In May pick off and burn leaves that are red and curled. In late June cut out and burn any branches that have silvered leaves (711). Syringe twice daily with clear water if red spider attacks the trees, especially under glass.

332. Greenhouse Management. Early trees can be started into growth in January by closing ventilators, watering border, and raising the temperature to 45° at night, 50°–55° by day. Most houses are not started until about a month later. Peaches and nectarines in unheated houses should not be hurried unduly and ventilation must be given freely until mid-March. All plants under glass must be well watered while in growth. Never encourage temperatures above 60° at night and 75° by day, and these only when fruit is set. Maintain a moist atmosphere by damping the paths and syringing the trees daily with tepid water, except while in flower and after fruit starts to ripen, when syringing should be discontinued.

333. Propagation. By budding during July and August in the same manner as for apples (210). Plum stocks (358), Brompton, Common Mussel and St Julien A, or seedling peaches are used for the purpose.

334. Varieties of Peach. Advance, Aug.; Alexander, July; *Amsden June, July; *Barrington, Sept.; *Bellegarde, Sept.; *Crimson Galande, Aug.; *Duke of York, July; *Dymond, Sept.; Early Grosse Mignonne, Aug.–Sept.; Goshawk, Aug.–Sept.; Golden Eagle, Oct.; *Hale's Early, July–Aug.; Lady Palmerston, Sept.–Oct.; Late Devonian, Sept.; Noblesse, Aug.–Sept.; *Peregrine, Aug.; Prince of Wales, Sept.; Princess of Wales, Sept.–Oct.; Rochester, Aug.; *Royal George, Sept.; *Sea Eagle, Sept.–Oct.;

Stirling Castle, Sept.; Thomas Rivers, Sept.; Violette Hâtive, Sept.; *Walburton Admirable, Sept.; *Waterloo, July.

335. Varieties of Nectarine. Cardinal, July; Darwin, Sept.; *Dryden, Aug.; *Early Rivers, July; *Elruge, Aug.; *Hardwick, Aug.; *Humboldt, Aug.; John Rivers, July; Lord Napier, Aug.; Pine Apple, Sept.; Rivers's Orange, Sept.; Spenser, Sept.; *Stanwick Elruge, Sept.; Victoria, Sept.; *Violette Hâtive, Aug.

May be planted outdoors.

PEARS

336. Soil and Situation. Pears require a warmer position and better drainage than apples, but in other respects are similar in their requirements. The preparation of the ground should be, within these limits, the same (189). If of a heavy nature, plenty of lightening material such as strawy manure, grit, or sand should be added, or it may be necessary to install land drains (34). Choice dessert varieties do best when planted against a south or south-west wall.

337. Planting. Times and methods are the same as for apples (190).

338. Forms of Training. The same as for apples (191), but standards and half-standards are not usually very satisfactory except for certain vigorous varieties, such as Beurré Clairgeau, Hessle, Chalk, and Jargonelle. Choice dessert varieties are excellent as horizontal-trained or single-cordon trees.

339. Pollination. As with apples, very few varieties of pear crop satisfactorily when planted alone, but require other pears to provide pollen. The table overleaf gives more details.

340. Pruning. Young trees are formed in exactly the same way as apples of the same type (194), (195), (196). As the trees become older and start to bear, summer and winter pruning should be practised as for apples (193), except that treatment

POLLINATION TABLE FOR PEARS

Early Flowering	Mid-season Flowering	Late Flowering
Beurré Clairgeau	*Beurré d'Amanlis	*Beurré Bedford
*Beurré Diel	Beurré Superfin	Beurré Hardy
Beurré Giffard	Conference	*Bristol Cross
Easter Beurré	Dr Jules Guyot	*Catillac
Émile d'Heyst	*Doyenné Bussoch	Clapp's Favourite
Louise Bonne of Jersey	Durondeau	Doyenné du Comice
*Marguerite Marillat	Fertility	Glou Morceau
Princess	Fondante d'Automne	Gorham
Seckle	*Jargonelle	Hessle
*Uvedale's St Germain	Merton Pride	Marie Louise
Vicar of Winkfield	Packham's Triumph	*Pitmaston Duchess
	Souvenire de Congrès	Winter Nelis
	Triomphe de Vienne	
	Thompson's	
	Williams's Bon Chrêtien	

*Varieties marked with an asterisk should not be planted alone or as pollinators for other pears. So far as possible, pollinators should be chosen from the same group so that their flowering periods coincide. Beurré d'Amanlis and Conference are incompatible with one another. Fondante d'Automne, Louise Bonne of Jersey, Seckle and Williams's Bon Chrêtien are also mutually incompatible varieties.

on the whole can be slightly more severe as most varieties form spurs readily. A few kinds, notably Jargonelle and Joséphine de Malines, produce fruit buds at the tips of side growths.

341. Thinning. This is necessary, especially with the larger-fruited varieties and the best dessert pears. The details are the same as for apples (197), except that final distance apart for best dessert varieties should be 5 in.; large cooking varieties slightly more.

342. Picking. Early pears such as Doyenné d Eté, Jargonelle, and Williams's Bon Chrêtien must be picked as soon as they are ripe and part from the tree readily. They will not keep. Later varieties can be left hanging until mid-October.

343. Storing. Pears require a drier and slightly warmer atmosphere than apples (199). They keep well in a spare room or airy, concrete-floored shed and are best laid in single layers on open-slat shelves, not placed in several layers in a box. They must be used as soon as ripe, which is indicated by softening of the flesh near the stem. Pears must be watched very closely, as some varieties go sleepy, i.e. rotten in the centre, within a few days of ripening.

344. Routine Feeding. The same as for apples (200), except that rather heavier dressings of well-rotted manure can be given in the spring, say 1 cwt. to 10–12 sq. yd., as pears require more nitrogen than apples.

345. Routine Pest Control. Spray at the end of December with tar-oil wash (703). In April spray with captan (649) when the flower buds show colour, but before they start to open. Add derris (662) or trichlorphon (708), if necessary, to kill caterpillars. Collect and burn all fruits attacked by pear midge (711) in early June. Spray with malathion (677) if aphid (711) appears. Place grease bands (187) round the trunks of the trees in September and keep them sticky until the following April.

346. Propagation. By grafting or budding at the same time and in the same manner as for apples (205), (210). The stocks used are free stock or seedling pear and quince. The former is variable and comparable with crab apple. It should be used only for standards of hardy varieties. Quince is best for all trained trees and bushes. Selected forms of quince have been obtained and are known under letter. Quince A is fairly vigorous and suitable for large bushes, etc. Quince C is moderately dwarfing and encourages early bearing. It is good for cordons and other trained trees. These stocks can be raised vegetatively by layering.

Old pears can be re-worked by rind grafting, or stub grafting, as described for apples (206), (207), (208).

347. Varieties of Pear. Admiral Gervis (D), Dec.

Bellissime d'Hiver (C), Nov.–Mar.; Bergamotte Esperen (D), Feb.–Apr.; Beurré d'Amanlis (D), Sept.; Beurré d'Anjou (D), Nov.–Jan.; Beurré Bedford (D), Oct.; Beurré Bosc (D), Sept.–Oct.; Beurré Clairgeau (C), Nov.–Dec.; Beurré Diel (D), Oct.–Nov.; Beurré Easter (D), Jan.–Mar.; Beurré Giffard (D), Aug.; Beurré Hardy (D), Oct.; Beurré Six (D), Dec.; Beurré Superfin (D), Oct.–Nov.; Blickling (D), Dec.–Jan.; Bristol Cross (D), Oct.

Catillac (C), Dec.–Apr.; Chalk (D), Aug.; Charles Ernest (D), Oct.–Nov.; Clapp's Favourite (D), Aug.; Colmar D'Été (D), Sept.; Comte de Lamy (D), Oct.; Conference (D) Oct.-Nov.

Directeur Hardy (D), Sept.; Dr Jules Guyot (D), Sept.; Doyenné Bussoch (D), Sept.; Doyenné d'Été (D), July–Aug.; Doyenné du Comice (D), Nov.; Durondeau (D), Oct.–Nov.

Easter Beurré (D), Feb.–Apr.; Émile d'Heyst (D), Oct.–Nov.; Fertility (D), Oct.; Fondante d'Automme (D), Oct.; Forelle

(Trout Pear) (D), Nov.–Jan.

Glou Morceau (D), Dec.–Jan.; Gorham (D), Sept.

Hessle (D), Sept.

Jargonelle (D), Aug.; Jersey Gratioli (D), Oct.; Joséphine de Malines (D), Dec.–Feb.

Knight's Monarch (D), Dec.–Jan.

Le Lectier (D), Dec.–Jan.; Louise Bonne of Jersey (D), Oct.

Maréchal de la Cour (D), Oct.–Nov.; Marguérite Marrilat (D), Sept.; Marie Louise (D), Oct.–Nov.

Nouvelle Fulvie (D), Nov.–Feb.

Olivier de Serres (D), Feb.–Mar.

Packham's' Triumph (D), Oct.–Nov.; Pitmaston Duchess (CD), Nov.; Princess (D), Nov.–Dec.

Record (D), Oct.–Nov.; Roosevelt (D), Oct.

Santa Claus (D), Dec.; Satisfaction (D), Oct.; Seckle (D), Oct.; Souvenir de Congrés (D), Sept.

Thompson's (D), Oct.–Nov.; Triomphe de Vienne (D), Sept. Uvedale's St Germain (C), Jan.–Apr.

Verulam (C), Oct.; Vicar of Winkfield (C), Dec.; Victor (D), Nov.

William's Bon Chrêtien (D), Sept.; Winter Nelis (D), Dec.–Mar.; Winter Orange (C), Feb.–Mar., Wonderful (D), Nov.

PLUMS AND DAMSONS

348. Soil and Situation. Succeed best on rather rich, loamy land. Plums and damsons require more nitrogen than apples and are therefore less suitable for grass orchards, though certain vigorous varieties, such as Blaisden Red and Pershore, succeed. Lime is beneficial. Sour, poor, and dry, sandy soils are unsuitable.

Plums flower early and are, in consequence, unsuitable for very exposed places in which the blossom is usually destroyed or fails to set. Choice dessert varieties may be trained against sunny walls. Some kinds, such as Belgian Purple, Czar, Oullin's Golden Gage, Rivers's Early Prolific, and Victoria, are also suitable for north walls.

349. Planting. This may be done at any time from late October till mid-March. Details are the same as for apples (190). For correct distances see table (22). Fan-trained trees should be 15 ft. apart.

350. Forms of Training. Plums are grown as cordons, fan-trained trees, bushes, half-standards, and standards. Cordons are not recommended as the very restrictive pruning necessary may cause bacterial canker (711). Choice dessert varieties, and particularly gages, should be fan trained against walls. The more vigorous, free-fruiting varieties, especially cooking plums and damsons, make excellent standards.

153

351. Pollination. Many varieties are completely self-sterile, while others set a very poor crop with their own pollen. Such should be planted with another variety of plum or damson that flowers at the same time. Self-fertile varieties may be planted alone.

POLLINATION TABLE FOR PLUMS

Early Flowering	Mid-season Flowering	Late Flowering
Allgrove's Superb	*Bountiful	*Belle de Louvain
Black Prince	Bryanston Gage	Blaisdon Red
Coe's Golden Drop	*Czar	*Bradley's King Damson
*Denniston's Superb	Early Laxton	Cambridge Gage
Diamond	*Goldfinch	Comte D'Althann's
Farleigh Damson	Kirke's Blue	Gage
Golden Transparent	Late Orange	Cox's Emperor
Jefferson	*Laxton's Gage	Early Orleans
Late Orleans	*Merryweather Damson	Early Transparent
*Monarch	*Pershore (yellow)	Frogmore Damson
President	Purple Gage	*Giant Prune
*Prince of Wales	*Purple Pershore	*Gisborne's
*Reine Claude de Bavay	*Severn Cross	Green Gage
Rivers's Early Prolific	Transparent Gage	Late Transparent
Utility	*Victoria	Marjorie's Seedling
*Warwickshire Drooper		Oullin's Golden Gage
		Pond's Seedling
		Red Magnum Bonum
		*Shropshire Damson
		Wyedale

*Varieties marked with an asterisk are fully self-fertile, and may be planted alone if desired. All others require cross pollination. So far as possible pollinators should be chosen from the same group, so that their flowering periods may coincide. Incompatibility occurs only in the following cases with the varieties mentioned: Allgrove's Superb, Coe's Golden Drop, and Jefferson fail to pollinate one another. Late Orange and President fail both ways; either may be pollinated by Cambridge Gage or Greengage, but the reverse cross is not satisfactory.

352. Pruning. Bushes and half- and full standards are treated very lightly after the first few years, during which the framework of the tree is built up in the same manner as that of an apple (194). Subsequently, all dead wood and any large branches that have been damaged, or are diseased, should be cut out in June. Further thinning of poor or ill-placed branchlets is done in late summer after the crop has been gathered. Leaders are shortened a little in March, to an upward-pointing bud for drooping varieties and an outward-pointing bud for those of upright habit.

All large wounds should be covered at once with Stockholm tar or a proprietary wound dressing.

Trained plums must be treated rather more severely. From June to August the tips of young side shoots are pinched out when they have made six to eight leaves. In September older shoots are shortened to fruit buds where these have formed. Leaders are shortened each September by about one-third of their length until the wall space is filled, after which they are cut right out.

353. Forming Fan-trained Trees. Maiden (i.e. one-year-old) trees are cut back in November to within 15 in. of ground level. The following spring about four new shoots are retained and trained equidistantly like the main ribs of a fan. The following November these main branches are shortened to about 15–18 in. each, and the thinning and training process repeated in the spring, with the result that the tree is provided with anything up to sixteen principal branches evenly spaced in one plane. The process may be repeated indefinitely until the whole available space is covered. Thereafter, pruning is the same as for established trees.

354. Thinning Fruits. This is usually unnecessary, except with choice dessert varieties against walls. Fruits on these may be reduced to one every 2 or 3 in. after stones are formed. A preliminary thinning to half distance may be given three or four weeks after flowering.

355. Picking. Should start as soon as the fruits are well coloured and juicy. Culinary varieties may be picked over several times, the first when the fruits are sizeable but still green. These can be used for cooking or bottling, so leaving more space for the remainder to grow. Plums cannot be stored but may be bottled or dried.

356. Routine Feeding. Nitrogen and potash are the two important elements but with more emphasis on the former than with apples. Give a good dressing of rotted dung (1 cwt. to 12 sq. yd.) each March, lightly forked in, followed by sulphate of ammonia, nitrate of soda, or Nitro-chalk, at 1½ oz. per square yard in May, and sulphate of potash at 1 oz. per square yard in October. Every alternate October give, in addition, basic slag at 6 oz. per square yard, or instead use fruit-tree fertilizer (97).

357. Routine Pest Control. Spray early each January with tar-oil wash. Cut out all dead wood or branches carrying silvered leaves (711) before the end of July and paint wounds with Stockholm tar. Spray repeatedly with malathion (677) if there is any sign of aphids (711).

358. Propagation. By budding in July or August exactly as for apples (210). Many stocks are used. Brompton is vigorous, suitable for standards and large bushes and is compatible with all varieties. Myrobalan B is vigorous and one of the most popular stocks for large trees but a few varieties such as Count Althann's Gage and Oullins Golden Gage will not grow on it. Common Mussel and Common Plum are semi-dwarfing and suitable for small trees and fan-trained plums but some varieties will not grow on them. St Julien A and Pershore are moderately dwarfing and suitable for small trees. They are compatible with all varieties.

A few varieties of plum are best propagated by suckers, a method usually too slow for nurserymen. These are Blaisdon Red, Pershore, and Warwickshire Drooper.

156

359. Varieties of Plum. Belgian Purple (CD), Aug.; Belle de Louvain (C), Aug.–Sept.; Blackbird (CD), Aug.; Black Prince (C), July; Blaisdon Red (C), Aug.; Blue Rock (D), Aug.; Blue Tit (D), Aug.; Bountiful (D), Aug.; Bradley's King (Damson) (CD), Sept.; Bryanston Gage (D), Sept.

Cambridge Gage (D), Aug.; Coe's Golden Drop (D), Sept.; Count Althann's Gage (D), Sept.; Cox's Emperor (CD), Sept.; Cropper (CD), Sept.; Czar (CD), Aug.

Denniston's Superb (D), Aug.; Diamond (C), Sept.

Early Laxton (C), July–Aug.; Early Orleans (C), July; Early Transparent Gage (D), Aug.; Evesham Wonder (C), Aug.

Farleigh Damson (Cluster or Crittenden) (C), Sept.; Frogmore Damson (C), Sept.

Gisborne's (C), Aug.; Giant Prune (C), Sept.; Golden Transparent Gage (D), Sept.; Goldfinch (D), Sept.; Green Gage (D), Aug.

Jefferson (D), Sept.; Jubilee (D), Aug.

Kirke's Blue (D), Sept.

Langley Bullace (C), Oct.–Nov.; Late Orange (C), Oct.; Late Transparent Gage (D), Sept.; Laxton's Gage (D), Aug.

Marjorie's Seedling (C), Oct.; Merryweather Damson (C), Sept.; Mirabelle (C), Aug.; Monarch (C), Sept.–Oct.

Oullin's Golden Gage (CD), Aug.

Pershore (C), Aug.; Pond's Seedling (C), Sept.; President (C), Oct.; Purple Gage (Reine-Claude Violette) (D), Sept.; Purple Pershore (C), Aug.

Reine Claude de Bavay (D), Sept.–Oct.; Red Magnum Bonum (C), Sept.; Rivers's Early Prolific (C), July.

Severn Cross (C or D), Sept.; Shepherd's Bullace (C), Oct.; Shropshire Damson (CD), Sept.–Oct.

Transparent Gage (D), Sept.; Utility (D), Aug.; Victoria (CD), Aug.–Sept.

Warwickshire Drooper (CD), Sept.; White Bullace (CD),

Oct.–Nov.; Wyedale (C), Oct.

QUINCE

360. Soil and Situation. Likes a sunny position and rich, rather moist soil. Well-rotted manure may be dug in freely before planting, especially on light, sandy soils.

361. Planting. As for apples (190).

362. Form of Training. Usually grown as bushes, but occasionally seen as small standards.

363. Pruning. As for pears (340).

364. Picking. Gather fruits towards the end of October and store as for pears (343). Very valuable for making into conserve or jelly.

365. Routine Feeding. As for pears (344).

366. Routine Pest Control. Usually unnecessary.

367. Varieties of Quince. Apple-shaped (English), Champion, Meech's Prolific, Pear-shaped, Portugal, Vranja.

RASPBERRIES

368. Soil and Situation. Raspberries succeed in most soils except those of a very light, dry nature. They appreciate moisture while in growth. Soil must be dug deeply and should be dressed with well-rotted manure at the rate of 1 cwt. to 12 sq. yd., and sulphate of potash at 1 oz. per square yard. Lime is not essential.

369. Planting. This may be done at any time from mid-October until the end of March. Autumn planting is best, but spring planting gives excellent results in some seasons. Canes should not be allowed to fruit the first year. They are spaced 18 in. apart in rows 6 ft. apart (22). The uppermost roots should be covered with about 1 in. of soil.

370. Training. Wires strained between posts, or a fence or trellis, must be provided to support the canes. The uppermost wire should be 5–5½ ft. from ground level. Each plant is allowed to form five or six canes and these are spread out fanwise on the support.

371. Pruning. After planting, cut all canes back to within 9 in. of ground level. In subsequent years summer-fruiting varieties are pruned as soon as the crop has been gathered. All canes that have borne fruit are cut out to ground level; strong young canes are trained in their places. Very long young canes are tipped in February, when they should be cut back to within about 6½ ft. of ground level. Autumn-fruiting varieties are pruned in February. All old canes are cut to within 6 in. of ground level. Perpetual-fruiting raspberries, such as Lloyd George, are pruned in both ways. Summer-fruiting canes are removed immediately after fruiting and autumn-fruiting canes cut back the following February.

NEW CANES, or suckers, are produced direct from the roots. Usually there are far more than are required. Retain five or six of the strongest nearest to the parent root. Canes appearing far from these should be cut out early in the summer or they become a nuisance. A few may be retained for propagation if necessary (374).

372. Routine Cultivation. Raspberry plantations become very weedy unless regularly hoed. Take care not to disturb the soil deeply, as most roots are near the surface. Forking and digging should not be attempted. Each May spread a mulch of well-rotted manure over the roots; each March give sulphate of potash at 1 oz. and sulphate of ammonia at ½ oz. per square yard.

373. Routine Pest Control. When raspberry beetle (711) is troublesome, dust or spray with derris (662) in June when the flowers begin to fall and repeat when the first fruits turn pink. Keep a sharp watch for mozaic (711) and remove any plants showing signs of this disease.

374. Propagation. Effected by digging up young canes

(suckers) in October or early November. Canes at some distance from the parent plants are most suitable, as they can be dug up with roots without injury to these plants. Replant at once in the ordinary manner.

375. Varieties of Raspberry. Lloyd George, June–Oct.; Malling Enterprise, June–July; Malling Exploit, June–July; Malling Jewel, July; Malling Landmark, July; Malling Promise, June–July; Norfolk Giant, July; September, Sept.–Oct.

STRAWBERRIES

376. Soil and Situation. Strawberries succeed best in rich soils. They will grow well in heavy loam if good winter drainage can be assured. Phosphates have a marked effect on growth. Soil should be deeply dug, enriched with manure or compost at 1 cwt. to 12–15 sq. yd., and dusted with basic slag at 6 oz. per square yard and sulphate of potash at $1\frac{1}{2}$ oz. per square yard. Lime is not essential.

ALPINE STRAWBERRIES do not as a rule make runners and are increased by seed. These are sown in March in a cool greenhouse (average temperature 55°) in ordinary seed compost (501). The seedlings are pricked off (502) into boxes as soon as they can be handled conveniently and then transferred to a frame and gradually hardened off for planting outdoors in early summer.

377. Planting. The best season is August and early September. Failing this, pot-grown runners (381) can be planted in March. These should not be allowed to fruit the first season. Space plants $1\frac{1}{2}$ ft. apart in rows $2\frac{1}{2}$–3 ft. apart (22). On heavy land, draw the soil into low ridges 2 ft. apart and plant along the summits of these. Be careful not to bury the crowns below the surface. Roots should be just covered and crowns on the surface.

378. Pollination. A few varieties produce no pollen and

consequently no fruits unless other pollen-bearing varieties are planted with them. Others are self-sterile, i.e. they produce pollen, but this is not effective for their own pollination. All these must be interplanted with other varieties. Few such varieties are cultivated in gardens nowadays, having been discarded in favour of self-fertile varieties, but Huxley Giant is grown commercially.

379. Routine Cultivation. All runners must be cut off during the summer months unless required for propagation (381). Soil should be kept clean by frequent hoeing, but digging or forking must not be attempted, because many roots are produced near the surface. Clean straw must be spread between plants in May to conserve moisture and preserve fruits from mud splashes, or strawberry mats may be used.

Each March top dress with a mixture of six parts by weight of superphosphate of lime, three parts of sulphate of potash, and two parts of sulphate of ammonia, at 3 oz. per sq. yd.

380. Routine Pest Control. Usually unnecessary, as foes are dealt with as noted. Dust with flowers of sulphur if mildew (711) appears; burn off straw on the beds when the crop has been gathered to destroy old foliage together with possible pests and fungi. This should be done on a dry, breezy day, so that the straw burns quickly. If red spider (711) or tarsonemid mite (711) is troublesome, spray with lime sulphur (675) at summer strength, about the third week in March. Use captan (649) or thiram (707) to control grey mould, but not if fruit is to be preserved in any way.

381. Propagation. Strawberries soon deteriorate, and beds are rarely worth keeping after their third year. Usual practice is to remake one-third of the bed each year, so that the whole plantation is renewed every three years. Propagation is effected by runners produced throughout the summer. These should be selected from the best plants only, chosen for health and good cropping. Retain five or six runners per plant. Pinch the tip out of each just beyond the first plantlet formed on it. Peg this plantlet firmly to the soil or fill a small flower pot with loamy soil, plunge to its rim near the parent plant and peg the runner into this. Propagation should be done in June or July. If kept moist, each plantlet will produce roots by the middle of August, when the runner joining it to the parent plant may be severed. A week or so later lift and replant in fruiting quarters, or, alternatively, pot and winter in a frame for spring planting.

The Alpine varieties of strawberry, which produce small fruits during most of the summer and early autumn, do not make runners and are usually raised from seed. The large-fruited perpetual strawberries produced by crossing Alpine varieties with normal large-fruited strawberries do make runners but not always very freely.

382. Forcing. Strawberries can be gently forced to fruit a month or more ahead of normal time. Strong runners should be rooted in June (381) and potted singly in 4- or 5-in. pots in August. Use an ordinary potting compost (505), place pots on ash base in a frame, shade for a week, but give no further protection till October. Then use lights to ward off extreme wet and snow, but ventilate freely whenever possible. Remove pots to a cool greenhouse (temp. 40°–50°) from January to March according to the time at which fruit is required. Water with increasing freedom as growth proceeds. Hand fertilize flowers with camel-hair brush. From the time plants come into flower, temperature may be increased gradually to a maximum of 70° to be reached as the fruit swells. Drop to 60°–65° for the last few days. Cooler conditions may be maintained throughout if it is not desired to hurry ripening unduly.

Cloches of the continuous barn type (520) may also be used to cover strawberry plants growing in the open. They should be placed in position about mid-February and may need to be lightly shaded with whitewash for the last few weeks if the weather is very sunny. Remove cloches as soon as crop has been gathered.

383. Varieties. Cambridge Favourite, mid-season; Cambridge Prizewinner, early; Cambridge Rival, early; Cambridge Vigour, mid-season; Gorella, early; Merton Herald, early; Redgauntlet, mid-season; Royal Sovereign, early; Talisman, late. Hampshire Maid, Red Rich, Sans Rivale, Gento and Triomphe are perpetual-fruiting varieties.

WALNUTS

384. Soil and Situation. Will succeed in most soils that are not waterlogged, or very poor and liable to dry out severely in summer. Prefer open, sunny places.

385. Planting. As for apples (190). Space trees at least 30 ft. apart.

386. Forms of Training. Almost invariably grown as standards. Often planted for ornament as well as utility.

387. Pollination. Male catkins and female flowers appear on the same tree and are compatible (183). Unfortunately, some varieties produce female flowers years before the male catkins start to appear, and are therefore unfruitful for an unnecessarily long period. Other kinds bear catkins early and are useful for pollination. Most walnuts grown in this country are seedlings and, in consequence, very variable. It is not possible to say in advance to which type they will belong. Where possible, selected varieties chosen for their early production of catkins should be planted.

388. Pruning. Practically unnecessary except for the removal of badly placed branches to improve the balance of the head. This may be done in November.

389. Picking and Storing. Leave the nuts to fall naturally or shake them from the tree. Remove outer skins, wipe with damp cloth and store in earthenware jars or crocks with a layer of salt over each layer of nuts. If desired, dry coconut fibre or peat may be mixed in equal bulk with the salt.

390. Routine Feeding and Pest Control. Unnecessary.

391. Propagation. Usually by seeds sown outdoors in March. Better results are obtained by budding or grafting seedling walnuts with selected varieties. Budding is done outdoors in May or June, using a special method known as patch budding. The bud is cut out with a circle or rectangle of bark and a similar piece of bark is removed from the stock to receive it. Alternatively, young seedlings potted for the purpose may be grafted in the greenhouse, usually in February or March. A temperature of 60°–65° must be maintained. Quicker results are obtained in a propagating case, temperature 70°–75°. The grafted plants must be carefully hardened off for transference to a frame in May or June and planting in a nursery bed in the autumn.

391a. Varieties. Franquette, Leeds Castle, Mayette, Northdown Clawnut and Stutton Seedling.

SECTION FIVE

THE ORNAMENTAL GARDEN

ALPINES

392. Description. Strictly a plant from a mountainous region but used loosely to cover all plants of dwarf habit suitable for planting in rock gardens. Most are hardy herbaceous perennials (451), some are biennials (429), others annuals (410), and a few are shrubs (476). There are evergreen and deciduous kinds (476).

393. Soil and Situation. Most alpines delight in a sunny situation and a rather gritty, well-drained soil. A few like shade and moisture. Detailed requirements, however, are very varied and some of the choicest varieties are difficult to grow. The moraine and scree are designed to meet the needs of these. These are beds, usually on a slope, filled with extremely gritty or stony compost. The moraine has an underground water supply; the scree has not. Specimen composts are for ordinary alpines – loam 6 parts, leaf-mould or peat 3 parts, stone chippings 1 part, sharp sand $\frac{1}{2}$ part. For peat lovers – lime-free loam 4 parts, leaf-mould and peat 3 parts, lime-free sand or grit 2 parts. For moraine or scree – loam 2 parts, leaf-mould or peat 2 parts, sand or grit 1 part, stone chippings 4 parts.

Contrary to popular belief, few alpines will grow on rocks with little soil. They are mostly deep-rooting plants and should have at least 18 in. of good soil. Sempervivums and a few sedums are practically the only kinds that will grow on roofs and similar bare places. Dry walls must have a core of soil in contact with the soil below so that plants can root through.

Good bottom drainage is most important. Is is usually advisable to spread a thick layer of brick ends or clinkers under the whole of the selected site. On top of this place the soil, which may be worked into irregular mounds to give a natural effect if so desired, though good results can be obtained from flat beds. The stone chosen should be fairly porous yet reasonably durable. Limestone and sandstone are most suitable, and the former can be obtained from hillside workings with natural weather and water marks on them. It is desirable to bed the stone well down into the soil, usually on its broadest face rather than to rear it up on the surface. Several rocks can be built together to form large spurs or outcrops. Crevices between such rocks can be suitably planted provided the crevice has an outlet to an ample body of soil behind or below. A good effect can often be obtained by arranging the stones to simulate a natural outcrop of rock such as may be seen on many hillsides.

394. Planting. Most nurserymen grow alpines in small containers. They can be transplanted from these with little or no root disturbance at any time of the year except when ground is frozen. Plants that are to be lifted from the open ground should be transplanted in March or April or, if they are in flower at that time, as soon as the flowers fade. Water freely until established. In general, small plants are to be preferred. When planting in the moraine or scree, shake all soil from the roots, spread these out and work the gritty compost around them. All alpines should be planted firmly.

395. Cultural Routine. Most varieties will benefit from the removal of faded flowers. With aubrietas, helianthemums, and iberis, this can be extended to a thorough trimming up with scissors or shears after flowering. A few plants may be left to carry seed if this is required for propagation (396). Apart from this the only cultural attentions required are to remove weeds, to cut back rampant plants which tend to smother others in their path, to remove fallen leaves, particularly tree leaves in the autumn, and to top dress with gritty soil in winter or early spring. This may consist of equal parts of coarse sand, stone chippings and loam, and should be worked between and among the shoots. In spite of the fact that most alpines grow in rocky places, they appreciate liberal watering in hot weather.

396. Propagation. Most alpines can be increased by division in similar manner to herbaceous perennials (454). This is best done in March–April or, if they are in flower at that time, immediately after flowering. Many varieties, particularly those of shrubby habit, can be increased by cuttings taken in July and August and treated in the same manner as summer shrub cuttings (481). The cuttings are naturally smaller, from $\frac{1}{2}$ to 2 in. in length. Seed provides a cheap method of increasing most kinds and should be sown in March in a frame or outdoors in May. In other respects, treatment is the same as for seed of hardy perennials (454).

397. Alpines for Shady Situations. *Anemone appenina, A. blanda, Arenaria balearica, Calceolaria polyrrhiza,* hardy cyclamen in variety, *Daphne blagayana, Gaultheria procumbens, Gentiana asclepiadea, Haberlea rhodopensis, Hepatica angulosa, Hutchinsia alpina, Iberis sempervirens, Linnaea borealis, Omphalodes verna, Oxalis enneaphylla, Primula denticulata* and varieties, *P. japonica, P. juliae, P. juliana* varieties, *Ramonda pyrenaica, Sanguinaria canadensis,* saxifraga (mossy varieties), *S. primuloides, Synthyris reniformis, Tiarella cordifolia, Viola cornuta* and varieties, *V. gracilis.*

398. Autumn- and Winter-flowering Alpines. Colchicums, *Crocus imperati, C. sieberi, C. speciosus, C. zonatus, Erica carnea* and varieties, *E. vulgaris* and varieties, *Galanthus byzantinus, G. cilicicus, Gentiana farreri, G. sino-ornata, G. macaulayi, Iris histrio, I. reticulata, Primula winteri, Sternbergia lutea.*

399. Alpines for Planting between Paving Stones. Acaenas, *Ajuga reptans* in variety, antennarias, *Arenaria balearica, Armeria maritima, Asperula gussonii, Calamintha alpina,* cotulas, *Frankenia laevis, Geranium pylzowianum, Herniaria glabra, Hypsela longiflora, Linaria aequitriloba, Mazus*

167

pumilio, *M. reptans*, *Mentha requienii*, *Mimulus radicans*, *Nierembergia rivularis*, *Raoulia australis*, *Saxifraga muscoides*, sedums, *Silene alpestris*, *Thymus serpyllum* in variety, *Veronica rupestris*.

400. Scree Plants. *Androsace arachnoidea superba*, *A. sempervivoides*, *Armeria caespitosa*, *Asperula suberosa*, *Calandrinia umbellata*, *Campanula allionii*, *C. arvatica*, *C. aucheri*, *C. cenisea*, *C. excisa*, *C. raineri*, *C. rupestris*, *C. stansfieldii*, *C. tommasiniana*, *C. wockii*, *Chrysanthemum alpinum*, *Dianthus alpinus*, *D. neglectus*, *Douglasia vitaliana*, *Draba imbricata*, *D. polytricha*, *D. pyrenaica*, *Erigeron leiomerus*, *E. trifidus*, *Erinus alpinus* (all varieties), *Erodium corsicum rubrum*, *Gentiana farreri*, *G. verna*, *Globularia incanescens*, *Gypsophila cerastioides*, *Helichrysum frigidum*, *Linaria alpina*, *Lychnis pyrenaica*, *Myosotis rupicola*, *Omphalodes lucilliae*, *Papaver alpinum*, *Penstemon rupicola*, *Phyteuma comosum*, *Polygala calcarea*, *Potentilla nitida*, *Ranunculus alpestris*, *R. glacialis*, *Raoulia australis*, saxifraga (all varieties of cushion and porphyrion types), *S. cochlearis minor*, *S. valdensis*, *Silene acaulis*, *Teucrium montanum*, *Wahlenbergia pumilo*, *W. serpyllifolia major*. All can also be grown in the moraine.

401. Easily Grown Alpine Plants. *Achillea tomentosa*, *Aethionema* Warley Rose, *Alyssum saxatile*, *Androsace lanuginosa*, *A. sarmentosa*, *Aquilegia caerulea*, *Arabis albida flore pleno*, *Arenaria montana*, *Armeria laucheana*, aubrietas, *Campanula carpatica*, *C. portenschlagiana*, *C. pusilla*, *Cotyledon simplicifolia*, *Dianthus caesius*, *D. deltoides*, *Erinus alpinus*, *Erodium hybridum roseum*, *Gentiana acaulis*, *G. lagodechiana*, *G. septemfida*, *Geranium sanguineum lancastriense*, *Gypsophila repens subcaulescens*, helianthemums, *Hypericum olympicum*, *Iberis sempervirens*, *I. saxatilis*, *Linum perenne*, *Oenothera missouriensis*, *Penstemon scouleri*, *Phlox divaricata*, *P. subulata*, *Potentilla tonguei*, *Primula denticulata*, *P. frondosa*, *P. juliana*, *P. marginata*, *P. rosea*, *Rosa roulettii*,

Saponaria ocymoides, Saxifraga aizoon, S. apiculata, S. cotyledon, S. elizabethae, S. granulata fl. pl., S. haagii, S. lingulata albertii, S. oppositifolia, S. primuloides Elliott's variety, all mossy saxifrages, sedums, sempervivums, *Silene alpestris, S. schafta, Sisyrinchium angustifolium, Thymus nitidus, T. serpyllum, Tunica saxifraga, Veronica prostrata, Viola cornuta, V. gracilis.*

ANNUALS (HALF-HARDY)

402. Description. Like hardy annuals (410) these complete their cycle of growth in one year, but, unlike them, they cannot be sown outdoors in early spring because of the danger of frost. Most must be raised under glass, but there are borderline varieties, nearly but not fully hardy, that may be sown outdoors in late April or early May. All can be grown outdoors without protection during the summer. Half-hardy annuals are also grown as pot plants for greenhouse decoration.

403. Soil and Situation. The same as for hardy annuals (411) with, if anything, more emphasis on good drainage and a sunny position. Nicotiana is one of the few exceptions which likes shade.

404. Sowing. Seed of most varieties can be sown in a warm greenhouse towards the end of February or in an unheated greenhouse or frame in March–April. Temperature of about 60° is required for germination. Seed is sown in well-drained pots, pans, or boxes in any good seed compost (501). It should be scattered very thinly, covered lightly with a sprinkling of finely sifted soil and then each receptacle covered with a sheet of glass and another of brown paper. The paper must be removed at the first signs of germination. A day later tilt the glass slightly with a pebble or stick, and two or three days after this remove altogether.

Soil must be kept moist. This is best done by holding each pan for a few moments almost to its rim in a bucket of water with the chill off. When the rising water darkens the surface of the soil, remove the pan and allow it to drain.

405. Pricking off. When the seedlings have made two or three leaves each, they must be transferred carefully to other trays or pans prepared in a similar manner (404). Lift carefully with a pointed stick, divide into single plants with as little injury to the roots as possible and replant with a round-ended dibber about as thick as an ordinary lead pencil. The seedlings should be planted about 2 in. apart each way. Make the soil firm round the roots, water freely overhead through a fine rose and return to the greenhouse or frame. Shade from strong sunlight for a day or so until growth resumes. Subsequently, give full exposure to sun and ventilate as freely as possible, consistent with a minimum temperature of 55° by day, 50° by night.

406. Hardening off. The seedlings must be gradually accustomed to the outdoor temperature. Those raised in the warm greenhouse should be transferred to a frame about mid-April. Ventilation must be further increased as weather permits until by mid-May lights are removed entirely except when frost threatens, as it may on clear, calm nights.

407. Planting. In some sheltered gardens half-hardy annuals can be planted out early in May, but in most localities it is not safe until the end of May or even until early June. Remove seedlings from the boxes or pans with as little soil disturbance as possible. This is most readily done if they have been well watered a few hours previously. Divide into separate plants and replant with a trowel. Make the soil thoroughly firm around the roots and water in freely. Small varieties should be 6 in. apart; those of medium height 9 or 12 in., large-growing kinds, $1\frac{1}{2}$ to 2 ft. (409).

408. Culture. The same as for hardy annuals (414). The trailing growths of *Phlox drummondii* should be pegged to the soil. Floppy varieties can be supported with bushy twigs (456).

409. A Table of Half-hardy Annuals

Name	Colour	Height	Planting Distance
*Ageratum	Mauve	6–12 in.	6–8 in.
*Antirrhinum	White, yellow, pink to crimson	6–36 in.	6–12 in.
Arctotis	White, yellow, orange, red, purple	1–2 ft.	12 in.
Aster	Blue, purple, pink, red, white	12–30 in.	12 in.
*Begonia semperflorens	White, pink to crimson	6–12 in.	9 in.
Celosia	Red, yellow	12–30 in.	12 in.
Cleome	Pink	3 ft.	18 in.
*Cosmea	White, pink to crimson, orange	2–3 ft.	12 in.
Dianthus sinensis	White to crimson	6–12 in.	6 in.
*Helichrysum	Yellow, orange, red, white	18–30 in.	9–12 in.
*Heliotrope	Purple	18–24 in.	12 in.
Impatiens	Red, pink, white	6–24 in.	9–12 in.
Kochia (summer cypress)	Green foliage, turning crimson	2–3 ft.	2 ft.
*Lobelia	Blue	6 in.–24 in.	6 in.
Marigolds (African and French)	Yellow, orange, and crimson	6 in.	6–12 in.
*Mesembryanthemum criniflorum	White, buff, pink to crimson	6 in.	6 in.
Nemesia	Various	9–12 in.	6–8 in.
Nicotiana	White, pink to crimson	1–3 ft.	12 in.
*Petunia	White, blue, pink, to purple	12–18 in.	8–12 in.
Phlox drummondii	White, scarlet to purple, etc.	6–18 in.	9 in.
Rudbeckia hirta	Yellow, red	18–36 in.	12–18 in.
Salpiglossis	Various	18–24 in.	12 in.
*Salvia splendens	Scarlet, purple	6–24 in.	6–12 in.
Statice sinuata	Blue, red, yellow, white	18 in.	12 in.
Stocks (ten weeks)	White, pink, red, purple	12–18 in.	12 in.
Ursinia	Orange	12–15 in.	9–12 in.
Venidium	Orange	2–3 ft.	18 in.
Zinnia	Red, pink, orange, yellow	6–36 in.	6–12 in.

*Strictly speaking, half-hardy perennials but usually treated as half-hardy annuals.

ANNUALS (HARDY)

410. Description. An annual completes its whole cycle of life, including the production of flowers and seed, within one year, and then dies. A hardy annual is, in addition, sufficiently resistant to cold to be sown outdoors without protection in the spring. Some hardy annuals can also be sown outdoors in the autumn and wintered without protection, but this does not apply to all (415).

411. Soil and Situation. Hardy annuals are extremely adaptable and there are few soils or places in which they will not grow. They prefer soils that are well drained and positions that are open and sunny, but godetias do tolerably well in shade also. Little preparation is required, beyond thorough forking to prepare a fine seed bed. Manure as a rule does more harm than good, tending to produce leaves at the expense of flowers.

412. Sowing. Seed may be sown at any time from March till May and, in the case of particularly hardy varieties, again in early September. September-sown plants will winter without thinning outdoors and start to flower in June the following year. March and April-sown annuals flower from July to September, while those sown in May flower from August to October. Seeds are sown where the plants are to flower. Some seedlings may be transplanted elsewhere later on if overcrowded, but the majority are left undisturbed. Taprooted annuals, such as godetias, eschscholzias, and Shirley poppies, do not transplant well. Seed may be sown broadcast or in drills, and should be covered very lightly with finely broken soil. Water if the soil is dry, not otherwise. Germination takes from one to three weeks according to variety and weather.

413. Thinning. If seedlings come up too thickly, they must be thinned as soon as they can be handled, except autumn-sown annuals, which are not thinned until the following spring. Small varieties should be thinned to 4 or 5 in. apart, kinds of medium growth to 8 to 12 in. and tall varieties to 18 in. or more (415).

414. Culture. Faded flowers should be removed before seed is formed unless it is intended to save some seed for the following year. If it is desired to save seed, a few good plants should be marked for the purpose early in the summer and all flowers retained. The seed pods are cut with a length of stem as soon as they turn yellow and start to split open or, with daisy-type flowers, as soon as the heads turn yellow and show signs of shedding their seeds. Ripening should be completed in clean, paper-lined trays in a sunny window or greenhouse. Different varieties of the same kind of annual, e.g. different colours of eschscholzias, cross readily and unless special precautions are taken seed will be mixed, i.e. the seedlings will produce flowers of many different colours.

Feeding is usually unnecessary. The only other routine measure is to keep beds free of weeds, by hoeing until the plants cover the ground, and then by hand weeding.

415. See pages 174, 175.

AQUATICS

416. Description. Any plants that grow wholly or mainly in water. Almost all are herbaceous perennials (451). There are hardy, half-hardy, and tender varieties. The first can be grown outdoors all the year; the second should have protection from frost in the winter; the third are suitable for cultivation only in indoor aquariums with warm water.

417. Soil and Situation. Most aquatics are sun-loving plants and for this reason ornamental pools should, if possible, be in the open, not under the shade of large trees. A few plants will grow in the water alone without soil, but the majority must have suitable compost. Medium to heavy loam is best. Manure and fertilizers should not be used for

415. Table of Hardy Annuals for Summer Beds

Name	Colour	Height	Distance to Thin
Alyssum (Sweet)	White	4–6 in.	4–6 in.
Amaranthus caudatus	Crimson and green	30 in.	12 in.
Bartonia	Yellow	18 in.	12 in.
†Calandrinia	Rose, crimson	9–18 in.	6–9 in.
*Calendula	Yellow and orange	12–18 in.	12 in.
Calliopsis (coreopsis)	Yellow and crimson	18–24 in.	12 in.
*Candytuft	White, lilac, and purple	6–12 in.	6–9 in.
*Chrysanthemum (annual)	White, yellow, scarlet to maroon	12–24 in.	12–18 in.
Clarkia	White, pink to crimson	18–24 in.	12 in.
Collinsia	White and purple	12 in.	6–9 in.
Convolvulus	Purple, crimson, and white	12–15 in.	9–18 in.
*Cornflower	White, blue, and rose	12–36 in.	9–12 in.
Dimorphotheca	Orange, salmon, etc.	12 in.	12 in.
Echium	Blue, lavender, pink, and white	12 in.	9 in.
Eschscholzia	Yellow, orange, carmine, and rose	9–12 in.	9 in.
Godetia	Pink to crimson and rose	6–24 in.	9–12 in.
*Gypsophila elegans	White, pink, and carmine	18 in.	9–12 in.
*Helipterum roseum	Pink and white	18 in.	6 in.
*Ipomoea purpurea	Blue, purple, pink, and white	Climbing	1–2 ft.
†Jacobaea	White, mauve, pink, and purple	18 in.	9–12 in.
*Larkspur	White, blue, pink, and scarlet	2–3 ft.	18 in.
†Lavatera	White and rose	3–4 ft.	18 in.–2 ft.
†Layia	Yellow and white	12 in.	9 in.
†Leptosiphon	Various	3–6 in.	3–4 in.
Limnanthes	Pale Yellow	6 in.	6 in.

Linum (scarlet flax)	Scarlet	9–12 in.	6 in.
Love-in-a-Mist (nigella)	Blue and white	18 in.	12 in.
Lupin	White, blue, pink to crimson	2 ft.	1 ft.
Malope	Purple, white, etc.	2–3 ft.	18 in.
Matthiola bicornis	Purple	9–12 in.	3–6 in.
Mignonette	Greenish yellow, white, and red	12 in.	6–9 in.
†Nasturtium	Yellow, scarlet, etc.	9–12 in. Also climbing.	9–15 in.
Nemophila	Blue	6 in.	4–6 in.
Phacelia	Blue	8 in.	9 in.
Poppy (Shirley and Cardinal)	White, pink, crimson, heliotrope, etc.	2–3 ft.	12–15 in.
Salvia horminum	Blue, pink and white	18–24 in.	9 in.
Saponaria	Rose	2 ft.	6 in.
Scabious (Sweet)	White, lavender, pink to maroon	18–24 in.	12–15 in.
Sunflower (annual)	Yellow and orange	3–10 ft.	2–3 ft.
*Sweet Pea	White, pink, blue, scarlet, etc.	6–10 ft.	4–9 in.
†Sweet Sultan	White, rose, and purple	18 in.	9 in.
†*Tagetes signata pumila*	Yellow	9–12 in.	6 in.
†*Tropaeolum canariense* (Canary creeper)	Yellow	Climbing	9–12 in.
Virginian Stock	White, yellow, pink to crimson	6 in.	3–4 in.
Viscaria	White, blue, pink to crimson	12 in.	6 in.

Most of these can be sown outdoors from March to May. Those marked with an asterisk may also be sown in September. Do not sow those marked † until mid-April.

fear of polluting the water. Spread soil to a depth of about 6 in. (more, if possible) over the bottom of the pool and cover with 1 in. of clean sand or gravel. Less depth is required in an aquarium. Alternatively, place compost in mounds with fine-meshed wire netting to hold it in place, or in plastic baskets or pots. Depth of water varies from 3 ft. for some of the strongest-growing water lilies to 3 in. for many marginal plants (421).

418. Planting. Plants with normal roots and crowns, e.g. water lilies, rushes, reed maces, etc., can be planted exactly like herbaceous perennials (453), if water can be emptied from the pool. If not, they are best planted in plastic baskets or pots and sunk in position. A simple way of planting oxygenating plants, i.e. plants which supply oxygen to the water, is to tie a stone to the bottom of each, and sink in position. No plants should be put into ice-cold water or water drawn direct from the main. It should be allowed to stand for a while to be warmed by the sun and acted upon by the atmosphere. It is better to fill pools gradually as plants grow than to plant in the maximum depth of water straight away. Late April and early May are the best times for planting outdoors. Indoor aquariums may be planted a little earlier.

Fishes, water snails, etc., should be introduced a few weeks after planting, when the water clears. It is always a little muddy at first.

419. Cultural Routine. All dead leaves must be removed in the autumn. Pond weed, etc., can be raked out from time to time. Algae (green scum on the surface) is removed by drawing a sack across the surface. In small quantity these weeds do no harm, but rather good. They can also be destroyed with copper sulphate, 23 grammes per thousand gallons of water. This treatment is not recommended, as an overdose may damage fish and water plants. A less dangerous method is to stir in a saturated solution of potassium permanganate at the rate of 1 teaspoonful of chemical to each gallon of water.

It is not necessary to change the water frequently, nor to grow plants in running water. Pools and aquariums properly stocked with water plants, including oxygenating plants (422), fish, water snails, etc., maintain a balance of life and do not become unpleasant. Water lost by evaporation should be made good with water at the same temperature as that of the pool or aquarium.

420. Propagation. Most water plants can be increased by division at the ordinary planting season (418), exactly like herbaceous perennials (454). As a rule they benefit from such division at intervals of five or six years, as this prevents overcrowding.

Some kinds can also be raised from seed sown in ordinary seed compost (501) in well-drained pans, which should then be supported on inverted flower pots or bricks at the edge of the pool so that their rims are about half an inch below water level. Seed is sown in the spring.

Most of the submerged oxygenating plants (422) can be increased by cuttings. Pieces 2 in. to 4 in. long will root readily in a sandy compost.

421. See next page.

422. Useful Oxygenating Plants. In all these the foliage is submerged and supplies oxygen to the water. Those preceded by an asterisk are tender and must be protected in winter. Apium (Marshwort), *Cabomba (Washington Grass), Callitriche (Water Starwort), Ceratophyllum (Hornwort), Chara, Elatine (Waterwort), Eleocharis (Needle Spike Rush), Elodea, Fontinalis (Willow Moss), Hottonia (Water Violet), *Myriophyllum hippuroides, Myriophyllum verticillatum (Water Millfoil), Oenanthe (Water Dropwort), Pilularia (Pillwort), Potamogeton (Pondweed), Ranunculus aquatilis (Water Crowfoot), Utricularia (Bladderwort), *Vallisneria (Tape Grass).

421. A Table of Aquatic Plants

Botanical Name	Popular Name	Ornamental Value	Depth of Water
Acorus	Sweet Flag	Sword-like foliage	3–5 in.
Alisma	Water Plantain	Broad foliage, pink flowers	3–5 in.
Aponogeton	Water Hawthorn	Pink flowers, floating leaves	6–18 in.
Butomus	Flowering Rush	Pink flowers	1–3 in.
Caltha	Marsh Marigold	Yellow flowers	Bog
Carex	Sedge Grass	Grassy foliage	Bog
Cyperus	Umbrella Grass	Rush-like foliage	Bog
Eriophorum	Cotton Grass	Rush-like foliage, cotton-like seeds	1–3 in.
Hydrocleis (Limnocharis)	Water Poppy	Yellow flowers	9–12 in.
Iris pseudacorus	Water Flag	Yellow flowers	3–5 in.
Juncus	Bog Rush	Narrow foliage	Bog
Limnanthemum (Villarsia)	Floating Heart	Yellow flowers	6–18 in.
Mentha	Water Mint	Aromatic foliage	Bog
Menyanthes	Buckbean	Floating foliage, white flowers	Bog
Mimulus	Water Musk	Yellow flowers	3–5 in.
Myosotis palustris	Water Forget-me-not	Blue flowers	Bog
Nuphar	Yellow Water Lily	Yellow flowers	2–3 ft.
Nymphaea	Water Lily	Flowers of many colours	½–3 ft.
Orontium	Golden Club	Glaucous foliage, yellow flowers	3–18 in.
Pontederia	Pickerel Weed	Heart-shaped leaves, blue flowers	1–3 in.
Sagittaria	Arrowhead	Foliage and white flowers	3–5 in.
Scirpus	Bulrush	Rush foliage	1–3 in.
Typha	Reed Mace	Rush foliage, cigar-like flower heads	1–3 in.

Note.—The depth of water is that which should cover the crowns.

BEDDING PLANTS (SUMMER)

423. Description. This is purely a garden term with no botanical significance. Some summer bedding plants are half-hardy annuals (402), some half-hardy perennials, i.e. plants which continue to live for many years, but may be damaged by frost, so cannot be left outdoors for the winter. Their sole link is that all may be planted out at the end of May or early in June to fill the garden with flowers in the summer. They are either thrown away in the autumn or lifted and wintered in a greenhouse, frame, or other frost-proof place. Treatment of half-hardy annuals has already been described (402 to 409); here only perennials are dealt with.

424. Soil and Situation. With few exceptions bedding plants thrive in well-dug but not over-rich soils and sunny positions. A few kinds, notably calceolarias and tuberous-rooted begonias, will succeed in shade.

425. Culture. This will vary according to the nature of the plant, and further particulars are given in a table (428). Summer treatment is similar to that of annuals except that it is rarely wise to save seeds, as these may give very disappointing results. Trailing plants, such as ivy-leaved geraniums, may be pegged to the soil or tied up to short stakes. Tall plants, e.g. standard fuchsias, heliotropes, abutilons, etc., are often spaced at regular intervals (dot plants) among dwarf kinds (ground plants) to give an attractive effect.

426. Propagation. Some kinds, such as geraniums (zonal and ivy-leaved pelargoniums), calceolarias, gazanias, fuchsias, marguerites, and penstemons, are increased by cuttings. These must be prepared from firm, non-flowering shoots. They should be 1 to 4 in. in length according to the nature of growth, severed immediately beneath a joint, and the lower leaves must be removed. Cuttings are inserted firmly $\frac{1}{2}$ to 1 in. deep in sandy soil round the edge of a well-drained flower pot or in a propagating frame (500). Spring cuttings root best with bottom heat; summer and autumn cuttings in an unheated frame or greenhouse. When well rooted, cuttings must be potted singly in 3-in. pots in an ordinary compost (505). Later it may be necessary to remove to 4-in. pots of a similar compost if the smaller pots become filled with roots before planting-out time arrives.

Other kinds, e.g. heliotrope, verbenas, etc., may be raised from seed as well as from cuttings. The seed should be treated in the same way as for half-hardy annuals (404).

Tuberous-rooted begonias can be raised from seed as above, or old tubers can be divided after starting into growth in spring (427). Cannas can be raised from seed in a temperature of 70° but are usually increased by division in spring.

427. Lifting and Wintering. If they are to be kept over the winter, either for replanting the following year or to supply cuttings in spring, bedding plants must be lifted and brought into a frost-proof place before cold becomes too intense. With all except tuberous-rooted plants this lifting should be done in September or early October, before foliage is damaged by frost. They are then potted in the smallest pots that will contain the roots and placed in a greenhouse. Water should be given sparingly throughout the winter, but soil must never become absolutely dry. Frost protection is sufficient for calceolarias, marguerites, and fuchsias. A slightly higher temperature is preferable for geraniums and heliotropes.

Tuberous-rooted plants such as begonias, cannas, dahlias, and *Salvia patens* are lifted as soon as foliage is blackened by frost. The tops are cut off, and the tubers stored in dry sand or peat in any dry, cool, but frost-proof place. They are re-started into growth from Jan. to April in moist soil or peat in a temperature of from 60°–65°.

428. See pages 182 and 183.

BIENNIALS (HARDY)

429. Description. Plants which complete their cycle of life within two years, i.e. are sown one year, flower the next year, produce seed, and then die. A few biennials can be induced to behave as annuals (410) if sown very early in a warm greenhouse. Monocarpic plants die in the same way as biennials and annuals after having flowered and produced seed, but complete their cycle in an indefinite number of years. The most important true hardy biennials are Canterbury bells, foxgloves, and some verbascums, but wallflowers, forget-me-nots, double daisies, hollyhocks, and sweet williams are often treated as such. (There are also half-hardy and tender kinds for the greenhouse, such as *Campanula pyramidalis* and *Humea elegans*) (534).

430. Soil and Situation. Most are adaptable plants, thriving in ordinary soils and sunny or partially shady positions. Soil should be prepared by thorough digging. A general garden fertilizer (104) can be used in the spring as a top dressing. Animal manure is not desirable.

431. Sowing and Planting. Seed must be sown every year to maintain a supply of flowering plants. The best time for sowing is May. Brompton stocks and forget-me-nots may be left until the end of June or early July. Seed may be sown outdoors in a sheltered border of finely broken soil, but the choicer kinds, such as Canterbury bell and Brompton stock, are best reared in an unheated frame in a semi-shady position. Transplant seedlings 3 to 4 in. apart in rows 8 in. apart into a bed of similar character as soon as they can be handled conveniently, usually between mid-July and mid-August. Plants can be transferred to flowering quarters in September–October or March. Details of planting are exactly the same as for herbaceous perennials (453).

432. Propagation. By seed as above.

428. A Table of Summer Bedding Plants

Name	Colour	Height	Distance Apart for Planting	Method of Propagation
Abutilons	Variegated leaves	2–4 ft.	3–4 ft.	Cuttings in spring
Alternanthera	Ornamental foliage	Creeping	4–6 in.	Cuttings in spring
Begonia (tuberous rooted)	Various	9 in.–1 ft.	9 in.–1 ft.	Seed in Feb. or division of tubers after starting in Feb. or Mar.
Calceolaria (shrubby)	Yellow, bronze	1–1½ ft.	9 in.	Cuttings in early autumn or spring
Calocephalus	Silvery leaves	2–3 ft.	1–1½ ft.	Cuttings in spring
Canna	Various	2–3 ft.	1–2 ft.	Division in spring or seed Jan.–Feb.
Cordyline	Ornamental foliage	2 ft. and upwards	3–6 ft.	Cuttings in spring, seed in Feb.
Dahlia	Various	18 in.–7 ft.	1–3 ft.	Cuttings in spring, seed in Feb. Mar.
Echevaria	Blue-grey rosettes	2–3 in.	6–9 in.	Division in spring

Fuchsia	Pink, red, purple, etc.	1–4 ft.	1–3 ft.	Cuttings in spring or late summer
Gazania	Yellow, orange, etc.	Trailing	6–9 in.	Cuttings in early autumn or spring
Heliotrope	Blue	9 in.–3 ft.	9 in.–4 ft.	Cuttings in spring
Marguerite	White, yellow	18 in.–2 ft.	1–1½ ft.	Cuttings in early autumn or spring
Mesembryanthemum (various)	Various	Trailing	1–2 ft.	Cuttings in spring or late summer
Pansies	Various	4–6 in.	6–9 in.	Seed in spring or early summer
Pelargonium (bedding geranium)	Pink, red, white, etc.	1–2 ft. and trailing	1 ft.	Cuttings in late summer or spring
Penstemon	Various	1½–2 ft.	1 ft.	Cuttings in early autumn
Salvia (blue)	Blue	1½–2 ft.	1 ft.	Cuttings in spring or division in spring
Senecio cineraria	Silver leaves	1½–2 ft.	2 ft.	Cuttings in early autumn or spring
*Verbena	Various	Trailing	9 in.–1 ft.	Cuttings in spring or seed in Jan.–Feb.
Violas	Various	4–6 in.	6–9 in.	Seed in spring or early summer or cuttings in late summer

*Note that these plants are often treated as half-hardy annuals (402).

433. Cultural Routine.. Practically non-existent except for hoeing and removal of weeds. If desired, some plants may be retained after flowering to ripen seeds. These are handled in the same way as annuals retained for seed (414). Other plants should be removed and burnt or placed on the compost heap as soon as they have finished flowering.

BULBS (HARDY)

434. Description. Botanically a bulb is built up of many fleshy or scaly segments, such as those of a lily. In this work the term is used more loosely to include many plants with thickened root stocks storing food to carry the plants over a dormant period. These plants are all perennials. There are also half-hardy and tender kinds (534).

435. Soil and Situation. Like hardy herbaceous perennials (451), bulbs are of many kinds and have varying requirements. Some thrive in shade, others in full sun, but in general most prefer open, well-drained, reasonably rich soils. Ground should be dug deeply and, if believed to be poor, should be enriched with manures such as bonemeal (59), basic slag (57), and hoof and horn (65), plus moderate dressings of well-rotted animal manure well worked in.

436. Planting. Spring-flowering bulbs are planted in late summer and autumn; summer-flowering bulbs in spring, and autumn-flowering bulbs in July and early August. Of the spring-flowering varieties, snowdrops and narcissi (daffodils) should receive first attention (August–September), while tulips and hyacinths may be left until last (October–November). For depths and distances see table (440). Planting may be done with a trowel, stout blunt-ended dibber, or spade. Never plant with a pointed dibber, as this may leave an air space beneath the bulb. A special tool (40) can be obtained for planting bulbs in grass.

Most lilies may be planted in autumn when dormant or

they may be moved in March or April like herbaceous perennials (453). Exception must be made for *Lilium candidum* (the Madonna lily) and *L. testaceum,* which should be planted in late July or early August. Moreover, these lilies and also *L. giganteum* are only just covered with soil. Stem-rooting lilies are planted most deeply, though often the holes are only half filled at first, more soil being added as the stems grow (437).

Gladioli should be put in successively during March and April to prolong the flowering season.

437. Cultural Routine. Beyond hoeing and weeding there is little that can be done while bulbous plants are in growth. Tall-growing kinds, e.g. lilies, or those with heavy spikes of blooms, e.g. gladioli, will require staking and tying. This should be done early. Some lilies form roots from the stems as well as from the bulbs. Soil may be drawn towards these while in growth or, better still, a mixture of soil and leaf-mould or peat can be spread around them in the spring to encourage formation of stem roots. Most bulbs can be fed with weak liquid manure (50) or a general fertilizer (104) applied during the spring for spring-flowering kinds and during the early summer months for gladioli.

438. Lifting and Storing. Spring-flowering bulbs may be lifted after the foliage has died down in summer. This will be in June or early July for narcissi (daffodils) and early tulips and in late June or early July for late tulips, hyacinths and Spanish, English and Dutch irises. In no case should foliage be removed before these times. If bulbs must be lifted earlier, they should be replanted (heeled in) at once, close together in trenches, to complete their growth.

After lifting, pull or cut off the dead leaves, sort the bulbs into sizes, place in shallow boxes, and store in a cool airy place, but not in full sunshine, until planting time. Small bulbs will not as a rule flower the following year but may be planted in a reserve bed to grow on.

Gladioli are lifted in September–October, about six weeks after flowering. Cut off the leaves at once about an inch above the corms (bulbs). Then remove and discard the old withered corms at the base of the new plump corms. Remove tiny cormlets which can be grown on to flowering size if desired. All are stored in shallow trays in an airy, frost-proof place.

Montbretias may be treated in the same way as gladioli, but it is better not to allow them to become fully dormant. Instead, lift in early November and replant close together in a frame, watering very moderately during the winter.

It is not necessary or desirable to lift and store all bulbs every year. Gladioli must come up because they are tender; tulips and hyacinths usually benefit from lifting. Lilies should be left undisturbed unless overcrowded, diseased, or in other ways in need of removal. Crocuses, snowdrops, muscari, bulbous irises, and narcissi (daffodils) can generally be left for several years undisturbed until a falling off in quality and quantity of bloom indicates overcrowding.

439. Propagation. Most bulbs can be increased by removing offsets or young bulbs which are formed alongside or above the old ones. This should be done at the usual lifting season (438) and the small bulbs should be replanted exactly like the large ones but at about two-thirds the depth and in a separate bed, as they will not flower the first year. Some kinds also make tiny bulbils or cormels; certain lilies have these bulbils in the axils of the leaves, while gladioli carry them round the new flowering corm. Like small bulbs, they must be grown on to flowering size but will take longer to attain this, possibly two to four years. Treatment is the same as for bulbs except that they must be covered with approximately their own depth of soil.

Bulbs can also be raised from seed sown in a frame or sheltered position outdoors in March. Choice varieties of lily, etc., are best sown in pans and germinated in a cool green-house. The seedlings are left undisturbed until they die down, when the tiny bulbs are unearthed and treated like bulblets or cormels. See above.

Most lilies can also be propagated by scales. These should be pulled from mature bulbs during the summer (July–Sept.), and laid fairly closely in trays half filled with peat moss or leaf-mould and sand. Cover with half an inch of the same mixture, moisten and keep in a cool place. Bulbs form on the scales and can be treated like bulblets or cormels. See above.

440. See pages 188 and 189.

CARNATIONS (BORDER)

441. Types. For exhibition purposes these are classified as selfs (flowers of one colour only); white-ground fancies (flowers with coloured markings on a white base); yellow-ground fancies (similar but with a yellow base); fancies, with markings on a base other than white or yellow; and picotees, flowers of one main colour with a narrow band of a con-trasting colour round the margin of each petal. Cloves are distinguished by their rich clove fragrance.

442. Soil and Situation. A fairly rich, rather limy or chalky, well-drained soil is most suitable. Digging should be thorough; only small quantities of animal manure or compost should be employed, but bonemeal (59) or basic slag (57) and hoof and horn meal (65) may be used. If lime is deficient, ground chalk or limestone should be forked in at 1 lb. per square yard. Situation should be open and sunny.

443. Planting. Can be done in September, October, or March. For autumn planting, rooted layers (445) can be lifted direct from the ground; for spring planting, potted layers wintered in a frame are best. Just cover topmost roots with soil and make very firm. Plant a foot apart each way,

440. A Table of Hardy Bulbs

Note—Figures in 'Colour and Season' column represent months e.g. 3 = March

Botanical Name	Popular Name	Colour and Season	Height	Planting Depth	Planting Time
Acidanthera	—	White and maroon, 8–9	3 ft.	3 in.	Apr.–May
Allium	—	Various, 5–7	1–4 ft.	4 in.	Autumn
Amaryllis belladonna	Belladonna Lily	Pink, 9–10	2–3 ft.	4–6 in.	Aug.
Anemone (St Brigid, Du Caen, fulgens)	Windflower	Various, 4–7	9–12 in.	2–3 in.	Oct.–Apr.
Antholyza	—	Orange, 8–9	3 ft.	3 in.	Mar.–Apr.
Calochortus	Butterfly Tulip	Various, 5–6	½–2 ft.	3 in.	Oct.–Nov.
Chionodoxa	Glory of the Snow	Blue, 3–4	4–6 in.	3 in.	Autumn
Colchicum	Autumn Crocus	Various, 9–10	7–8 in.	1 in.	Aug.
Convallaria	Lily of the Valley	White, 4–5	6 in.	1–2 in.	Nov.–Mar.
Crinum	—	White pink, 8–9	3–4 ft.	9 in.	Mar.
Crocus	—	Various, 10–3	3–6 in.	3–4 in.	Aug.–Oct.
Cyclamen	—	White to crimson, 10–5	4–6 in.	½ in.	Aug.–Sept.
Eranthis	Winter Aconite	Yellow, 1–2	2 in.	2 in.	Autumn

		Colour, flowering months	Height	Depth	Planting time
Erythronium	Dog's-tooth Violet	Various, 3–5	6–12 in.	3 in.	Autumn
Fritillaria imperialis	Crown Imperial	Yellow, red, 5	2–3 ft.	4–5 in.	Autumn
Fritillaria meleagris	Snakeshead Fritillary	Various, 4–5	6–12 in.	2–3 in.	Autumn
Galanthus	Snowdrop	White, 11–2	4–8 in.	4 in.	Autumn
Galtonia	Spire Lily	White, 7–8	2–3 ft.	6 in.	Autumn
Gladiolus	—	Various, 6–9	2–5 ft.	4 in.	Mar.–Apr.
Hyacinthus	Hyacinth	Various, 4–5	9–15 in.	5–6 in.	Oct.–Nov.
Iris (bulbous rooted)	—	Various, 1–7	½–2½ ft.	3 in.	Autumn
Ixia	—	Various, 6	2 ft.	2 in.	Autumn
Leucojum	Snowflake	White, 1–5, 10	4–18 in.	3 in.	Aug.–Sept.
Lilium	Lily	Various, 6–9	1½–12 in.	1–8 in.	Autumn
Montbretia	—	Yellow to crimson, 8–9	2–3 ft.	2–3 in.	Mar.–Apr.
Muscari	Grape Hyacinth	Blue, 4–5	4–8 in.	2–3 in.	Autumn
Narcissus	Daffodil	White, yellow, orange, 2–5	4–24 in.	3–6 in.	Autumn
Ornithogalum	Star of Bethlehem	White, 5–6	1–1½ ft.	4 in.	Autumn
Puschkinia	—	Blue and white, 4	6 in.	3 in.	Autumn
Ranunculus (Turban French)	—	Various, 5–6	9 in.	2 in.	Nov.–Mar.
Schizostylis	Caffre Lily	Pink, scarlet, 10–11	18 in.	3 in.	Mar.–Apr.
Scilla	Squill, Bluebell	Blue, white, pink, 3–6	3–15 in.	3–6 in.	Autumn
Sparaxis	Harlequin Flower	Various, 5–6	1 ft.	2 in.	Autumn
Sternbergia	Lily-of-the-Field	Yellow, 10–11	4 in.	4 in.	Aug.
Tigridia	Tiger Flower	Various, 7–8	18 in.	2 in.	Apr.–May
Tulipa	Tulip	Various, 3–5	6–30 in.	4–5 in.	Autumn
Watsonia	Bugle Lily	Various, 8–9	3–4 ft.	3 in.	April

but rather more space will be needed for exhibition plants.

444. Cultural Routine. Keep beds regularly hoed throughout the spring and summer; top dress with carnation fertilizer (102) in April. Tie flower stems to bamboo canes, making uppermost tie 4 or 5 in. below flower bud so that this arches over in a natural manner and does not collect rain as it opens. Remove from half to two-thirds the number of side flower buds that form below the terminal (tip) bud. Usually plants are not worth keeping after their second year and should be replaced by young rooted layers. Syringe occasionally during the summer with a good systemic insecticide to keep down greenfly. For other foes, see Section 8.

445. Propagation. By layering in July. Layers are prepared from young, non-flowering growths. An upward-sloping incision is made through a joint at a point 2 or 3 in. from the base where the shoot can be bent readily to soil level. The incision is then opened and the stem pressed into the soil. It is fixed in position with a wire or wooden pin and more soil is heaped over it. The extremity of the shoot is tied to a small stake. A number of layers may be pegged down round each parent plant. If kept moist, roots will be formed in a few weeks. Layers can be severed from the parent in September and planted a week or so later.

DAHLIAS

466. Types. The principal types grown today are decorative, sub-divided into giant, large, medium, small and miniature flowered; cactus, with the same divisions, single flowered, anemone, collerette, peony, ball, pompon and bedding.

447. Soil and Situation. Dahlias require a deep, rich, well-watered soil. Digging should be thorough. Animal manure or compost may be added at 1 cwt. to 8 sq. yd. Lime is not necessary. The situation should be sunny but not too exposed.

448. Planting. Dahlias are very tender and must not be

planted out until all danger of frost is past. This is usually in late May in the south, a week or so later in the north. Plant all except bedding varieties 3 ft. apart each way. Bedding kinds may be 15 to 18 in. apart. Tubers should be covered with about 2 in. of soil and this made moderately firm.

449. Cultural Routine. Staking is necessary for all except bedding kinds. Stakes must be strong and driven well into the ground, as growth is heavy. For exhibition purposes growths of large-flowered decoratives and large cactus varieties are reduced to one to three per plant according to strength. All flower buds except the main terminal buds on each stem are removed. Water freely during dry weather, mulch with strawy manure or grass clippings and feed every ten days or so with weak liquid manure (50). Sprinkle leaves with pepper dust during August and September and place inverted flower pots stuffed with hay on dahlia stakes to drive off or trap earwigs. For other foes, see Section 8.

As soon as growth is blackened by frost (usually in October), tops are cut off an inch or so above ground level, tubers are lifted, all soil shaken off, and they are then stored in dry peat in any dry, cool, but frost-proof place.

450. Propagation. Best results are obtained from cuttings. Tubers stored as above are placed in boxes or large pots in February, March, or April and covered with old potting soil. They are watered moderately, placed in a greenhouse or frame with average température 60°–65°. Shoots appear freely and are severed nearly to the tuber when 2 in. long. Remove lower leaves, trim each cutting cleanly just below a joint and insert $\frac{1}{2}$ in. deep in sandy soil in a propagating frame (500) within the greenhouse, preferably with bottom heat. Water freely and shade from direct sun. Pot singly in ordinary potting compost (505) as soon as each cutting has rooted. Remove to a frame in May and harden them off for planting out.

POT-TUBERS, i.e. small tubers for planting out from pots in June, are produced from late cuttings taken in May or June and inserted singly in 3-in. pots. The rooted cuttings are grown in the same small pots all summer and are gradually dried off in September–October. The following spring they are watered again and kept in a sunny greenhouse or frame till planting-out time.

Alternatively, old tubers can be started into growth in a frame in April, split into several pieces when shoots appear and be planted out in early June. Yet another method is to plant tubers in early May where they are to flower, covering shoots with cloches or inverted flower pots at night if they appear too early in the season and there is likely to be danger from frost.

HERBACEOUS PERENNIALS (HARDY)

451. Description. Plants which continue to live for a number of years irrespective of whether they flower or not, have a comparatively soft, as distinct from woody, growth, and are hardy enough to be grown outdoors all the year round.

452. Soil and Situation. There are hardy herbaceous perennials suitable for every imaginable soil and situation from light sands to heavy clays, and from full sun to dense shade. Many are extremely adaptable (458). Ground should be prepared by thorough digging and all weeds of a perennial nature (33) should be removed, as little further cultivation will be possible for some years. For the same reason, if soil is believed to be poor, organic manure (44), compost (45), or slow-acting fertilizers, such as bonemeal (59), basic slag (57), or hoof and horn meal (65) should be worked in prior to planting.

453. Planting. All can be planted in the spring, from early March to the end of April. Many kinds can also be planted in late September and October, especially if the soil is warm and well drained. It is not advisable to transplant *Scabiosa caucasica*, *Aster amellus*, pyrethrums, or *Chrysanthemum leucanthemum* in the autumn. Bearded (German) irises can, in addition, be transplanted immediately after flowering, at the end of June. Planting should be done with a trowel or spade, not a dibber. Holes must be wide enough to allow roots to be spread out naturally; deep enough to permit crowns to be just covered with soil. The rhizomes of flag irises should be barely covered; later they will work out on top, their natural position. The soil mark on the plant, or the difference in colour (green above ground, whitish below), usually gives a reliable guide to planting depth. Distance will vary according to habit and height, ranging from 6 in. for low-growing plants to 3 ft. for the tallest varieties. See table (458).

Plant very firmly. Water in freely if the soil is dry, and continue to water until growth recommences.

454. Propagation. Almost all can be increased by division, i.e. by pulling the roots and crowns to pieces, either by hand or with the aid of pointed sticks or small forks thrust back to back through the plant and levered apart. A knife may be required to cut through hard pieces, but should be used as little as possible. When dividing old plants the younger, outside portions are to be preferred; old woody centres should be discarded unless stock is short. Each piece of growth must have roots attached. It is no use planting shoots without roots or vice versa. Division can be done at the usual planting season, but in general the best time is spring, when growth is just beginning.

Some herbaceous perennials can be increased by cuttings, e.g. anthemis, delphiniums, lupins, *Scabiosa caucasica*, and *Coreopsis grandiflora*. These are prepared from firm young shoots 3–5 in. in length taken in spring as growth begins. They should be severed as low down as possible. Trim just below a joint, remove lower leaves and insert firmly in sandy soil in a frame or under a handlight (518), (520). Water moderately and shade from strong sunshine until growth recommences, when discontinue shading and gradually increase ventilation. Rooted cuttings may be planted out in June or July and should be watered freely until established.

A few kinds, e.g. anchusas, gaillardias, oriental poppies, phloxes, romneyas, and verbascums can be increased by root cuttings. These are taken at any time during the winter. The thicker roots are cut into pieces 1–2 in. in length, strewn thinly on ordinary potting compost (505) in well-drained pots or boxes, and covered with $\frac{1}{2}$ in. of the same material. An alternative method is to dibble them in 1 in. apart right way up with the tops just beneath soil level. They are placed in an unheated greenhouse or frame and watered moderately. Shoots will be formed in the spring and the plants can be planted out in June or July.

Most herbaceous perennials can be increased by seed, but seedlings of highly developed garden races (e.g. delphiniums, phloxes, lupins) are liable to vary considerably from their parents. Seed may be sown in a greenhouse or frame in March or outdoors in May or early June. Seed beds should be as fine as possible with extra peat and sand if needed. If sown in frames, prick off (405) as soon as possible and harden off (406) for planting out during July or August. If sown outdoors, prick off into another similar bed, placing the seedlings 3 or 4 in. apart, in rows 6 or 8 in. apart, so that they can grow into sturdy plants for removal to their permanent flowering quarters the following spring. Germination of some perennials is extremely slow and such are best sown in pots, pans or boxes. These should not be discarded as failures for two or three years.

The double-flowered forms of *Gypsophila paniculata* are propogated by grafting young shoots in spring or early summer on to seedling roots of the single gypsophila. The shoot is cut to form a wedge, the root is slit vertically, the wedge is inserted in this, bound in position and the whole potted and placed in a propagating frame (500).

Most perennials are improved by division or renewal from cuttings every four or five years, some even more frequently, but this does not apply to paeonies or Christmas roses (helleborus), which resent root disturbance.

455. Thinning. Better results are often obtained by thinning the shoots in the spring. This is particularly true with delphiniums and Michelmas daisies. Thinning should be done early and the best shoots only retained. The number will depend upon the age of the plant and the purpose for which flowers are required. Thus with young delphiniums needed for exhibition, only one shoot will be kept per plant; two-year-old plants might carry two or three shoots; three-year-old, five or six shoots.

456. Staking. Most tall herbaceous perennials require staking. So far as possible, allow one stake to each main growth; thrust into the ground firmly near the base of the plant and allow the stakes to lean outwards at the top like a shuttlecock to open growth rather than crowd it together. Plants of medium height that are liable to flop about, e.g. gaillardias, erigerons, etc., are most readily supported by thrusting bushy twigs into the ground round them while still young; they will grow up through the twigs and find their own support.

457. Cultural Routine. Most herbaceous perennials will benefit from annual feeding. This may be done by spreading animal manure (44) or compost (45) around them in April or May, and by sprinkling a good compound fertilizer (104) around them occasionally during the spring or summer and hoeing in. Watering of established plants is usually unnecessary unless the weather is exceptionally dry, or special results, e.g. exhibition flowers, are required. When flowers fade they should be cut off, but leaves should not be removed unnecessarily until the autumn, when growth dies down. Then all shoots can be removed an inch or so above ground level, except from plants with evergreen leaves, e.g. kniphofias, bearded irises, etc., which must be allowed to retain all healthy foliage. Dead or diseased leaves may be removed at any time.

A few hardy perennials require some winter protection, especially if the soil is wet and heavy. The two most important are *Gunnera manicata* and all kinds of eremurus. The first can be protected by placing a low tunnel of fine-mesh wire netting over the crowns, after the dead leaves have been removed in November, piling dead leaves, straw or bracken on top and pegging more netting on top to keep in position. The leaves, etc., must not be heaped directly on the crowns or they may cause decay. Eremuri can be protected by heaping sharp sand or boiler ashes over the crowns in November. This can be left in position till the shoots grow through the following spring. Christmas roses (helleborus) may be protected in November and December with cloches (520) or frames, but solely to protect the blooms from mud splashes, not because the plants lack hardiness.

458. See pp. 197–199.

LAWNS

459. Soil Preparation. Ground should be dug at least one spit deep and may be enriched with animal manure (44) or compost (45) in moderate quantity if believed to be poor. Bonemeal (59) may also be applied, but lime should not be used unless ground is really acid. It tends to produce growth of clover and the coarser grasses at the expense of fine grass. Drainage (34) must be improved if ground tends to lie

458. Table of Hardy Perennials

Name	Height	Colour	Distance Apart to Plant	Position to Plant	Flowering Period
Acanthus	3–4 ft.	Orange, pink	9 in.	Sun	July
Achillea	4–24 in.	White, yellow, crimson	6 in.–1 ft.	Sun	May–Sept.
Alstroemeria	3–5 ft.	Orange, pink	9 in.	Sun	July
Anchusa	2–4 ft.	Blue	2 ft.	Sun	June
Anemone japonica	3 ft.	White, pink	1½–2 ft.	Sun or shade	Aug.–Oct.
Anthemis	1½–3 ft.	Yellow	18 in.	Sun	June–Sept.
Aquilegia	5 ft.	Various	1 ft.	Sun or semi-shade	May–June
Artemisia lactiflora	6 in.–6 ft.	White	2½ ft.	Sun or semi-shade	Aug.–Sept.
Aster (Michaelmas daisy)		Various	1–3 ft.	Sun or shade	Aug.–Oct.
Astilbe	1–3 ft.	White, pink to crimson	18 in.	Sun or shade	July–Aug.
Auricula	6 in.	Various	6 in.	Sun	May–June
Bergenia	1 ft.	Pink, crimson	1 ft.	Sun or shade	Mar.–May
Campanula	6 in.–4 ft.	Blue, white	6 in.–2 ft.	Sun or semi-shade	May–July
Carnations (border)	2 ft.	Various	1 ft.	Sun	July
Centaurea	1½–4 ft.	Yellow, pink, blue	1–2 ft.	Sun	June–Sept.
Centranthus	2 ft.	Pink, red, white	1 ft.	Sun	June–July
Chrysanthemum maximum	2½–3 ft.	White	18 in.	Sun	June–Aug.
Coreopsis	2–3 ft.	Yellow	18 in.	Sun	June–Sept.
Delphiniums	3–6 ft.	Blue, white	2–3 ft.	Sun	June–July
Dicentra	1–2 ft.	Pink, red	9–12 in.	Sun or shade	May–June
Dictamnus	2½ ft.	Purple, white	18 in.	Sun or shade	July–Aug.
Echinacea	3 ft.	Purple	2 ft.	Sun	Aug.–Sept.
Echinops	3–5 ft.	Blue	2 ft.	Sun	July–Aug.
Eremurus	3–8 ft.	White, pink, yellow	3 ft.	Sun	May–June

TABLE OF HARDY PERENNIALS – *continued*

Name	Height	Colour	Distance Apart to Plant	Position to Plant	Flowering Period
Erigeron	1–2 ft.	Blue	1 ft.	Sun	June–July
Eryngium	2–3 ft.	Blue, white	18 in.	Sun	July–Sept.
Euphorbia	1–2 ft.	Yellow, orange	1 ft.	Sun	April–May
Gaillardia	2 ft.	Yellow and scarlet	1 ft.	Sun	June–Oct.
Geranium	1–3 ft.	Crimson, pink, blue	1 ft.	Sun	June–Sept.
Geum	1–2 ft.	Red, yellow, orange	1 ft.	Sun	May–Oct.
Gypsophila paniculata	2–3 ft.	White	2 ft. 6 in.	Sun	July–Aug.
Helenium	2–5 ft.	Yellow, crimson	1½–3 ft.	Sun	July–Sept.
Helianthus	4–7 ft.	Yellow	2–4 ft.	Sun	July–Oct.
Heliopsis	3–4 ft.	Yellow, orange	2 ft.	Sun or semi-shade	July–Aug.
Helleborus	12–18 in.	White, pink to crimson	1 ft.	Sun or shade	Nov.–Apr.
Hemerocallis	2–3 ft.	Yellow	2 ft.	Sun or semi-shade	June–July
Heuchera	1½–2½ ft.	Pink, scarlet	1 ft.	Sun or semi-shade	June–Aug.
Hollyhock	5–8 ft.	Various	3 ft.	Sun	July
Hosta	1½–3 ft.	White, mauve	12–18 in.	Sun or shade	July
Incarvillea	1½–3 ft.	Pink, carmine	1 ft.	Sun	May–June
Iris	2–5 ft.	Various	6 in.–2 ft.	Sun	May–June
Kniphofia	2–8 ft.	Yellow to scarlet	1½–3 ft.	Sun	June–Oct.
Liatris	1½–3 ft.	Purple	9–12 in.	Sun or semi-shade	July–Aug.
Ligularia	4–5 ft.	Yellow	3 ft.	Sun or semi-shade	July–Sept.
Limonium	1–2 ft.	Blue, pink	18 in.	Sun	Aug.–Sept.
Lupinus	3–4 ft.	Various	2 ft.	Sun	June
Lychnis	1–3 ft.	Scarlet, crimson	1 ft.	Sun	July–Aug.
Lysimachia	3–4 ft.	Yellow	18 in.	Sun or shade	July–Aug.
Meconopsis	1–5 ft.	Blue, yellow, orange	9–18 in.	Semi-shade	May–Aug.
Monarda	3 ft.	Scarlet	2 ft.	Sun or semi-shade	July–Aug.
Nepeta	1 ft.	Blue	9 in.	Sun	June–Sept.

Oenothera	1½–3 ft.	Yellow	1–1½ ft.	Sun	June–Oct.
Paeonia	2–3 ft.	White, pink-crimson	2 ft.	Sun	May–June
Papaver orientale	2–3 ft.	Scarlet, pink, white	18 in.	Sun	June
Phlox	1–4 ft.	White, pink to scarlet, purple	12–18 in.	Sun or semi-shade	July–Sept.
Phygelius	3 ft.	Orange	2 ft.	Sun	July–Sept.
Physalis	1½ ft.	Orange pods	9–12 in.	Sun	July–Oct.
Physostegia	1½–3 ft.	Pink, white	9–12 in.	Sun or semi-shade	Aug.–Oct.
Pinks	9–18 in.	White, pink-crimson	6 in.–1 ft.	Sun	June–Aug.
Platycodon	12–18 in.	Blue, white	9 in.	Sun	July–Aug.
Polemonium	1½ ft.	Blue, white	9 in.	Sun or shade	May–June
Polyanthus	6–9 in.	Various	9 in.	Sun or shade	Mar.–Apr.
Polygonatum	2–3 ft.	White and green	9 in.	Shade	May–June
Potentilla	6–24 in.	Yellow, scarlet, crimson	6 in.–1 ft.	Sun	June–Sept.
Primrose	6 in.	Various	6–9 in.	Sun or shade	Mar.–Apr.
Pulmonaria	6–18 in.	Blue, purple, red	9 in.	Shade	Mar.–Apr.
Pyrethrum	3 ft.	White, pink-crimson	1½ ft.	Sun	June
Rodgersia	3 ft.	Pink, white	2 ft.	Sun or shade	July–Aug.
Romneya	5–6 ft.	White	3 ft.	Sun	July–Sept.
Rudbeckia	2–7 ft.	Yellow	1½–3 ft.	Sun	July–Sept.
Salvia superba	3 ft.	Blue	1½–3 ft.	Sun	July–Aug.
Santolina	1 ft.	Yellow	1 ft.	Sun	July–Aug.
Scabiosa caucasica	2–3 ft.	Blue, white	1 ft.	Sun	July–Oct.
Sedum spectabile	18 in.	Pink to crimson	1 ft.	Sun	Sept.–Oct.
Sidalcea	2–4 ft.	White, pink-crimson	18 in.	Sun	July–Aug.
Solidago	2–5 ft.	Yellow	2–3 ft.	Sun or semi-shade	Aug.–Oct.
Spiraea	2–5 ft.	White, pink-crimson	1½–3 ft.	Sun or shade	July–Aug.
Sweet william	2 ft.	Various	1 ft.	Sun or semi-shade	June–Aug.
Thalictrum	3–6 ft.	Yellow, mauve, white	2 ft.	Sun	June–Aug.
Trollius	1–2 ft.	Yellow	1 ft.	Semi-shade	May–June
Verbascum	3–8 ft.	White, yellow, pink	1–3 ft.	Sun or shade	July–Aug.
Veronica	1–6 ft.	Blue, pink, white	1–3 ft.	Sun or shade	July–Aug.
Viola	6 in.	Various	6 in.	Sun or shade	May–Aug.

waterlogged in the winter. It is a great advantage to leave ground fallow for a month or so prior to sowing so that weed seeds may germinate and the weed seedlings be destroyed by hoeing before the grass is sown. Break the surface down as finely as possible with fork and rake prior to sowing or turfing. Either tread or roll to secure even firmness throughout. A fairly firm seed bed is essential.

460. Sowing. This can be done in April or September. Seed is sown broadcast at 1–2 oz. per square yard, and is either raked in or covered with a light sprinkling of soil. If seeds are properly covered, no further protection from birds is necessary; small birds do not scratch but simply pick up the seeds from the surface. Proprietary dressings can be obtained to make seeds unpalatable for birds and ready dressed seed is also available. Do not sow when ground is very dry or wet; it should be slightly moist.

The finest lawns are formed from certain species of agrostis and festuca, particularly New Zealand Brown Top (*Agrostis tenuis*) and Chewing's fescue (*Festuca rubra fallax*). A drawback to these is that they germinate slowly and take a considerable time to give a good cover to the ground. In consequence, unless the lawn site has been well fallowed to get rid of weeds, there is a danger that these will get the upper hand. Perennial rye grass grows quickly at the outset and smothers weeds well but tends to die out after a few years of close mowing. A mixture of several fine grasses but without rye grass is best for most purposes. The wood meadowgrass (*Poa nemoralis*) may be used in shady places.

461. Aftercare of Seedling Lawns. Seedling grass should be cut for the first time when 3 in. high. Cut with a sharp scythe or a sharp mower, with blades set high at first but gradually lowered at each subsequent cutting. Roll lightly before the first cutting, but never use the roller when the surface of the ground is very wet.

462. Turfing. Turves may be laid at any time from October to April, when the ground is not frozen or waterlogged. Turves are cut in two sizes, 3 ft. by 1 ft. (supplied rolled up), and 1 ft. square (supplied flat). The latter make a more even lawn, but are usually more expensive and take longer to lay. Plantains, dandelions, etc., should first be cut out with a knife. Lay lengthwise in straight rows but stagger joints in alternate rows like bricks in a wall. Bed turves evenly and beat them down gently with the back of a spade or a wooden turf beater. Scatter fine soil lightly on the surface and brush into crevices with a stiff besom.

Never lay small portions of turf at the edge of a lawn either when making new lawns or repairing old ones. If pieces are required to complete a row, lay a whole turf on the edge and use the pieces inside. When repairing worn patches, first remove a rectangle of old turf to the thickness of new turf, then rake bottom level and lay turves in the ordinary way.

463. Cultural Routine. Established lawns, whether formed from seed or turf, require the same treatment. Mow regularly throughout the year, but at less frequent intervals during autumn and winter than in spring and summer and with blades set higher. Very close mowing and heavy rolling are undesirable except for lawns used for sport. For ordinary purposes, set the cutting edge about $\frac{1}{2}$ in. off the ground. Use the roller only when the surface is moist, not when sodden or quite dry. Lawns which get heavy wear may be aerated each autumn by pricking all over with a fork, special perforating tool or spiked roller. Brush in sharp sand or flint grit to improve drainage.

In spring and early summer give occasional top dressings of peat or leaf-mould mixed with equal parts of well-decayed manure and loam, all passed through a $\frac{1}{4}$-in.-mesh sieve. No top dressing must exceed $\frac{1}{4}$ in. in depth. Lawn fertilizer (107) is best used in April or May. Weeds can be killed either by watering with selective lawn weed-killer (see Section 8) or by dusting with lawn sand (108). Both treatments are most effective in spring or when growth is strong.

Moss on lawns can be dragged out with a spring-toothed rake or killed with calomel (648). The growth of moss is usually an indication of bad drainage or poor soil, which should be rectified.

464. Cumberland Turf. This is obtained from coastal regions and is actually washed by sea water at high tide. It is exceptionally fine and valued for bowling greens, etc., but is not recommended for lawns generally as it is difficult to maintain in inland gardens. An early spring application of agricultural salt, $\frac{1}{2}$ oz. per square yard, is beneficial, otherwise treatment is as for ordinary lawns.

PANSIES AND VIOLAS

465. Description. Pansies and violas are closely allied but differ in habit and type of colouring. Violas are in the main more tufted and flowers are either of one colour or else, if of two colours, these are not so clearly defined and strongly contrasted as those of pansies. Both pansies and violas are subdivided into two groups – exhibition and bedding. The former are characterized by the size and quality of the flowers, while the latter are freer flowering and of more compact habit.

466. Soil and Situation. All delight in a deep, cool, rather rich soil. Dig thoroughly and work in animal manure (44) or compost (45) freely. Peat or leaf-mould can be employed to improve moisture-holding qualities of light soil. A partially shaded position, but not beneath large trees, gives the best results, but all are adaptable.

467. Planting. This is done in April and May. For bedding, plants are set 6–9 in. apart; for exhibition 1 ft. apart. Other details are the same as for herbaceous plants (453).

468. Cultural Routine. For bedding, it is only necessary to remove faded flowers and keep down weeds. For exhibition, each plant is restricted to one or two main stems at a time. These are replaced, when old, with young shoots. Selected growths are tied to short stakes, and plants are fed freely during the summer months with weak liquid manure (50) or a general garden fertilizer (104). Syringe occasionally with a good systematic insecticide to keep down greenfly. For other foes, see Section 8.

469. Propagation. Bedding violas and pansies are usually raised from seed sown in a warm greenhouse in February, in a frame in March, or outdoors in May. Early seedlings will flower the same year, late seedlings the following year. When grown in this way the plants are generally discarded after flowering as many may die from soil-borne diseases in winter and those that survive are apt to get straggly. However, this does not apply to *Viola cornuta, V. gracilis* and their varieties which will usually survive for years.

Specially selected exhibition varieties are increased by cuttings taken from August to October. A few selected plants are cut back almost to the roots in July or early August and a little sifted potting compost (505) worked around them. Young shoots form freely, and these are severed to the base when about 2 in. in length and inserted ½ in. deep and 2 in. apart in sandy soil in a frame. Once rooted, the frame lights will be required only during frosty weather or heavy rain.

ROSES

470. Types. The principal types of roses grown for garden display are hybrid tea, floribunda, shrub, climber and rambler. Hybrid teas produce the finest individual flowers but floribundas produce the greatest quantity of bloom. These and the so-called perpetual-flowering climbers flower in flushes from June to September. Most ramblers and some shrub roses flower only once each summer. There are also polyantha pompon roses of bushy habit with large clusters of small rosette flowers like those of ramblers, and miniature roses, which may be anything from 6 to 15 in. high with small leaves and flowers.

Bush roses branch from ground level. Standard roses have a head of branches on a bare main stem three or four feet in height. These are especially useful in giving a second tier of flowers above bush roses. Climbers and ramblers have long, whippy stems which need to be tied to supports such as wires, trellis work, arches, pergolas, pillars, screens or walls. Ramblers produce small to medium-sized flowers in large clusters and most have a rather short flowering season in July and August. Climbers have flowers of various types and sizes. Some are more or less continuous flowering and some flower once only each summer. Shrub roses branch from ground level but are bigger than bush hybrid teas or floribundas and more suitable for planting as individual specimens or for mixing with other shrubs than for massing in beds together.

471. Soil and Situation. All like an open situation, though most will tolerate some shade. They like a well-cultivated, rich soil. Animal manure or compost may be dug in at 1 cwt. to 8 sq. yd. and bonemeal at 4–6 oz. per square yard. Turves, dug in grass side downwards, are very useful. Lime is not required; excess lime causes yellowing of the foliage (known as chlorosis).

472. Planting. Early November is the best planting time, though work can be continued during any open weather until the end of March. Container-grown roses can be planted at any time. Plant in wide, rather deep holes with roots spread outwards and downwards. The soil mark on the stems gives best indication as to correct depth; it should be just covered.

Other planting details are the same as for trees and shrubs (478). All standards must be securely staked.

473. Pruning. After planting, all roses, except climbing 'sports', must be pruned severely. Cut strong growths to within three dormant growth buds of soil level (or the main stem in standards of all types), weaker growths to one or two buds and remove thin shoots altogether. Climbing 'sports', which always have the word 'Climbing' before their name, e.g. Climbing Etoile de Hollande, should have strong growths shortened by one-third, medium growths by two-thirds, weak growths removed. In subsequent years, pruning will vary according to type and requirements. These 'sports' arise spontaneously from bush varieties which they resemble in size and colour of flowers. They differ in their much more vigorous growth and most do not flower as freely as their parent varieties.

HYBRID TEAS are pruned most severely. First of all old, diseased, damaged, very thin, or worn-out branches are removed completely. Then strong young growths are shortened to between two and four dormant buds and medium growths to one or two buds. This work is best done during March or early in April in very cold gardens. The severest pruning is required for exhibition work; lighter pruning for garden decoration. After first flowering in summer, faded blooms are removed with two-thirds of their stems.

FLORIBUNDAS are pruned at the same time and in a similar manner to hybrid teas, etc., but less severely. Strong growths may be left with six or eight buds, medium three or four buds, weak one or two.

POLYANTHA POMPONS AND MINIATURES are also pruned in March. Remove thin, weak, and worn-out growths and then shorten remaining stems by about half.

CLIMBING SPORTS are so known because they have been derived as 'sports' (i.e. chance variations from the normal type) from bush roses. They are pruned at the same time as hybrid teas, but lightly. Shorten strong growths by almost one-quarter, medium growths by one-half, weak by two-thirds or more. An occasional sturdy shoot may be cut back to within 1 ft. of ground level to maintain basal growth.

RAMBLERS make a great deal of new growth from the base and are pruned as soon as possible after flowering, when the old flowering stems are cut right out to make way for young growth.

Weeping standards are produced by growing rambler roses on a long base stem so that their flexible stems hang down all round. They are pruned like other ramblers, but rather more severely. Growths retained are tied spirally downwards on crinoline-like wire trainers fixed to stakes.

CLIMBERS other than climbing sports are pruned moderately in February or March when all old, diseased and worn-out stems are removed and good young stems short-end from a third to two-thirds according to the room available.

SHRUB ROSES can be pruned at any time from October to March. They only require thinning, and particularly the removal of old, diseased and worn-out stems.

Make all cuts cleanly just above growth buds. On bushes and standards these should point outwards, away from the centre of the tree. Suckers must be cut out as soon as noted from roses budded on a stock (475), but not from those raised from cuttings. Note that in standard and half-standard roses the main stem is formed by the stock and therefore any growths which appear on this below the head of branches will be suckers. Note also that some ramblers produce strong basal growths which must not be mistaken for suckers.

474. Cultural Routine. Mulch with well-rotted manure (44) or compost (45) each spring at about 1 cwt. to 12 sq. yd. and fork in later. A mulch of long grass clippings may be maintained throughout the summer; it assists growth and keeps down black spot (711). Use a good rose fertilizer (103) or a general garden fertilizer (104) in early April. Garden roses will require no further feeding, but exhibition roses may be fed with liquid manure (50) or a general garden fertilizer (104) occasionally during the summer. Exhibition roses are also disbudded, i.e. side flower buds are removed at an early stage and only the terminal bud on each stem is allowed to mature.

It is advisable to spray occasionally between the months of May and September with a fungicide and an insecticide to keep pests and diseases under control. For further information on this subject, see Section 8, 'Pests, Diseases and Weeds'.

475. Propagation. Rambler roses, shrubs, and some vigorous bushes can be increased by cuttings 1 ft. to 15 in. in length prepared from well-ripened young growths in October or November. Sever each beneath a joint and insert 4 in. deep in rather sandy soil and sheltered position outdoors. Cuttings should be rooted and ready for removal to flowering quarters by the following autumn.

Most choice varieties of other types are propagated by budding. In the main, details are the same as for budding apples (210), but for bush roses buds are inserted just below soil level where stem and root join. Soil is scraped away immediately before budding to allow this to be done.

Brier stems which are intended for use as root stocks for standards are allowed to form side growths at the height desired for the head of branches ($3\frac{1}{2}$ ft. for full standards, $2\frac{1}{2}$ ft. for half-standards), and one bud is enserted near the base of each such shoot. Buds are inserted direct on to the main stem of rugosa standard stocks at the required height. Whichever stock is used, it is usual to have three buds per standard.

Budding is carried out from the end of June until early

207

September while the bark peels readily from the wood. Buds are cut from half-ripened young shoots. A test is to break off the thorns. They should snap off cleanly but have a moist scar. Stocks are left unpruned until March following budding, when all growth is cut off about 3 in. above the bud. This final 3 in. is cut off a month or so later when the bud has started into growth.

Numerous stocks are used, including brier, rugosa, Manetti, laxa, and multiflora. The two first are the commonest. Brier gives long life, but rugosa makes a big plant more rapidly. Briers for bush stocks are usually raised from seed sown outdoors in March, but can also be reared from cuttings treated like those of garden roses. Rugosa should always be raised from cuttings. Standard brier stems are cut with roots attached from hedgerows and thickets in autumn.

Roses can also be raised from seed, but in practice this method is adopted only for the 'fairy' roses (*Rosa lawranceana*) species and when raising new varieties. Ripe hips are gathered in the autumn and placed in shallow seed trays filled with sand. These are stood in the open and exposed to frost. In March the hips and sand are rubbed between the palms of the hand, to separate the seeds, and then the whole contents of the tray are sown thinly in drills $\frac{1}{2}$ in. deep and 2 ft. apart in the open. Seedlings are not disturbed until they have flowered.

TREES, SHRUBS, AND CLIMBERS (HARDY)

476. Description. All plants of fully woody character that can be grown outdoors summer and winter. Some varieties are evergreen, i.e. retain their foliage throughout the winter, others are deciduous, i.e. lose their foliage in autumn. There are also half-hardy and tender kinds which can be grown by enthusiasts in a greenhouse (534), (535).

477. Soil and Situation. Requirements are very varied. Kinds may be found for practically every conceivable soil and position. (See tables 482, 483, 484). Ground must always be well dug prior to planting. If believed to be poor, it may be enriched with moderate quantities of organic manure (44), compost (45) and slow-acting fertilizers such as bonemeal (59) and hoof and horn meal (65). Little beyond surface cultivation will be possible once trees and shrubs are established.

478. Planting. Deciduous trees and shrubs, with one exception, may be planted at any time while bare of leaves, roughly from early November to mid-March. The exception is magnolia, deciduous forms of which are best planted in late April or early May. Evergreen conifers, e.g. pines, firs, spruces, cedars, junipers, cypresses, etc., may be planted at the same time as deciduous shrubs. Early November and March are usually the most favourable months. Other evergreen trees and shrubs should be transplanted in October, April, or early May, not in winter, though container-grown trees and shrubs can be planted at any time.

Plant in wide, rather shallow holes so that roots can be spread out fully and the uppermost covered with 2 or 3 in. of soil. Work fine soil between the roots and make thoroughly firm. Stake and tie all newly planted trees securely, also large bushes. Water freely if the soil is dry. Evergreens moved in the spring should be syringed nightly with water if the weather is hot. Screens of sacking, hurdles, or evergreen boughs will help if the weather is windy. Roots must not be damaged unnecessarily, nor allowed to dry.

Certain shrubs, e.g. brooms, *Berberis darwinii*, and *cupressus macrocarpa*, resent root disturbance at any time and are usually supplied in containers. From these they may be planted at any time, early autumn and spring being the most favourable. Similar remarks apply to most climbing shrubs such as clematis, jasmine, and honeysuckle. Remove the container carefully and plant with ball of soil and roots intact.

Edging box is sold by the yard as measured along the rows in the nursery beds. The plants are divided and replanted 4 in. apart so that they occupy approximately three times the room, i.e. 1 yard of purchased box edging will plant 3 yards.

479. Cultural Routine. Surface hoeing to keep down weeds and light forking in the autumn or winter are the only attentions required by established trees and shrubs. For the first few years grass should not be allowed to grow over the roots. Later the ground may be grassed over if desired. Trees and shrubs can be fed with a good compound fertilizer (104) or a mulch of organic manure (44), or compost (45), either applied in spring. For treatment of suckers see (481).

480. Pruning. Most trees, shrubs, and climbers require little regular pruning, but sometimes it is essential to check growth to keep plants within bounds or prevent overcrowding. All diseased or damaged branches must be removed. In general, trees and shrubs which flower before mid-summer are best pruned immediately the flowers fade; those which bloom after that date are pruned in late winter or early spring. All cuts should be made cleanly either close to a main branch or just above a growth bud or side branch. Large wounds should be coated with Stockholm tar or a proprietary wound dressing.

Established wisterias are summer and winter pruned. Side growths are cut back to five leaves in July and further shortened to one or two buds in November.

Evergreen shrubs grown for their foliage, also evergreen hedges, should not be cut in winter. Hard pruning and topping, when necessary, is best done in May. Trimming may be carried out at any time during the summer. Deciduous hedges may be trimmed during the summer but any hard cutting is best left until winter.

For further details see tables (482), (483), (484), and (485).

481. Propagation. Many kinds can be increased by cuttings. These are of two principal types: summer cuttings prepared during July and August from half-ripened young shoots, and autumn cuttings prepared during October and November from fully ripened young shoots. Both types may either be severed immediately beneath a joint or be pulled off with a heel of older wood which is then trimmed up closely. Clematis cuttings are severed between joints.

SUMMER CUTTINGS must be rooted quickly or they will flag and die. They are smaller than autumn cuttings, varying from 1 to 4 in. in length according to the nature of growth. Insert in very sandy soil or pure silver sand in a frame or under mist, and give no ventilation until they are rooted, except that the light is lifted and wiped daily, and returned immediately. Water freely and dispense with shading so far as possible, but do not allow severe flagging. Root-forming hormones (111) may be used to hasten rooting. When the cuttings start to grow, ventilation is given, and a few weeks later they are potted singly in ordinary potting compost (505) and slowly accustomed to normal atmospheric conditions.

AUTUMN CUTTINGS do not flag so readily and can root comparatively slowly. They will be from 4 to 15 in. in length and are treated exactly like cuttings of black currants or other fruit bushes (259). Choice varieties, particularly evergreens, may be inserted in a frame, but should be ventilated fairly freely except during severe weather.

Many shrubs and climbers, especially those with pliable branches that can be bent to soil level, can be increased by LAYERING. This is done in the spring or autumn. One- or two-year-old branches or vines are most suitable. Slit half-way through at a joint (with clematis between joints) where the shoot touches the ground, and peg this portion firmly

211

Layering. If the tips of young branches are pegged into the soil as shown they will soon form roots and can be detached from the parent plant.

to the soil or weight with a stone. Cover with more soil and water thoroughly if dry. Tie the extremity of the shoot to a stake. Roots will be formed in anything from three to fifteen months, after which the layer can be severed from the parent plant and transferred to new quarters at the normal planting season (478). AIR LAYERING is another form of layering and is done without bringing the shoots to ground level. An incision is made in the branch or stem to be layered and the cut is dusted with hormone rooting powder. Moist sphagnum moss is placed around the cut and enclosed in a sleeve of polythene film, tightly tied at each end. Roots are formed into the moss and when there are plenty of these the layer is severed and, after removal of the polythene, is potted or planted. Air layering can be done at any time but is usually most effective in spring or early summer.

Some choice varieties of trees and shrubs, notably ornamental cherries, plums, crab apples, double-flowered hawthorns, lilacs, and rhododendrons, are GRAFTED or BUDDED on to suitable stocks. The methods in general are the same as those for fruit trees (205, (206), (209), (210), but rhododendrons are usually grafted in a warm greenhouse. Clematises are raised commercially in the same way, but cuttings or layers produce sturdier plants.

SUCKERS can be detached with roots attached at the normal planting season (478), provided the shrub is not grafted or budded (see above). If it is, the sucker will be from the stock and will not reproduce the garden shrub grafted upon it. Such suckers must be traced to their source and removed or they may choke the plant. This can be done at any time of the year.

Almost all trees and shrubs can be raised from SEED, but results are sometimes unreliable, especially with choice garden forms and hybrids, as seedlings may differ considerably from their parents. Seeds of the choicest kinds should be sown in well-drained pans filled with ordinary seed compost (501), and germinated in a cool greenhouse or frame. Seeds can be covered with their own depth of soil. The commoner varieties can be sown in drills $\frac{1}{4}$–1 in. deep made outdoors in March or April. Seedlings are transplanted, when large enough to handle, at the normal planting season (478). They should be placed a few inches apart each way in a nursery bed to grow on until big enough for removal to permanent quarters. Kinds that are difficult to transplant (478) should be potted. Berries and other fleshy fruits should be treated like rose hips (475).

213

482. A Table of Hardy Deciduous Trees and Shrubs

Name	Height in Feet	Ornamental Value	Flowering or Fruiting Months	Position	Soil	Pruning
Acer (maple)	6–40	Foliage	—	Sun	Ordinary	(a)
Aesculus (horse chestnut)	30–40	White or pink flowers	5–7	Sun	Ordinary	(a)
Ailanthus	60	Foliage	—	Sun	Ordinary	(a) or (b)
Amelanchier	25	White flowers	4	Sun	Ordinary	(a)
Artemisia abrotanum	3	Silver foliage	—	Sun	Light	(a)
Azalea (except amoena and indica)	4–8	Flowers of many colours	5–6	Sun or shade	Peaty	(f)
Berberis	3–8	Flowers and foliage	5–6	Sun	Ordinary	(g)
Betula (silver birch)	40	Foliage and silver bark	—	Sun or semi-shade	Ordinary	(a)
Buddleia globosa	10–12	Orange flowers	5–6	Sun	Ordinary	(a)
Buddleia davidii	6–12	Purple flowers	7–9	Sun	Ordinary	(c)
Caryopteris	2–3	Lavender flowers	9–10	Sun	Light	(c)
Catalpa	30	Foliage	—	Sun	Ordinary	(a) or (b)
Ceanothus azureus and hybrids	5–8	Blue or pink flowers	7–9	Sun	Ordinary	(c)
Ceratostigma (plumbago)	2–3	Blue flowers	8–9	Sun	Light	(c)
Cercis (Judas tree)	15–20	Purple flowers	5	Sun	Light	(a)
Chaenomeles	6–10	Scarlet, pink, or white flowers	3–5	Sun or shade	Ordinary	(e)
Chimonanthus (winter sweet)	7–9	Yellow flowers	1–2	Sun or semi-shade	Ordinary	(e)
Colutea	9	Yellow flowers, inflated pods	6–9	Sun	Light	(a)

						(a) or (b)
Cornus alba spaethii	5–7	Foliage and bark	—	Sun or shade	Ordinary	(a) or (b)
Cornus kousa	12–16	Cream flowers	5–6	Sun	Ordinary	(a)
Corylus	10	Foliage	—	Sun or shade	Ordinary	(a)
Cotoneaster (some are evergreen)	½–15	Scarlet or black berries	10–12	Sun or semi-shade	Ordinary	(a)
Crataegus (hawthorn)	15–20	Flowers and berries	5–6, 10–12	Sun	Ordinary	(a)
Cytisus (broom)	1–12	Flowers of various colours	5	Sun	Light	(e)
Daphne mezereum	3	Purple flowers	2–3	Sun or semi-shade	Ordinary, moist	(a)
Deutzia	4–8	White or purple flowers	5–7	Sun	Ordinary	(d)
Enkianthus	5–7	Creamy flowers	4–5	Shade	Peaty	(a)
Eucryphia	12–20	White flowers	10–15	Semi-shade	Peaty	(a)
Euonymus europaeus	6–8	Orange and red fruits	9–11	Sun	Ordinary	(a)
Exochorda	6–7	White flowers	5	Sun	Ordinary	(a)
Fagus (beech)	60	Foliage	—	Sun	Ordinary	(a)
Forsythia	6–8	Yellow flowers	3–4	Sun	Ordinary	(e)
Fuchsia (hardy varieties)	1–5	Variously coloured flowers	6–10	Sun or semi-shade	Ordinary	(c)
Genista	2–10	Yellow flowers	5–6	Sun	Light	(a)
Ginkgo	30–60	Foliage	—	Sun	Ordinary	(a)
Gleditschia	15–20	Foliage	—	Sun	Light	(a)
Hamamelis	6–12	Yellow flowers	12–2	Sun or shade	Ordinary	(a)
Hedysarum	4	Magenta flowers	6–9	Sun	Light	(a)
Hibiscus	8	Flowers of various colours	9–10	Sun	Ordinary	(a)
Hippophaë (sea buckthorn)	15	Orange berries (on female)	9–11	Sun	Light	(a)
Hydrangea macrophylla	3–6	Blue, pink, or white flowers	7–8	Sun or shade	Ordinary	(f)

215

A TABLE OF HARDY DECIDUOUS TREES AND SHRUBS—*continued*

Name	Height in Feet	Ornamental Value	Flowering or Fruiting Months	Position	Soil	Pruning
Hydrangea paniculata	3–6	White flowers	8–9	Sun or shade	Ordinary	(b)
Hypericum patulum	3–5	Yellow flowers	7–9	Sun or semi-shade	Ordinary	(h)
Kerria	6–8	Yellow flowers	4–5	Sun or shade	Ordinary	(e)
Koelreuteria	15–20	Yellow flowers	7–8	Sun	Ordinary	(a)
Kolkwitzia	6–8	Pink flowers	6	Sun	Ordinary	(d)
Laburnum	15–20	Yellow flowers	5–6	Sun	Ordinary	(a)
Leycesteria	6	Claret flowers	7–9	Sun or shade	Ordinary	(e)
Liquidambar	30–50	Autumn foliage	9–11	Sun	Ordinary	(a)
Magnolia (except *M. grandiflora*)	6–20	White to purple flowers	3–4	Sun	Peaty	(a)
Malus (crab apple)	15–25	White to crimson flowers, followed by fruits	4–5, 9–11	Sun	Ordinary	(a)
Metasequoia	40–60	Foliage	—	Sun	Ordinary, moist	(a)
Perowskia	4	Blue flowers	8–9	Sun	Light	(c)
Philadelphus (mock orange)	3–12	White flowers	6	Sun or semi-shade	Ordinary	(d)
Populus (poplar)	40–60	Foliage	—	Sun	Ordinary	(a) or (b)
Potentilla fruticosa	2–4	Yellow flowers	7–9	Sun	Light	(a) or (b)
Prunus (almond, cherry, plum, peach)	15–30	Pink or white flowers	3–4	Sun	Ordinary	(a)
Pyrus salicifolia	15–20	Foliage	—	Sun	Ordinary	(a)
Quercus (oak)	20–60	Foliage	—	Sun	Ordinary	(a)
Rhus (sumach)	6–10	Autumn foliage	—	Sun	Light	(a)
Ribes sanguineum (flowering currant)	7	Pink to carmine	3–4	Sun or shade	Ordinary	(d)

Robinia (false acacia)	White flowers	30–40	5–6	Sun	Light	(a)
Rubus	White or rose flowers	4–8	7–8	Sun or shade	Ordinary	(c)
Salix (willow)	Catkins and foliage	8–40	2–3	Sun	Ordinary, moist	(a) or (b)
Sambucus	Foliage	8–12	—	Sun or shade	Ordinary, moist	(b)
Sorbaria	White flowers	6–10	7–8	Sun	Ordinary	(b) or (h)
Sorbus (mountain ash, whitebeam etc.)	Flowers and berries	15–30	5–6, 9–10	Sun	Ordinary	(a)
Spartium (Spanish broom)	Yellow flowers	9	6–9	Sun	Light	(e)
Spiraea (early flowering)	White	4–6	4–5	Sun or semi-shade	Ordinary	(h)
Spiraea (summer flowering)	Cream to crimson	3–8	6–8	Sun or semi-shade	Ordinary	(b)
Symphoricarpos (snowberry)	White berries	6	9–12	Sun or shade	Ordinary	(h)
Syringa (lilac)	White to purple flowers	6–15	5–6	Sun	Ordinary	(f)
Tamarix	White or pink flowers	5–10	7–9	Sun	Ordinary	(a) or (b)
Taxodium	Foliage	30–40	—	Sun	Ordinary, moist	(a)
Tilia (lime)	Foliage	60–80	—	Sun	Ordinary	(a)
Ulmus (elm)	Foliage	20–60	—	Sun	Ordinary	(a)
Viburnum	White or pink flowers	4–6	4–6	Sun	Ordinary	(a)
Weigela (diervilla)	White to crimson flowers	7	5–6	Sun	Ordinary	(d)

217

PRUNING INSTRUCTIONS

(a) No regular pruning required. Remove badly placed, damaged, or diseased branches in February.
(b) Cut back severely in February.
(c) Cut back severely in April.
(d) Shorten flowering branches to growth buds or side growths after flowering.
(e) Shorten flowering branches nearly to base after flowering.
(f) Remove faded flower trusses.
(g) Thin out oldest growths every third or fourth year.
(h) Thin out moderately and shorten young growths a little in February.

483. A Table of Hardy Climbing Plants

Name	Ornamental Value	Flowering or Fruiting Months	Position	Support	Pruning
Ampelopsis (Parthenocissus)	Foliage	—	Sun or shade	Wall	(a)
*Azara	Yellow flowers	2	Sun or shade	Wall	(b)
Campsis	Orange-scarlet flowers	8–9	Sun	Wall	(a)
*Ceanothus (evergreen vars.)	Blue flowers	5–6	Sun	Wall	(c)
Celastrus	Yellow and scarlet fruits	9–11	Sun	Screen, low roof	(a)
Clematis	Flowers of various colours	4–9	Sun	Trellis, pole, arch, etc.	(d)
Cotoneaster horizontalis	Scarlet berries	9–12	Sun or shade	Wall	(a)
*Cotoneaster microphylla	Scarlet berries	9–12	Sun or shade	Wall	(b)
Chaenomeles speciosa japonica	Scarlet, pink or white flowers	2–4	Sun or shade	Wall	(c)
*Escallonia	White to crimson flowers	6–7	Sun	Wall	(c)
Forsythia suspensa	Yellow flowers	3–4	Sun or shade	Wall	(c)
*Hedera (ivy)	Foliage	—	Sun or shade	Wall	(b)
Humulus (hop)	Foliage	—	Sun	Trellis, pole, arch, etc.	(a)
Hydrangea petiolaris	White flowers	6–7	Sun	Wall	(a)

Jasminum nudiflorum (winter jasmine)	Yellow flowers	11–2	Sun or shade	Wall	(c)
Jasminum officinale (summer jasmine)	White flowers	6–9	Sun	Trellis, arch, etc.	(a)
Kerria	Yellow flowers	4–5	Sun or shade	Wall	(c)
Lonicera (honeysuckle)	Yellow or red flowers	6–8	Sun	Trellis, pole, arch, etc.	(a)
*Magnolia grandiflora	White flowers	7–9	Sun	Wall	(b)
Polygonum baldschuanicum (Russian vine)	Pinkish-white flowers	7–9	Sun	Trellis, pergola, tree	(a)
*Pyracantha	Orange or scarlet berries	9–11	Sun or shade	Wall	(c)
Solanum crispum	Lavender flowers	7–9	Sun	Wall or trellis	(a)
Vitis (vine, Virginian creeper)	Foliage	—	Sun or shade	Pergola, trellis	(a)
Wisteria	Mauve flowers	5–6	Sun	Wall	(f)

* Evergreen foliage.

PRUNING INSTRUCTIONS

(a) Thin in February when overcrowded.
(b) No regular pruning. Shorten straggly growths in April–May.
(c) Shorten flowering growths when flowers fade.
(d) *Clematis jackmannii* and varieties, cut back young vines to one pair of eyes in February; or cut to within 1 ft. of ground level. *C. montana*, thin lightly after flowering. Other kinds, thin out oldest vines and shorten young vines a little in February.
(e) Thin out weak or worn-out growths after flowering.
(f) Shorten side growths to five leaves in July; two dormant buds in November.

484. A Table of Hardy Evergreen Trees and Shrubs

Name	Height in Feet	Ornamental Value	Season	Position	Soil
Andromeda	1½	Pink flowers	May	Sun or semi-shade	Peaty, moist
Arbutus unedo	15–25	White flowers, orange fruits	Oct.–May	Sun or shade	Ordinary
Aucuba	7	Foliage and scarlet berries	All year	Sun or shade	Ordinary
Azalea (evergreen vars.)	3	Flowers of various colours	May–June	Sun or semi-shade	Lime free
Azara	8–20	Yellow flowers	Feb.	Sun or shade, sheltered	Ordinary
Berberis (some species are deciduous)	3–10	Yellow or orange flowers	Apr.–June	Sun or shade	Ordinary
Buxus (box)	1–15	Foliage	All year	Sun or shade	Ordinary
Calluna (ling)	1¼–3	White to crimson flowers	Aug.–Sept.	Sun	Lime free
Ceanothus (evergreen vars.)	6–10	Blue flowers	May–July	Sun, sheltered	Ordinary
Cedrus (cedar)	60–70	Foliage	All year	Sun	Ordinary
Chamaecyparis	¼–50	Foliage	All year	Sun or semi-shade	Ordinary
Choisya	5–6	White flowers	Apr.–May Sept.	Sun, sheltered	Ordinary
Cistus	2–4	Flowers of various colours	June–July	Sun, sheltered	Ordinary
Cotoneaster (some are deciduous)	6	Scarlet berries	Autumn	Sun or semi-shade	Ordinary
Cryptomeria	15–50	Foliage	All year	Sun	Ordinary
Cupressus	60	Foliage	All year	Sun or semi-shade	Ordinary

Daboëcia	2	Purple or white flowers	July–Oct.	Sun or semi-shade	Lime free
Elaeagnus	8–12	Foliage	All year	Sun	Ordinary
Erica (heather)	¼–6	White to crimson flowers	All year	Sun	Lime free
Escallonia	5–10	White to crimson flowers	June–July	Sun	Ordinary
Euonymus	1–10	Foliage	All year	Sun or shade	Ordinary
Garrya	6–8	Green catkins	Nov.–Feb.	Sun, sheltered	Ordinary
Gaultheria	¼–3	White flowers, red berries	May and late summer	Shade	Lime free
Hypericum calycinum	¼–1	Yellow flowers	July–Sept.	Sun or shade	Ordinary
Ilex (holly)	40	Foliage and berries (on female)	All year	Sun or shade	Ordinary
Juniperus	1–15	Foliage	All year	Sun	Ordinary
Kalmia	6	Pink flowers	June	Sun or semi-shade	Lime free
Lavandula (lavender)	1–3	Lavender flowers	July–Aug.	Sun	Light
Mahonia	3–5	Yellow flowers	Feb.–May	Sun or shade	Ordinary
Magnolia grandiflora	20	White flowers	July–Sept.	Sun	Lime free, sheltered
Olearia	4–8	White flowers	July–Aug.	Sun	Ordinary, sheltered
Osmanthus	6–8	White flowers	April	Sun	Ordinary
Pernettya	3–4	Coloured berries	Autumn	Sun	Peaty
Phlomis fruticosa	3	Yellow flowers	June–July	Sun	Light
Picea (spruce)	2–60	Foliage	All year	Sun	Ordinary
Pieris	6–8	White flowers	Mar.–Apr.	Sun or semi-shade	Peaty
Pinus (pine)	6–60	Foliage	All year	Sun	Light
Prunus laurocerasus (laurel)	20	White flowers	Apr.–May	Sun or shade	Ordinary
Prunus lusitanica (Portugal laurel)	15–20	White flowers	June	Sun or shade	Ordinary
Pyracantha	6–8	Orange or scarlet berries	Autumn	Sun or semi-shade	Ordinary

A TABLE OF HARDY EVERGREEN TREES AND SHRUBS—continued

Name	Height in Feet	Ornamental Value	Season	Position	Soil
Rhododendron	1–20	Flowers of various colours	Apr.–July	Sun or shade	Lime free
Rosmarinus (rosemary)	1–5	Blue flowers	May	Sun	Light
Ruscus (butcher's broom)	2–3	Red berries	Autumn	Shade	Ordinary
Santolina	2	Grey foliage, yellow flowers	July–Aug.	Sun	Light
Senecio	2–3	Yellow flowers	July	Sun, sheltered	Ordinary
Sequoiadendron (wellingtonia)	50–100	Foliage	All year	Sun	Ordinary
Skimmia	1–3	Scarlet berries (on female in S. japonica)	Autumn	Sun or shade	Lime free
Taxus (yew)	3–15	Foliage	All year	Sun or shade	Ordinary
Thuja	3–60	Foliage	All year	Sun or semi-shade	Ordinary
Ulex (gorse)	4–6	Yellow flowers	April–May	Sun	Light
Viburnum tinus	8–10	White flowers	Nov.–May	Sun or semi-shade	Ordinary
Vinca	½–1	Blue flowers	March–May	Sun or shade	Ordinary
Yucca	3–8	White flowers	July–Aug.	Sun	Light

Note.—When grown as bushes in the open none of the above requires regular pruning. If they become too large or overcrowded, they may be thinned in May or, if in flower then, as soon as flowers fade. For pruning when trained against walls, etc., see 'Table of Hardy Climbers' (483).

485. A Table of Shrubs for Hedges

Name	Height in Feet	Planting Distance (feet)	Pruning	Remarks
Beech	6–10	1–1½	(a)	Retains autumn foliage
Berberis darwinii and *B. stenophylla*	6–8	1½–2	(c)	Orange or yellow flowers
Box	1–6	1–1½	(b)	Very neat habit
Chamaecyparis	6–10	2–2½	(b)	There are numerous varieties
Cotoneaster simonsii	5–8	1½	(a)	Scarlet berries
Cupressocyparis	6–12	2–3	(b)	Very fast growing
Escallonia	4–6	1½–2½	(c)	Rather tender
Euonymus japonicus	3–8	1½	(b)	Some have variegated leaves
Holly	4–12	1½–2	(a)	Slow growing
Hornbeam	6–10	1½–2	(a)	Like beech
Laurel (cherry)	6–10	1½–2	(b)	Prune with secateurs
Laurel (Portugal)	6–12	2–3	(b)	Makes thick hedge
Lonicera nitida	3–5	1–1½	(b)	Can be trimmed very thin
Myrobalan plum	5–10	1–2	(a)	Makes thick hedge
Privet (golden)	3–5	1–1½	(b)	Very bright colour
Privet (green)	3–8	1–1½	(b)	Grows anywhere
Quick (hawthorn)	4–8	¾	(a)	Grows anywhere
Thuja	6–12	2–3	(b)	Like chamaecyparis
Yew	3–12	1½–2	(b)	Slow growing

PRUNING INSTRUCTIONS

(a) Trim in summer. Head back in February if necessary.
(b) Trim in summer. Head back in May if necessary.
(c) Trim after flowering.

VIOLETS

486. Types. There are two main groups, the Parma violets, with double flowers, and the singles. These latter may be further split up into 'hardy' for flowering outdoors in winter, and 'large flowered' for flowering in frames. A few singles have petaloid centres to the blooms and are termed 'semi-double.'

487. Soil and Situation. A cool, rich, rather heavy soil suits all violets best and they like a sheltered position shaded from the noonday sun. Manure or compost can be used freely in the preparation of the summer quarters (44), (45).

488. Propagation. New stock should be raised every year, either from cuttings, taken in Aug–Sept., or by offsets (young rooted pieces) pulled from old clumps in March–April. Cuttings are prepared from the ends of runners, but in other ways are made, inserted, and treated in exactly the same manner as those of violas or pansies (469).

489. Cultural Routine. Rooted cuttings or offsets are planted out in March–April, singles 1 ft. apart in rows 18 in. apart, doubles 6 in. apart in rows 1 ft. apart. Water in freely if weather is dry. Subsequently keep hoed, feed with dilute liquid manure (50) frequently during the summer and spray with derris (662) or malathion (677) occasionally to keep down red spider.

490. Frame Culture. Make up beds of loamy soil, with plenty of leaf-mould or peat and a little sharp sand, to within 6–9 in. of the glass. Transfer clumps to these in September with large balls of roots and soil and plant so that leaves are just touching. Ventilate freely at first, more sparingly as weather becomes cold. Water moderately. Stir soil occasionally with a pointed stick.

SECTION SIX

GREENHOUSE, FRAME, AND CLOCHE

GREENHOUSE, FRAME, AND CLOCHE

491. Types and Position. There are four main types of greenhouse. A SPAN-ROOFED HOUSE has a ridge-shaped roof, both sides of which are of equal length. The roof stands on walls which may be all masonry or wood, partly or entirely glass. The height of these walls varies from about 1 ft. to $5\frac{1}{2}$ ft.

A LEAN-TO HOUSE has a roof sloping in one direction only, the back being formed by a wall. In other respects it is similar to the span-roofed type.

A THREE-QUARTER SPAN HOUSE is midway between these two types. The roof is in the form of a ridge, but one side is only about one-quarter the length of the other, and rests against a wall like the lean-to.

The fourth type is THE FORCING HOUSE or PIT, which has a span roof coming right down to soil level. The floor is excavated about 3 ft. below soil level and borders may be built up on this to within a foot of the base of the glass. These houses retain warmth especially well and are useful for forcing crops under high temperatures. Sometimes ordinary span-roofed houses on solid masonry walls are used as forcing houses.

Where possible, span-roofed and forcing houses should have the ridge running north and south; lean-to and three-quarter span houses should face south, the ridge running east and west. Only houses intended for ferns and certain tropical foliage plants should be in an entirely shaded place. All houses should be glazed with clear, 21-oz. glass.

492. Temperatures. These may be varied within wide limits, but roughly there are four main groupings.

Cold houses are unheated, and in winter the temperature may fall below freezing point, though the average will be in

225

the neighbourhood of 45°. This will rise in summer to 60°, or considerably more with direct sun heat.

The cool house is artificially heated in winter to a minimum of 45°, average 50°–55°. In summer it is not heated.

The temperate house has a winter minimum of 55° and summer minimum of 60° and the hothouse has a minimum of 65° winter and 70° summer. Both may need some artificial heat even in summer.

Cold houses can be used in winter only for hardy plants, but many tender plants can be grown in them during the summer. Cool and intermediate houses are the most generally serviceable for the majority of popular greenhouse plants. Hothouses are for really tender plants from tropical regions and for forcing plants into early growth or flower.

493. Heating. Hot-water boilers connected to water pipes and burning coal, coke or oil are commonly used for all large houses and many small ones. Pipes may be 2 or 4 in. in diameter; the latter are preferable. They must have a steady rise from the boiler to an expansion tank at the highest point and a similar fall back to the boiler. Pipes are usually accommodated at the side of the house, low down beneath the stages, if any. Sometimes in carnation houses, where heat is required more to circulate than to warm the atmosphere, the pipes are slung on brackets about a foot below the glass, midway between ridge and eaves.

Coke, coal and oil Heating are still the most economical, but small boilers are sometimes difficult to control. Improvement is effected by placing the boiler in a pit or shed so that it is not directly exposed to the wind. Automatic stokers are obtainable for large coke and coal boilers.

A single 4-in. flow and return down one side is sufficient for cool greenhouses not exceeding 8 ft. in width. For wider houses, pipes may be continued across one end, while if over 12 ft. in width they should be on three sides. For hothouses,

226

the number of pipes is increased. Often the return pipes are in duplicate.

The precise length of piping required to maintain any particular temperature will depend upon the position and structure of the house, but as a rough guide the following table may be of service. It is based on an outside temperature of 32° F. (freezing point):

For 45–50° F. provide 36 ft.
     50–55° F.   ,,   42 ft.
     55–60° F.   ,,   50 ft. of 4-in. pipes for each 1,000
     60–65° F.   ,,   55 ft. cu. ft. of space.
     70–75° F.   ,,   60 ft.

Hot-water boilers can also be obtained to be heated by gas. Care must be taken that there is no leakage of gas or escape fumes into the greenhouse. In other respects, details of installation are similar.

Houses can also be heated directly with oil lamps without water pipes. These should be specially designed to give off no fumes. Blue-flame lamps are more economical than those of the white-flame type, but are more liable to give off harmful fumes if out of adjustment. Cleanliness is of vital importance and only high-grade paraffin should be used. Oil heaters are more serviceable for occasional use, to keep out frost from otherwise unheated or slightly heated houses, than for constant operation.

Electrical heating is very reliable and satisfactory, but comparatively costly unless current can be obtained at a reasonable price. Ordinary domestic heaters are not satisfactory, as the source of heat is too concentrated. Low-temperature radiators, low-voltage strip heaters or fan-assisted heaters should be used. Special greenhouse installations are made by many manufactuers of electrical equipment, and expert advice should always be obtained regarding their installation.

Thermostatic control can be applied very easily both to electrical heaters and to gas-heated boilers. The instrument is set to keep the heat of the greenhouse constant within certain limits, usually three or four degrees. Thermostatic control cannot prevent rises of temperature caused by sun heat.

494. Capacity of Electrical Heaters. This is expressed in terms of the watts or kilowatts (1000 watts or units) of electricity the heater consumes. Approximately 10 watts is required for every square foot of glass and 5 watts for every square foot of masonry or woodwork to raise the inside temperature of a greenhouse 25° above the outside temperature. Since this is about what is required in cool greenhouses in winter in most parts of Britain, except the coldest and most exposed, it is a useful formula upon which to base calculations.

Make all measurements in feet or in fractions of feet. Measure each section of sides, ends and roof separately. Multiply the length and width of each section to obtain its area in square feet. Add together all the sections composed of glass and multiply by 10. Add all sections made of masonry or wood and multiply by 5. The sum of these two figures will give the number of watts required in a heater adequate to maintain cool house temperatures. This may need to be doubled for an intermediate house and tripled, or even quadrupled, for a hothouse. It can be reduced a little if frost protection only is required.

495. Staging. This is essential in houses with solid side walls more than 2 ft. in height and is useful in all houses in which pot plants or seedlings are to be grown. Its object is to keep plants near the glass where the light intensity is greatest and also to bring them close to hand so that they can be easily inspected, watered and tended.

Staging may be permanent or removable. If the latter, it

is usually made of wood; if the former, it may be of wood, brick, or concrete. Open-slat staging is best for plants that like a dry atmosphere and free circulation of air, e.g. pelargoniums and perpetual-flowering carnations. Solid staging covered with clean gravel or small, sifted cinders is to be preferred for moisture-loving plants, e.g. tuberous-rooted begonias and gloxinias.

496. Ventilation. Ventilators should be fitted in the ridge of every house – on both sides in the case of span-roofed houses – about 2 ft. in depth and in total length equivalent to at least half the total length of the house. Houses with part glass and part brick or wood sides should have ventilators of large size in the glass and it is an advantage if they can have small box ventilators with hinged or sliding wooden doors in the brick walls also. Greenhouses standing on brick or wood sides only should certainly have such box ventilators every 3 ft. along these walls.

The purpose of ventilation is to allow as free a current of air as possible, without severe draughts, to assist in the control of temperature and humidity. As a rule, top ventilators alone are used in winter, and then only by day when the weather is reasonably fine. They may be opened an inch or so for three or four hours around midday, according to outside conditions. In summer, when the weather is really hot, top and side ventilators may be opened widely to let currents of air pass through the house from bottom to top. Automatic ventilator openers are available which can be adjusted to operate at required temperatures. An alternative is to use extractor fans, which can be thermostatically controlled, usually fitted high up in the end walls of small greenhouses.

In unheated or moderately heated houses it is often possible to trap enough sun heat to keep the air warm throughout the night if all ventilators are closed an hour or so before sundown. Note that in the spring a clearing sky and falling wind towards evening is usually a warning sign of a sharp frost.

497. Atmospheric Moisture. This is required in very varying degree by different plants. Cacti like a comparatively dry atmosphere, whereas most tropical plants need one that is saturated with moisture. The majority of popular greenhouse plants stand midway between these extremes. Excessive humidity will encourage mildew (711), damping off (711), and other fungal diseases. Excessive dryness will result in scorching of the leaves and stems, often mistaken for disease. Scorched leaves develop brown patches which are dry and parchment-like without any sign of mould. Ventilation usually increases the dryness of the air especially if combined with some artificial heat.

The necessary moisture is maintained in three ways: by syringing the plants themselves, by damping down the paths, walls, and stages, and by placing water in shallow evaporating trays over the hot-water pipes.

SYRINGING must be practised only with plants known to like moisture and should be discontinued while plants are in flower or are ripening fruits. As a rule it is done in the morning when the temperature has begun to rise, but before the sun is shining fiercely. In some cases several syringings may be required each day. Avoid syringing late in the evening, as this lowers the temperature and encourages condensed moisture on the foliage early in the morning which, in turn, causes scorching. Tepid water is to be preferred to cold.

Damping down can be done with any plants if moisture is required. Again it is advisable not to work late in the evening nor to use very cold water.

Evaporating trays are used mainly in hothouses and vineries, and have much the same effect as damping down, except that the moisture is given off night and day.

498. Watering. Plants require varying quantities of water according to their nature and period of growth. In a general way plants with very small leaves, e.g. heaths, require less water than those with large leaves, e.g. caladiums, while cacti and succulents require less water than those of ordinary character. The maximum quantity of water is required while plants are in full growth and producing flowers and fruit. Most plants have a resting season when little or no water is required. It is most marked in plants with bulbous or tuberous roots, many of which can be kept completely dry for several months each year after their foliage has died down.

No hard-and-fast rules can be given regarding the quantity of water required. This will depend upon many changing factors, such as the weather, time of year, state of growth, and type of soil. It is never wise to wet the surface soil and leave lower layers dry. When water is given it must be in sufficient quantity to moisten the soil right through. If top watering is being practised with watering-can or hose, application usually should not be repeated until there are definite signs of dryness. To tell this the pot may be lifted and its weight judged, since damp soil weighs more than dry, but usually a little experience will enable the gardener to judge requirements by sight alone.

Automatic watering systems are also available of which one of the easiest to install is the capillary bench. This is a 1-in. deep layer of sand and pea gravel on a perfectly level, water-retentive surface such as polythene film, kept constantly wet so that pot plants placed on it draw water upwards by capillary attraction as they require it. Various devices are available for feeding water to such beds.

Water may be applied from a watering-pot either with or without a rose which should be used only when watering seed pans, seedlings, or freshly potted plants. The drawback is that water flows slowly, the surface becomes deceptively wet and foliage is unnecessarily splashed. Established greenhouse plants are almost invariably watered direct from the spout, which should be held close to the soil to prevent splashing.

Watering by complete immersion of the pot in a tub of water is useful for established plants which require abundant moisture, e.g. hydrangeas. Watering by partial immersion, i.e. by holding the pot or pan almost to its rim in a tub of water so that water rises from below through the drainage hole, but does not flow over the surface, is useful for seed receptacles, especially if they contain very small seedlings liable to be disturbed by top watering. Partial immersion should be continued until the surface of the soil is darkened by the rising moisture.

499. Shading. Only ferns and a few foliage plants require permanent shading, but many greenhouse plants, even normally sun-loving varieties, may require temporary shading from strong sunlight in the summer. This is particularly so in small houses which are heated rapidly by the sun and may become excessively hot in summer even with maximum ventilation.

Shading is of two types, semi-permanent and temporary.

SEMI-PERMANENT SHADING is obtained by painting or spraying the glass with lime wash or one of the proprietary shading compounds. If lime wash is applied outside (the usual method), it should be rendered adhesive by adding a little size to it. Lime wash is made by slaking quick lime or fresh hydrated lime in sufficient water to give it the consistency of milk.

TEMPORARY SHADING is obtained with blinds of hessian or chain laths. These are attached to rollers fixed to the outside ridge of the house so that they can be pulled down over the glass as required. As a rule such shading is needed on the south side only. Alternatively plastic blinds may be fitted inside the house or muslin may be attached to the roof rafters to provide a screen.

500. Propagating Frames. Some seedlings and cuttings

need a hotter or moister atmosphere than that of the green-house. To obtain this a propagating box or frame is used. In its simplest form this is a box of any convenient size and about 1 ft. in depth placed over the hot-water pipes or heating apparatus at the warmest end of the house and covered with panes of glass. The box is half filled with sand or granulated peat in which pots containing the seeds or cuttings are plunged. The purpose of the fibre is to retain heat and moisture. More elaborate propagators and propagating frames contain their own heating or soil-warming devices.

501. Seed Raising under Glass. It is not necessary to employ numerous composts for raising seeds of different plants. One good mixture will serve for all. That known as the John Innes Seed Compost (JIS for short) is as follows:

> 2 parts by loose bulk of medium loam.
> 1 part by loose bulk of good peat.
> 1 part by loose bulk of coarse silver sand.

To each bushel of this mixture add:

$1\frac{1}{2}$ oz. of superphosphate (16% phosphoric acid) (88).
$\frac{3}{4}$ oz. of ground limestone or chalk.

Pass all ingredients through a $\frac{1}{4}$-in. mesh sieve. It is an advantage if loam is first sterilized by steam or electricity (639). An alternative to loam-based compost is peat-based or all-peat compost of which various brands are available.

Seeds may be sown in earthenware or plastic pans 2–3 in. deep and of any diameter, pots, usually 4 or 5 in. diameter, and in wooden boxes or plastic trays $1\frac{1}{2}$–2 in. deep. All must be well supplied with drainage holes or slits, and these must be covered with crocks (broken pots), and small rubble or sphagnum moss. Make soil firm (except for pure peat compost) but do not fill within $\frac{1}{2}$ in. of the rim. Smooth surface with a planed block of wood and scatter seeds evenly. Cover with a sprinkling of finely sifted compost. A good guide is to cover seeds with twice their own depth of soil; very fine seeds, such as those of begonia and gloxinia, are not covered at all, simply pressed into the surface. Cover seed pans with panes of glass and sheets of paper. Directly seedlings appear, remove paper. A day later tilt the glasses on pebbles or wooden tallies, and a day or so after that remove altogether. Most seeds will germinate more rapidly if placed in a propagating frame (500), but excessive temperatures are detrimental for some seedlings and may cause damping off (711). Seeds of most popular greenhouse plants germinate well in a temperature of from 60°–70°.

Soil in which seeds are to be sown should be moist but not wet. It must not be allowed to become dry while seeds are germinating. Further water may be required and should be given by semi-immersion (498).

502. Pricking Off. Almost all seedlings must be pricked off, i.e. transplanted to other receptacles, as soon as they can be handled conveniently. Exceptions are mainly for bulbous-rooted plants, which may be sown extra thinly and allowed to grow on undisturbed for the first year.

Prick off into compost and receptacles similar to those used for sowing (501). Seedlings are lifted carefully with a sharpened stick, singled out (except with certain annuals) and dropped into dibber holes about 2 in. apart each way. A dibber the thickness of a stout lead pencil is used. Make soil firm round roots (but not for pure peat composts) and, finally, water freely through a fine rose. Seedlings should be shaded and given reduced ventilation for a few days until established. Subsequently, most kinds may be stood on staging or a shelf near the glass.

503. Cuttings under Glass. Greenhouse stem cuttings, like those taken outdoors (454), (481), are of three main classes, soft, half-ripe, and hard wooded. The first are prepared from young shoots of herbaceous plants or shrubs, the second and third from half-grown and fully grown shoots respectively of shrubs and half-shrubby plants only. Young cuttings must be rooted quickly. For this reason they are usually best in a propagating frame (500), and shaded until rooted. Cuttings are prepared in the same way as those of outdoor plants (454), (481). Bottom heat, i.e. heat coming from below through the soil (as in a propagating box), is of particular service in helping soft cuttings to root quickly. Root-forming hormones (111) may be used with the same object. Various automatic misting devices are also available and, if used, cuttings need not be shut up in a frame or propagator (735).

Composts for cuttings are usually very sandy and no fertilizers should be included.

504. Leaf Cuttings. The leaves of certain plants, e.g. gloxinias, *Begonia rex*, streptocarpus, and achimenes, will root. Well-developed leaves are pegged or weighted to the surface of sandy soil in a propagating frame (500), and are kept moist and shaded. Sometimes incisions are made across the main veins. Plantlets are formed at these incisions and at the leaf base. Plantlets also form along the fronds of some ferns, e.g. *Polystichum angulare* and *Asplenium bulbiferum*, if these are pegged firmly to the soil round the parent plant without being detached.

505. Potting. It is not necessary to make a different compost (mixture of soils) for each kind of plant since one general compost will serve for the majority of greenhouse plants. That known as the John Innes Potting Compost (or JIP.1 for short) is prepared as follows:

> 7 parts by loose bulk of medium loam.
> 3 parts by loose bulk of good peat.
> 2 parts by loose bulk of coarse silver sand.

To each bushel of this mixture add $\frac{3}{4}$ oz. of ground limestone or chalk and 4 oz. of base fertilizer prepared from 2 parts by weight of superphosphate (16% phosphoric acid) (88); 2 parts by weight of hoof and horn meal (12·75% nitrogen)

(65); and also 1 part by weight of sulphate of potash (87).

For many strong-growing greenhouse plants these quantities of fertilizers and chalk may be doubled when they are moved into pots larger than $4\frac{1}{2}$ in. in diameter, and trebled for 8-in. pots or larger. These stronger composts are often called JIP.2 and JIP.3 respectively.

The limestone or chalk may be omitted for plants known to dislike lime, e.g. azaleas, rhododendrons, and ericas.

Ingredients should be passed through a sieve only for the smaller plants. For final potting of chrysanthemums, etc., use it pulled and chopped to pieces so that the largest fragments are about as big as a pullet's egg. Soil should be moist but not wet, and must be at the same temperature as the greenhouse. It is an advantage if loam is first sterilized by steam or electricity (639). Alternatively, proprietary peat-based or pure peat composts are available.

Pots must be clean. New earthenware pots should be soaked to take the kiln dryness out of them. Drainage holes may be covered with crocks (pieces of broken pot) or special wire 'stoppers', but no such extra drainage should be used if pots are to stand on a capillary bench (498).

Most plants are potted just as they start to grow. Firm potting is necessary as a rule, but not for ferns, which grow best in soil only moderately consolidated, nor for plants grown in all-peat potting composts. A potting stick made from an old broom handle is used to press down the soil.

When repotting plants, do not disturb the roots unnecessarily. Tap them out of the old pot, remove drainage crocks from the bottom, and then repot.

It is seldom wise to pot direct from small into large pots. As a rule, one size increase is sufficient at first, two sizes later, e.g. plants in 3-in. pots will be moved to 4- or $4\frac{1}{2}$-in. pots, then to 5- or 6-in., then to 7- or 8-in. Water rather sparingly for a few days, and shade from strong sunlight.

506. Blueing Hydrangeas. Blue flowers on hydrangeas are obtained by growing pink varieties in a rather acid compost (pH 4·0–6·0) treated with alum. Good results have been obtained with the following mixture:

> 3 parts by bulk of acid loam.
>
> 1 part by bulk of oak leaf-mould.

To each 1 cwt. add $2\frac{1}{2}$ lb. of aluminium sulphate.

Pot plants in this mixture as soon as they come from the propagating frame.

Outdoor plants can be 'blued' by top dressing the soil in February with aluminium sulphate at approximately $\frac{1}{4}$ lb. per stem, but it is practically impossible to get any result on highly alkaline soils. Markedly acid soils produce blue flowers without treatment.

507. Bulbs in Fibre. A special compost made with 6 parts by bulk of peat, 2 parts of oyster shell, and 1 part of crushed charcoal is used when bulbs are grown in bowls without drainage holes. This compost will not become sour, but it contains little or no nutriment and the bulbs lose quality in consequence. It is essential to moisten this fibre before bulbs are planted in it as, when dry, water tends to run off it and not soak in. Subsequently, water must be given occasionally to keep the fibre moist. Bulbs in fibre must be kept in a cool, dark place for at least eight weeks to form roots.

508. Bulbs in Soil. All bulbs may also be grown in ordinary compost in boxes or pots if these are drained in the ordinary way (505). In particular, early narcissi, early tulips, hyacinths, and *Iris tingitana* are frequently so grown and forced into flower between December and March. Bulbs should be potted in August or September. They may be almost shoulder to shoulder and just covered with soil. They are then placed outdoors in a cool, sheltered place and covered with 4 in. of sand or ashes. They must remain in this plunge bed for at least eight weeks before they are introduced to a greenhouse. Even then temperature should not exceed 60° at first. Later, when flower stems appear, it may be raised to as much as 75° to rush bulbs into flower.

509. Plunging Plants. During the summer months many greenhouse plants, e.g. azaleas, deutzias, genistas, etc., are better in the open in a sunny, sheltered position. To prevent rapid drying out of the soil, the pots are plunged to their rims in a bed of ashes, sand, or peat.

510. Resting Plants. All plants have a season of rest when they make little or no growth, but this is much more marked with some kinds, notably those with bulbous or tuberous roots. Water supply must be adjusted accordingly (498) and as a rule temperature can be reduced considerably. This can often be effected by moving plants to a different part of the house.

511. Starting Plants. When growth is about to recommence (or earlier if it is desired to hurry the plant), temperature is raised (see above) and water supply gradually increased. With begonias and gloxinias it is best to arrange the tubers almost shoulder to shoulder in shallow boxes filled with damp peat and then transfer them from these to pots filled with ordinary potting soil (505) when they have made two or three leaves each.

512. Pruning Greenhouse Plants. Shrubby, half-shrubby, and climbing plants often need to be pruned to prevent them from becoming straggly or occupying too much space. This is usually done in February or March unless plants are then in full growth or flower, when it is deferred until after this. An exception is made for regal and show pelargoniums, which are pruned in early August. Method of pruning will depend upon requirements and type of growth. Climbers can, as a rule, have some of the oldest growths removed if overcrowded, and others shortened a little. Most shrubby plants can be cut back severely if it is desired to restrict size, but hard cutting must be avoided with hydrangeas, as it limits flowering.

FRAMES

513. Types. Frames may be permanent or portable and they may have span or lean-to roofs as in greenhouses. The pitch of the frame light (covering glass) is usually much less than that of the greenhouse, but must never be quite flat. The standard light measures 6 ft. by 4 ft. or 3 ft. by 4 ft., but other sizes can be obtained. Depth of frames varies greatly according to requirements but is not as a rule less than 9 in. at the lowest point or more than 3 ft. at the highest.

514. Maintaining Temperature. An unheated frame, known as a cold frame, will not be proof against frost in winter. In consequence, tender plants cannot be kept in it with complete safety. Matters can be improved by covering it heavily with sacks or mats during frosty weather, but these are mainly of use at night, for if kept on for long by day, plants will become drawn through lack of light.

Heating can be effected by running hot-water pipes through the frames, placing small electrical or oil heaters in them, or by heating the air or soil with electrical warming cables. The cable is attached to the inside walls of the frame or buried a few inches deep in the soil. Alternatively the frame may be placed on a hotbed, i.e. a heap of decaying manure. Fresh manure is required and should be turned once or twice as for mushroom beds (157). As it starts to ferment it will heat. When the temperature in the centre of the heap has subsided to 75°–80°, it is trodden into a pit at least 18 in. deep and a little larger than the frame, or alternatively it is built up into a rectangular mound of this size and 18–24 in. high. Six inches of soil is placed on top and then the frame is set in position. Seeds can be sown or cuttings inserted either in the soil or in boxes and pots plunged in it.

515. Ventilation. This can be given in three ways, by sliding the lights, by tilting them, or by removing them altogether. All are useful according to weather and condition of growth. When tilting lights, always do so on the side away from the wind. Frames are especially useful for hardening off half-hardy plants. This is done during April and May, and ventilation is gradually increased until the lights are removed altogether by day and finally by night as well.

516. Watering. General rules are the same as for watering in greenhouses (498). During rainy weather it is often wise to remove the lights for a time and let the plants get their moisture naturally, but do not do this if the rain is very cold or the plants of a kind that do not like moisture on their foliage.

517. Seed Raising in Frames. General rules are the same as for greenhouses, but seeds may be sown direct in a bed of soil prepared in the frame instead of in boxes or pots, if preferred. As a rule this is desirable only with strong-growing plants, such as vegetables and herbaceous perennials. February and March are the two months when the frame is most in use for seed sowing, but it may also be required in June and again in August–September.

518. Cuttings in Frames. General remarks regarding cuttings in greenhouses (503) apply. Frames are particularly serviceable for cuttings of hardy plants which need a close atmosphere, e.g. spring and summer cuttings, or those that appreciate shelter, e.g. evergreen shrubs. No attempt should be made to strike tender cuttings in frames unless they can be moved before cold weather arrives or the frames can be heated.

519. Frames in Summer. From June to September inclusive, frames can be used for many greenhouse plants that do not like high temperatures. A shaded frame will be serviceable for cyclamen, greenhouse primulas, calceolarias and cinerarias, and a sunny one for perpetual-flowering carnations, pelargoniums, etc. For some of these plants it may be necessary to increase the height of the sides.

CLOCHES AND HANDLIGHTS

520. Types. There are bell glasses, which are made entirely of glass and are shaped like a bell; handlights of varying pattern, but usually rectangular with span or pyramidal top glazed with glass or glass substitute, and continuous cloches which are open ended, and so may be placed end to end to cover a row of any length. These continuous cloches are the most useful for rearing seedlings and growing crops. Bell glasses and handlights are superior for striking summer cuttings, as the atmosphere within them is closer.

Continuous cloches can be made of sheets of glass held together by special wire frames or clamps. They can be dismantled easily and stored flat when not required. Breakages are easily made good. These cloches can be had in several forms, the two most important being the tent, made of two panes of glass set together like an inverted V, and the barn, made of four pieces set together like the end view of a barn. Plastic cloches of many different patterns are also available and yet another method is to stretch lengths of polythene film over wire supports to make long, tunnel-like protectors held in place by wooden pegs.

521. Ventilation. Bell glasses and handlights are ventilated by tilting them on a block of wood. Continuous cloches may be ventilated in two ways according to the weather and needs of plants: by leaving the ends of the row of cloches open, or by spacing the cloches out a little. In this way a great range of ventilation can be obtained. There are also special designs of cloches in which provision is made to open the sides or tops for ventilation.

522. Watering. Seeds and plants in cloches or handlights must not be allowed to get dry, but as a rule they do not require watering as freely as those in frames because water runs down the glass and then soaks in from the surrounding soil. Cloches may be placed fairly close together over ground in late winter and early spring, to enable the surface to dry off and so make seed sowing possible.

523. Plants to Grow in Cloches. In spring they are serviceable for early seedlings of flowering plants and vegetables and for early crops of salad vegetables, tomatoes, and strawberries. In summer they are used for cuttings of all kinds; in autumn for more cuttings, seedlings of hardy annuals, broad beans, brussels sprouts, and cauliflower, for ripening tomatoes and also crops of lettuce, endive, parsley, and radish. In winter cloches are useful as protection for small plants of doubtful hardiness such as some alpines and bulbs, also on the seedling crops already raised under them in the autumn.

CARNATIONS (PERPETUAL-FLOWERING)

524. Propagation. Cuttings may be taken at any time from December to March. They are rooted in pure silver sand or very sandy soil in a propagating frame, temperature 60° F. Cuttings are prepared from side growths on the flowering stems. Those mid-way up these stems are the best ones to take. They are simply pulled off with a heel attached and this is then trimmed up.

525. Potting. Cuttings are potted singly in 3-in. pots as soon as they are rooted. Subsequently, they are potted on as necessary until by May or early June they reach the 6- or 7-in. pots, in which they will flower. At first use an ordinary potting compost such as JIP.1 (505). For the later potting use JIP.2. Alternatively carnations may be grown in rings of soil on an aggregate base (733). Pot firmly.

526. Stopping. This is first done when the cutting has made seven joints. The top joint is broken off to encourage side growths to form.

242

The plants are stopped a second time when side growths resulting from the first stopping have made about eight joints. Two joints are broken out. Complete this second stopping by early July if flowers are required by Christmas.

527 Routine Cultivation. From October to May plants must have the protection of a greenhouse, but during the summer they may be placed in a frame and ventilated freely. Stand the frame on bricks to give height and allow air to enter from below as well as above. Cool, airy treatment is necessary throughout. Even in winter, heat is used more to dry than to warm the atmosphere, but frost must be excluded. By taking cuttings over a long period (524) plants may be had in flower most of the year. Water moderately in summer, sparingly in winter. Excessive heat encourages thrips and red spider (711).

CHRYSANTHEMUMS

528. Types and Classification. There are annual and hardy perennial chrysanthemums which are dealt with elsewhere (415 and 458). Here we are only concerned with the florist chrysanthemums developed over many centuries from plants of Chinese and Japanese origin. For garden purposes these are broadly divided into three main groups, Early Flowering or Border which normally flower in the open before October 1st, October Flowering or Mid-season and Late Flowering or Indoor which normally flower under glass between November and January. The controlling body for classification in Britain is the National Chrysanthemum Society.

Within each division the varieties are classified according to flower characteristics. Singles have up to five rows of petals and a button-like disk. Anemone-centred varieties are similar except that a low, soft cushion of very short petals replaces the button-like centre. Doubles have so many petals that no central disk is visible until the flower fades.

Doubles are split into three groups according to the form of the petals. In Incurved varieties these all curl inwards making a ball-like flower. Reflexed varieties have outward or downward-curling petals. Intermediate varieties have the inner petals curling inwards and the outer petals curling outwards. For exhibition purposes there are further sub-divisions of each group according to the normal size of the flower.

There are also some other special classes. Pompons have very small fully double flowers produced freely in clusters. Thread petalled or Rayonante are doubles with petals rolled lengthwise like thin quills. In Spoon-petalled varieties petals are partly rolled but open out at the end like little spoons. Cascade varieties have lax growth and can be trained as hanging plants. Charm varieties are very branching, compact and have numerous small single flowers. Korean and Rubellum varieties have very numerous single or semi-double flowers but are relatively hardy and may be grown outdoors all the year in mild places and on light soils. All other chrysanthemums, even the Early Flowering or Border varieties, are likely to need winter protection in most parts of Britain.

529. Propagation. Though chrysanthemums can be raised quite easily from seed, seedlings are very variable in quality and this method is therefore hardly ever adopted, except with Cascade and Charm (small single-flowered) varieties. Seed is sown in February in a warm greenhouse and subsequent treatment of seedlings is similar to that of half-hardy annuals (405 to 408).

Cuttings are almost invariably employed for other chrysanthemums and selected Cascades. These are taken from November until May; the earliest cuttings for exhibition varieties and especially those to be flowered on second crown buds (531), and the latest cuttings for dwarf plants. With the exception of late cuttings, which are often prepared from the tops of plants rooted earlier in the year, all cuttings are made from sucker growths, i.e. shoots coming direct from the roots through the soil. Shoots growing from the old, woody flower stems will not make good cuttings. Cuttings are 2–3 in. in length, trimmed below a joint and the lower leaves are removed. They are inserted $\frac{1}{2}$–1 in. deep in sandy soil, usually in pots or boxes, and are rooted on the cool greenhouse staging or in a propagating frame (500). Great heat is undesirable as it encourages disease.

530. Potting. As soon as cuttings are rooted and growing, they are potted singly in 3-in. pots and ordinary potting compost (505). Pot rather firmly and shade for a day or so until established. Subsequently, grow on in full sun and average temperature of 55°–60°. Pot on as smaller pots become moderately full of roots, using similar compost throughout but coarser in texture as plants get bigger. For final potting in late May or June into 8-9 in. pots loam may be in lumps as large as a small hen's egg. To this final compost, basic chrysanthemum fertilizer (100) should be added instead of the general potting fertilizer. Pot firmly throughout. Early-flowering and Korean chrysanthemums are not usually potted beyond 3-in. pots, in which they are hardened off (515) in a frame and planted outdoors 1 ft. apart in rows 2 ft. apart in early May.

531. Stopping. This means pinching out the growing tips of the plants. It is practised for two distinct reasons: (i) to make the plants more bushy, and (ii) to obtain buds and flowers at the right time. The first purpose is necessary only for decorative varieties, singles grown for decoration, late-flowering varieties grown as large specimen plants, early-flowering types grown for garden decoration or small flowers in sprays, and Koreans. As a rule two stoppings are then given, the first when the young plants are 6 or 7 in. in height and the second when the side growths produced as a result of the first stopping are about 8 in. long. For exhibition purposes, early-flowering chrysanthemums are usually grown with one stopping only during the first half of May.

When stopping to time blooms for exhibition, each variety must be treated according to its peculiarities. Catalogues issued by trade specialists usually give instructions which may need to be modified to suit the locality. Left to itself the cutting will, after a few weeks, produce a flower bud at the tip of the stem. This bud prevents further extension of the main stem and forces the plant to produce side growths. It is, in consequence, known as a BREAK BUD. Some time later the side growths will produce flower buds, known as FIRST CROWN BUDS. Further shoots appear below them, themselves

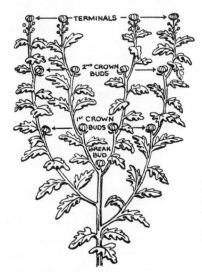

Chrysanthemum Terminology. The ultimate object in 'stopping', and the position of the buds is illustrated.

terminating in flower buds some weeks later. These are SECOND CROWN BUDS. Again, the process is repeated, but the third batch of side growths will end in clusters of flower buds, not in one flower bud surrounded by further shoots. The plant has reached the end of its development and these buds are in consequence known as TERMINAL BUDS. By pinching out the tips of shoots a little before each stage in this sequence would occur naturally, the next stage can also be advanced by a few days. Since the sequence of growth and bud formation is controlled by the interaction of warmth and day length it is subject to modification according to the time at which cuttings are taken. It can also be modified by artificial control of temperature and by the use of blackouts or lighting to shorten or lengthen the days, and it is by these means that commercial growers are able to produce chrysanthemum cut flowers throughout the year. However, not all varieties respond equally well or in a similar manner and for good results it is essential to be able to control the lighting and heating very accurately.

A special system of stopping and training is necessary for Cascade chrysanthemums. After the first stopping of the rooted cutting, the uppermost new shoot is tied to a bamboo cane sloping downwards at an angle of 45° towards the north, and is not stopped again. The plant must be stood on a shelf or raised bench both in the greenhouse and when outdoors from June to September (533). All other growths are stopped after the fourth leaf. If they form secondary growths, these are stopped in turn at the fourth leaf. No growths are stopped after the middle of September. When the plants are brought into the greenhouse the main stems are lowered so that they hang perpendicularly.

532. Bud Taking. This signifies the gardener's decision that the particular flower bud just formed will develop into a bloom at the right time and so must be kept. All other buds

247

or side growths surrounding or immediately beneath it are rubbed out. Usually buds of intermediate or reflexed varieties required for exhibition about the second week in November should be taken between the middle and end of August, while incurves may be a week or fortnight later. Buds that appear a little too soon can be retarded by leaving side growths round them for a week or fortnight.

Bud selection is also sometimes determined by the type of flower required since first crown buds tend to produce flowers with more petals than second crown buds which, in time, have more petals than do flowers from terminal buds (531).

533. Cultural Routine. Chrysanthemums are almost hardy but the flowers and flower buds of all kinds except the very hardy Korean varieties may be damaged severely by frost. They require cool greenhouse (492) protection from early October until the end of May. During the remaining months they are best outdoors in a sunny position. Old roots are discarded and only the rooted cuttings retained. These are watered moderately at first, but more freely as weather becomes warmer. In summer, water is supplied freely. Feed with chrysanthemum summer fertilizer (101) from mid-July till flower buds show colour.

When plants are stood outdoors, pots should be placed on boards, slates, or a gravel or ash base to assist drainage and to keep out worms. Stake and tie each plant securely.

Alternatively, decorative varieties may be planted out in late May in ordinary well-dug soil, 18 in. apart in rows $2\frac{1}{2}$ ft. apart. They are then lifted with good balls of soil in the autumn and replanted in the greenhouse either in beds or boxes. Planting of border and Korean varieties has already been described (530). These may be left in the open all the winter in well-drained soil, but a few plants should be lifted in October into a frame with old potting soil to give cuttings. After flowering, cut down all plants to within about 4 in. of soil level. Chrysanthemums can be grown successfully by the ring culture method (733).

Chrysanthemums are frequently attacked in summer by aphids and capsid bugs and flowers may be damaged by earwigs. All can be kept under control by occasional spraying with suitable insecticides (see Section 8). Diseases include rust and mildew, also grey mould (botrytis) which is particularly likely to damage expanding flowers, causing them to decay. This disease thrives in a cold, damp atmosphere and is best controlled by good ventilation coupled with some artificial heat to dry the air and keep it on the move. Other diseases can be controlled by occasional spraying or dusting with fungicide (see Section 8).

534. A Table of Green-

Note.—Letters indicate habit

An, Annual, or treated as such (410).
Bn, Biennial (429).
Hb, Herbaceous (451).
Sh, Shrubby (476).
HSh, Half-shrubby.
Cl, Climbing.
Tr, Trailing.
Bl, Bulbous or tuberous.
Su, Succulents.
Lc, Leaf cutting.

Numbers indicate months,

* Other methods of propagation : d, division ;

Name	Colour	Season
Abutilon	Various	1–12
Acacia	Yellow	2–4
Achimenes	Various	6–9
Aechmea *	Red and blue	8–9
Agapanthus	Blue or white	6–9
Agathaea	Blue	5–10
Allamanda	Yellow	4–9
Allium neapolitanum	White	5–6
Anthurium	Red or pink	5–9
Aristolochia	Various	7
Arum (Zantedeschia)	White or yellow	12–4
Astilbe	White to crimson	5–6
Auricula	Various	3–4
Azalea indica	White to crimson	12–3
Balsam	Various	6–10
Begonia (fibrous)	White to crimson	6–10, 11–2
Begonia (tuberous)	Various	6–9
Beloperone	Pink and white	6–8
Billbergia	Pink and green	6–8
Bougainvillea	Rose, crimson, orange	6–10
Bouvardia	White to scarlet	9–1
Browallia	White and blue	7–12
Brunfelsia	Blue	1–12
Calceolaria (herbaceous)	Various	4–6
Calceolaria (shrubby)	Various	6–9
Calystemon	Red	3–7

house Flowering Plants

and treatment as follows:

> U, Cold (unheated) house ⎫
> C, Cool house   ⎬ (492)
> T, Temperate house ⎪
> H, Hothouse   ⎭
>
> D, Dry atmosphere   ⎫
> I, Intermediate atmosphere ⎬ (497)
> W, Wet atmosphere   ⎭
>
> R, No water during resting period   ⎫
> G, Water moderately during resting period ⎬ (498), (510)

e.g. 3 = March.

g, grafting or budding; 1, layering.

Habit	Treatment	Propagation			Potting
		Seed	Cuttings	Etc*	
Sh, Cl	CIG	3	3–7	—	3
Sh	CIG	3	6–7	—	5–6
Bl, Tr	TIR	1–2	4, 7	d 2	1–4
Hb	TWG	—	—	d 3	3–4
Hb	CIG	—	—	d 3	3
HSh	TIG	3–6	9–10	—	3–10
Cl	HIG	—	3	—	3–4
Bl	CIR	—	—	d 10–11	10–11
Hb	HWG	—	—	d 3	—
Cl	H or TIG	3	6–7	—	3
Bl	C or TWR	—	—	d 8	8
Hb	U or CIG	—	—	d 10	9–10
Hb	CIG	3 or 6	—	d 6	6
Sh	CIG	—	6–7	g 3	4
An or Hb	CWG	3–5	4–5	—	3–7
Hb	TIG	2–3	2–4	—	3–4
Bl, some Tr	C or TIR	1–3	—	d 3–4	3–5
Hb	C or TIG	—	4	—	3–4
Hb	C or TIG	—	—	d 3–4	3–4
Cl	C or TIG	—	6–7	—	2
Sh	T or HIG	—	3–4	—	3
An	TI	2–3	—	—	4–5
Sh	T or HIG	—	6–7	—	3–4
An	TI	5–6	—	—	8–2
Sh	CIG	3	9–10	—	4–6
Sh	CDG	—	7–8	—	9

A TABLE OF GREENHOUSE

Name	Colour	Season
C .mellia	White to crimson	1–4
Campanula isophylla	Blue, white	6–9
Campanula pyramidalis	Blue, white	6–7
Canna	Yellow to red	7–10
Carnation (perpetual)	Various	1–12
Cassia	Yellow	6–10
Celosia	Yellow, red	7–9
Celsia	Yellow	4–10
Chrysanthemum	Various	10–1
Cineraria	Various	11–5
Clerodendrum fallax	Scarlet	5–8
Clerodendrum (others)	White, red	7–9
Clianthus puniceus	Red or white	5–6
Clivia	Yellow, orange	3–5
Cobaea	Purple	7–10
Coronilla	Yellow	5
Crinum	White, pink	7–8
Cuphea	Scarlet	6–8
Cyclamen	White to crimson	11–2
Daphne odora	Pink	2–3
Datura	White, orange	6–7
Deutzia gracilis	White	2–5
Dicentra	Rose	4–5
Diplacus	Orange to red	5–9
Dipladenia	White to pink	5–9
Eccremocarpus	Orange	7–10
Epacris	White to red	11–1
Erica	White to red	10–6
Eucharis	White	1–4
Euphorbia fulgens	Scarlet	11–2
Exacum	Lavender	8–12
Francoa	White and red	7–9
Freesia	Various	12–3
Fuchsia	White, red, purple	5–10
Gardenia	White	1–12
Genista	Yellow	3–4
Gerbera	Yellow to red	5–9

FLOWERING PLANTS – *continued*

Habit	Treatment	Propagation			Potting
		Seed	*Cuttings*	*Etc**	
Sh	U or CIG	3	6–7	1, 3, 9 g 3	4–5
Tr	U or CIG	—	3–4	—	3–5
Bn	U or CIG	2–3	—	—	4–10
Bl	TIR	2–3	—	d 2–3	2–3
Hb	CDG	2–3	11–3	—	3–6
Cl	C or TIG	—	3–6	—	3–4
An	C or TI	2–3	—	—	4–6
Hb	CIG	3 or 7	3–4	—	3–6
HSh	CDG	2–3	11–5	—	3–6
An	CI	4–6	—	—	7–10
Hb	T or HIG	3	—	—	4–6
Cl	T or HIG	—	1–3	—	3
Sh	CDG	3	6–7	—	3–4
Bl	TIR	2–3	—	d 2, 6	2
Cl	CIG	2–3	7–8	—	3–5
Sh	CIG	—	4 or 8	—	3
Bl	CDR	3	—	d 3	3
Hb	TIG	—	4–7	—	3
Bl	CIR	8	—	—	3–10
Sh	U or CIG	—	9–10	—	3–4
Sh	TWG	3	3–4	—	3
Sh	U or CIG	—	6–7	—	5
Hb	U or CIG	—	—	d 3	3, 9
Sh	CIG	—	4–7	—	3
Cl	T or HWG	—	3	—	3–4
Cl	U or CIG	2–4	—	—	3–4
Sh	CDG	—	5–6	—	3
Sh	CDG	—	4–7	—	3, 9
Bl	T or HIG	—	—	d 5	5–6
Hb	T or HIG	—	4–5	—	3
An	U or CI	3–9	—	—	4–10
Hb	U or CIG	3–4	—	d 3	3
Bl	CIR	3–6	—	d 8	8
Sh	U or CIG	3	3, 9	—	3–4
Sh	T or HWG	—	1–4	—	3–4
Sh	U or CIG	3–4	6–7	—	5
Hb	CDR	3–4	—	—	3–4

253

A TABLE OF GREENHOUSE

Name	Colour	Season
Gloxinia	Various	5–9
Haemanthus	Red or white	12–4
Hedychium	White, yellow, red	7–8
Heliotrope	Mauve	6–9
Hibiscus rosa-sinensis	Yellow to crimson	5–9
Hippeastrum	Red to white	11–6
Hoya	Pink	7–8
Humea elegans	Brown	7–10
Hydrangea	White, pink, blue	5–7
Ipomoea	Various	7–10
Jacobinia (Justicia)	Various	10–1
Jasminum	White, yellow	11–3
Kalanchoë	Red to white	1–12
Lachenalia	Yellow, orange	2–4
Lantana	Various	6–10
Lapageria	White to crimson	6–10
Lilium	Various	3–10
Luculia	Pink	12–1
Nerine	White to scarlet	9–11
Nerium (oleander)	Pink or white	6–8
Orchids, cattleya	White to purple	3–6
,, cymbidium	White, pink, buff, etc.	3–5
,, cypripedium	Blush, green, chocolate	1–4
,, dendrobium	Yellow, pink, mauve	2–5
,, miltonia	White, crimson	4–7
,, odontoglossum	White, yellow to maroon	2–5
,, oncidium	Yellow to brown	2–7
Pancratium	White	6–8
Passiflora	Various	7–9
Pelargonium (geranium)	White to crimson	4–10
Plumbago	Blue	7–10
Poinsettia	Scarlet, pink	11–1
Primula malacoides	Pink, red, mauve	2–4
Primula obconica	Various	10–4
Primula sinensis	Various	12–3
Rehmannia	Rose	5–8
Rose	Various	1–12
Saintpaulia	Violet, pink, white	1–12

FLOWERING PLANTS—*continued*

Habit	Treatment	Propagation			Potting
		Seed	Cuttings	Etc*	
Bl	TWR	1–2	—	—	1–5
Bl	TIR	—	—	d 4	4
Bl	T or HIR	—	—	d 3	3
Hb	C or TIG	2–3	4, 9	—	3
Sh	T or HWG	—	3–4	—	3–4
Bl	C or TIR	8	—	d 1–3	1–3
Cl	TIG	—	3–5	1 6–7	3
Bn	CIG	4–7	—	—	3–10
Sh	U or CIG	—	4–7	—	3
Cl, An	CI	2–6	—	—	4–7
Hb	H or TIG	—	4	—	2
Cl	T or HIG	—	4	—	4
Su	CDR	3	5–9	—	3–4
Bl	CDR	3	—	d 8–9	8–9
HSh	CIG	2–3	3, 8	—	3–6
Cl	CIR	—	—	1 3, 9	—
Bl	U or CIR	2–3	—	d 9–10	9–10
Sh	CIG	5–6	4–5	—	4
Bl	CDR	—	—	d 8	8
Sh	CIG	—	7–8	—	3
—	H or TIR	3–4	—	d 3–4	3–4
—	C or TIR	3–4	—	d 5	5
Hb	C or TIG	3–4	—	d 4	4
—	H or TIR	3–4	—	d 4–5	4–5
—	T or HIR	3–4	—	d 3	3
—	TIR	3–4	—	d 4–5	4–5
—	TIR	3–4	—	d 4	4
Bl	CIR	—	—	d 3	3
Cl	C or TIG	2–3	3–4	—	3
HSh	CDG	2–3	7–9	—	3–4
Cl	CIG	4–5	5–6	—	3–4
HSh	HWR	—	4–5	—	4–5
An	CI	4–7	—	—	6–10
An	CI	3–6	—	—	6–10
An	CI	3–6	—	—	6–10
Hb	CIG	2–3	—	d 3	3
Sh, Cl	U or CIG	—	—	g 6–8	11
Hb	H or TIG	2–3	—	Lc 6–8	3

A TABLE OF GREENHOUSE

Name	Colour	Season
Salvia	Scarlet, blue	8–11
Schizanthus	Various	4–10
Smithiantha	Yellow to red	7–9
Solanum capsicastrum	Red berries	11–1
Solanum jasminoides	White	7–8
Sparmannia	White	1–12
Statice	White, pink, blue	8–10
Stephanotis	White	1–12
Strelitzia	Blue and orange	5–6
Streptocarpus	Various	9–6
Streptosolen	Orange	4–7
Thunbergia alata	Orange	6–9
Thunbergia (others)	Various	5–10
Tibouchina	Violet	5–10
Trachelium	Blue	6–9
Tropaeolum	Yellow to scarlet	6–10
Tuberose	White	7–10
Vallota	Scarlet	8–9
Veltheimia	Yellow and red	11–4
Vinca rosea	Pink, white	1–12

FLOWERING PLANTS – *continued*

Habit	Treatment	Propagation			Potting
		Seed	Cuttings	Etc*	
Hb or HSh	CIG	2–3	3–4	—	3–6
An	U or CI	1–9	—	—	3–6
Bl	C or TIR	2–3	—	d 2–3	2–3
Sh	C or TIG	2–3	—	—	4–9
Cl	CIG	—	6–8	—	3
Sh	CIG	—	4–7	—	3–4
Hb and An	U or CIG	2–3	3–4	—	3–6
Cl	HWG	—	3–4	—	2–3
Hb	T or HIG	—	—	d 3–4	3–4
Hb	C or TIG	2–6	—	d 3	3
Cl	CIG	—	4–7	—	3
An	U or CI	3–4	—	—	5–7
Cl	HWG	3–4	3–6	—	3
Sh	C or TIG	—	4–7	—	3
An	CI	3, 7	—	—	4–10
Cl	CIG	3	3–4	—	4–6
Bl	T or HIR	—	—	d 2	2–4
Bl	CDR	—	—	d 3	3
Bl	CIR	—	—	d 8–9	8–9
HG	T or HIG	2–4	—	—	3–4

535. A Table of Greenhouse Foliage Plants

For abbreviations see (534)

Name	Description	Habit	Treatment	Seed	Cuttings	Etc.	Potting
Aralia	Green, bronze	Sh	T or HIG	—	6-8	—	3
Araucaria excelsa	Green	Sh	CIG	3	—	—	3
Asparagus plumosus	Ferny, green	Hb	CIG	3	—	d 3	3
Asparagus sprengeri	Trailing, green	Hb	CIG	3	—	d 3	3
Aspidistra	Green and white	Hb	CIG	—	—	d 3	3
Begonia rex	Marbled	Hb	C or TWG	3-4	—	d 3	3
Caladium	Marbled	Hb	HWR	—	—	d 3	3
Chlorophytum	Green and white	Hb	CIG	—	—	d 3	3
Cissus	Purple, green, variegated	Cl	C or TIG	—	4-7	—	3-4
Coleus	Green, crimson, yellow, etc.	Hb	C or TIG	2-3	7-8	—	3
Croton (codiaeum)	Green, yellow, orange, etc.	Sh	HWG	—	5-6	—	3
Dracaena	Red, orange, green, etc.	Sh	TIG	3	3-4	—	3
Fatsia	Green	Sh	UIG	—	6-7	—	3
Ferns	Green	Hb	U to HWG	6	—	d 3	3
Ficus	Green and yellow	Sh	TIG	—	4-6	—	3
Grevillea	Green	Sh	CIG	2-3	—	—	3
Palms	Green	Sh	C or TWG	3	—	—	3
Pandanus	Green and white	Hb	TWG	—	—	d 3	3
Sansevieria	Marbled	Hb	T or HIG	—	—	d 3	3
Selaginella	Green, bronze, etc.	Hb	CWG	—	—	d 3	3
Smilax	Green	Cl	CIG	3	—	—	3
Tradescantia	Variegated, trailing	Hb	TIG	—	3-6	—	3

Note.—All the above with the exception of caladiums are evergreen

SECTION SEVEN

CALENDAR OF GARDEN OPERATIONS

GARDEN OPERATIONS

WORK FOR JANUARY

536. Seeds to Sow in Warmth. VEGETABLES: french beans, cress, shorthorn carrots, leeks, lettuces, mustard, onions, radishes, tomatoes. FLOWERS: antirrhinums, begonias, cannas, gloxinias, scarlet salvias, streptocarpus, sweet peas, verbenas.

537. Plants to Start in Warmth. FLOWERS: achimenes, tuberous begonias, clivias, gloxinias, hippeastrums, hyacinths, bulbous irises, lilies, narcissi, pot-grown roses and shrubs, tulips. FRUITS: early vines, peaches, and nectarines. VEGETABLES: chicory, early potatoes, rhubarb, seakale.

538. Vegetables to Force Outdoors. Rhubarb, seakale.

539. Cuttings to Take in Warmth. Perpetual-flowering carnations, greenhouse chrysanthemums.

540. Root Cuttings to Take in Frame. Anchusas, gaillardias, perowskia, oriental poppies, *Phlox decussata*, romneyas, perennial statices, perennial verbascums.

541. Pruning Outdoors. Apples, apricots, cherries, currants, gooseberries, nectarines, peaches, pears, plums.

542. Pruning under Glass. FLOWERS: *Plumbago capensis*, passion flowers (passiflora). Also climbing roses. FRUITS: late vines.

543. Miscellaneous. VEGETABLES: dig, trench, work in bulky and slow-acting manures and fertilizers, mulch asparagus beds with dung, protect broccoli curds. FRUIT: spray fruit trees with tar-oil wash, protect fruit buds from birds.

WORK FOR FEBRUARY

544. Seeds to Sow in Sheltered Places Outdoors. Onions, parsley, parsnips, early peas, turnips.

545. Seeds to Sow in Warmth. VEGETABLES: french beans,

broad beans, brussels sprouts, shorthorn carrots, cress, cucumbers, celery, cauliflowers, leeks, lettuces, mustard, onions, radishes, tomatoes. FRUIT: melons. FLOWERS: antirrhinum, ageratum, anagallis, begonias, brachycome, balsams, cobaea, cosmeas, cannas, celsia, celosia (including cockscomb), *Clerodendrum fallax*, carnations, dahlias, *Dianthus heddewigii*, eccremocarpus, fuchsias, gloxinias, *Impatiens holstii*, *I. sultanii*, kochia, lobelia, marigolds (tagetes), marguerites, mimulus, nicotianas, nemesias, *Phlox drummondii*, petunias, pelargoniums, *Rehmannia angulata*, streptocarpus, scarlet salvia, sweet peas, salpiglossis, schizanthus, annual statices, ten-week stocks, trachelium, verbenas.

546. Planting Outdoors. VEGETABLES: Jerusalem artichokes, chives, spring cabbage, garlic, onion sets, autumn-sown onions, early potatoes (in very sheltered place), shallots. FRUITS: apples, apricots, blackberries, cherries, currants, figs, grape vines, gooseberries, loganberries, medlars, mulberries, nectarines, nuts, pears, plums, peaches, raspberries. FLOWERS: tuberous-rooted anemones, lilies (except *Lilium candidum* and *testaceum*), roses, ranunculuses, deciduous trees and shrubs (except magnolias).

547. Plants to Start in Warmth. FLOWERS: achimenes, tuberous begonias, clivias, cannas, dahlias, gloxinias, hyacinths, hippeastrums, bulbous irises, lilies, narcissi, pot-grown roses and shrubs, tulips. FRUIT: apricots, nectarines and peaches, mid-season vines. VEGETABLE: seakale.

548. Planting and Potting under Glass. FLOWERS: autumn-sown annuals for the greenhouse, started begonias and gloxinias, rooted chrysanthemums, border chrysanthemums, perpetual-flowering carnations.

549. Cuttings to Take in Warmth. Winter-flowering begonias, greenhouse chrysanthemums, border chrysanthemums, perpetual-flowering carnations.

550. Pruning Outdoors. Late-planted fruit trees, cobnuts and filberts, autumn-fruiting raspberries. FLOWERS: *Cornus alba*, clematises of the jackmanii, lanuginosa and viticella types, *Hydrangea paniculata, Hypericum moserianum, Spiraea aitchisonii, arborea, ariaefolia, bullata, japonica, lindleyana, menziesii* and *salicifolia, Tamarix pentandra*.

551. Pruning under Glass. Bougainvilleas, *Diplacus glutinosus*, fuchsias, gardenias, zonal and ivy-leaved pelargoniums.

552. Miscellaneous. VEGETABLES: dig, trench, work in bulky and slow-acting manures and fertilizers, break down surface of rough dug ground, protect broccoli curds, lift and store parsnips, protect fruit buds from birds, harden off vegetable seedlings in frames, prick off early seedlings under glass. FRUIT: pollinate early flowers in vinery and orchard house, and spray outdoor peaches and nectarines with lime sulphur.

WORK FOR MARCH

553. Seeds to Sow Outdoors. VEGETABLES: broccoli, brussels sprouts, broad beans, early carrots, cabbages, cauliflowers, lettuces, leeks, onions, peas, parsnips, parsley, radishes, summer spinach, spinach beet, turnips. FLOWERS: annual alyssum, bartonia, calendulas, annual candytuft, annual chrysanthemums, clarkias, collinsia, *Convolvulus tricolor*, annual coreopsis, cornflowers, eschscholzias, godetias, annual gypsophila, larkspurs, *Lavatera rosea,* limnanthes, linums, annual lupins, malopes, nemophilas, nigellas, phacelias, cardinal and Shirley poppies, annual rudbeckias, roses, annual saponaria, annual sunflowers, Virginia stock, ornamental trees and shrubs, viscarias.

554. Seeds to Sow under Glass. VEGETABLES: brussels sprouts, broccoli, cress, celery, celeriac, cucumbers, cauliflowers, herbs, mustard, radishes, tomatoes. FRUITS: melons. FLOWERS: as February. Also asters, hardy annuals (for pot culture in greenhouse), coleus, exacum, herbaceous perennials, *Solanum capsicastrum*, zinnias.

555. Planting Outdoors. VEGETABLES: brussels sprouts, spring cabbages, pickling cabbages, cauliflowers, chives, garlic, mint, onion sets, autumn-sown onions, potatoes, horse-radish, rhubarb, shallots, seakale. FRUITS: as February. Also strawberries. FLOWERS: Alpines, hardy climbers, border carnations, Canterbury bells, double daisies, forget-me-nots, gladioli, montbretias, herbaceous perennials, polyanthuses, sweet peas, roses, ornamental trees and shrubs (deciduous and evergreen), tigridias, wallflowers.

556. Planting and Potting under Glass. VEGETABLES: early cucumbers and tomatoes. FLOWERS: *Asparagus plumosus*, *A. sprengeri*, aspidistras, begonias, coleus, crotons, cacti and succulents, chrysanthemums, perpetual-flowering carnations, ferns, fuchsias, gloxinias, heliotropes, marguerites, palms, pelargoniums (geraniums), smilax. Bedding plants.

557. Plants to Start in Warmth. FLOWERS: as February. FRUITS: apricots, nectarines, peaches, vines.

558. Cuttings to Take in Warmth. FLOWERS: as February. Also ageratum, dahlias, fuchsias, heliotropes, lobelias, marguerites, pelargoniums, scarlet salvias.

559. Cuttings to Take in Frame. Delphiniums, perennial coreopsis, lupins, perennial scabious.

560. Pruning Outdoors. FLOWERS: *Buddleia davidii*, hardy fuchsias, hybrid tea, floribunda and climbing roses. Clip ivy on walls.

561. Spraying Outdoors. FRUIT: apples, pears and plums with petroleum oil wash against capsid bugs and with thiocyanate against red spider, capsid bug, aphids, etc.; loganberries, raspberries, and blackberries with lime sulphur against cane sopt.

562. Miscellaneous. VEGETABLES: prick off seedlings raised under glass as soon as they can be handled. FRUIT: train and pinch young growths of grape vines. Pollinate grapes, peaches, and nectarines in bloom. Protect early blossom outdoors. Graft apples and pears. FLOWERS: increase herbaceous perennials by division, stop Japanese and incurved chrysanthemums and perpetual-flowering carnations, turf lawns.

WORK FOR APRIL

563. Seeds to Sow Outdoors. VEGETABLES: asparagus, globe artichokes, globe beetroot, broad beans, broccoli, sprouting broccoli, brussels sprouts, cabbage, carrots, cauliflowers, cress, endive, kale, kohl rabi, lettuce, mustard, parsley, peas, radishes, salsify, savoy, spinach beet, turnips. FLOWERS: hardy annuals as March. Also, late in the month, nicotianas, aster, calandrinia, canary creeper, dahlias, dimorphotheca, jacobaea, layia, leptosiphon, *Mesembryanthemum criniflorum*, nasturtiums, salpiglossis, sweet sultan, *Tagetes signata pumila*, ursinia, venidium, zinnias, lawn grass seed.

564. Seeds to Sow under Glass. VEGETABLES: french beans, runner beans, celery, cucumbers, vegetable marrows, tomatoes. FRUITS: melons. FLOWERS: cinerarias, coleus, exacum, *Primula kewensis*, *P. obconica*, *P. sinensis*. Annuals (hardy and half-hardy for flowering in pots).

565. Planting Outdoors. VEGETABLES: asparagus, artichokes, broad beans, cauliflower, leeks, lettuces, onions, peas, potatoes. FLOWERS: alpines, antirrhinums, evergreen shrubs, gladioli, herbaceous perennials, montbretias, pansies, penstemons, sweet peas, violas, violets.

566. Planting and Potting under Glass. VEGETABLES: celery, cucumber, tomato. FLOWERS: achimenes, azaleas, annuals or plants treated as such sown in February and March, begonias, bedding plants generally, carnations, chrysanthemums, camellias, cyclamen, dahlias, eupatorium, gloxinias, haemanthus, jasminum, luculia, pelargoniums.

567. Plants to Start in Warmth. FLOWERS: as February. FRUITS: late vines.

568. Cuttings to Take in Warmth. As March. Winter-flowering begonias of the Lorraine type, poinsettias.

569. Cuttings to Take in Frames. As March.

570. Pruning Outdoors. As March. Also evergreen foliage shrubs, forsythias, *Leycesteria formosa*, *Perowskia atriplicifolia*, romneyas, willows grown for bark.

571. Pruning under Glass. Azaleas, deutzias, genistas.

572. Spraying Outdoors. Blackcurrants and gooseberries with lime sulphur against mildew and big bud; apples and pears with lime sulphur or captan against scab.

Training cucumbers. The fruit-bearing laterals have been stopped some time previously by pinching out their tips. Further laterals are allowed to form all up the stem which is stopped when it reaches the ridge.

573. Miscellaneous. VEGETABLES: train and top dress cucumbers, lift celery and leeks, feed spring cabbages, protect early potatoes, harden off celery. FRUITS: Train and pollinate melons, train and stop vines, thin and disbud peaches and nectarines, graft fruit trees, remove grease bands from fruit trees. FLOWERS: sow grass seed, apply fertilizer to roses, harden off bedding plants and half-hardy annuals, stake sweet peas, feed lawns and apply selective lawn weed-killer if necessary.

WORK FOR MAY

574. Seeds to Sow Outdoors. VEGETABLES: french beans,

haricot beans, runner beans, beetroots, chicory, cress, ridge cucumbers, endive, kohl rabi, lettuces, vegetable marrows, mustard, peas, radishes, spinach, turnips. FLOWERS: Asters, hardy annuals (as April), zinnias and other half-hardy annuals for autumn flowering.

575. Seeds to Sow under Glass. FLOWERS: Calceolarias, cinerarias, humea, greenhouse primulas.

576. Planting Outdoors. VEGETABLES: french beans, early broccoli, brussels sprouts, cauliflowers, celeriac, leeks, onions, peas, potatoes. FLOWERS: alpines, antirrhinums, aquatics, bedding plants (towards end of month), border chrysanthemums, dormant dahlia tubers, magnolias, pansies, penstemons, seedling hardy perennials, violas, violets.

577. Planting and Potting under Glass. VEGETABLES: cucumbers, tomatoes. FRUITS: melons. FLOWERS: begonias, perpetual-flowering carnations, chrysanthemums, gloxinias, streptocarpus, spring-rooted cuttings of pelargoniums, fuchsias, etc.

578. Pest Control Outdoors. VEGETABLES: spray onions and peas with dinocap if mildew appears; spray with derris if any vegetables are attacked by aphids (greenfly, black-fly, etc.) or caterpillars; dust soil around onion and cabbage seedlings with lindane dust to kill eggs of onion and cabbage flies. FRUIT: apples with derris against codling moth, nicotine against apple sawfly, and lime sulphur or captan against scab; pears with captan against scab; raspberries, loganberries and blackberries with lime sulphur (twice summer strength) against cane spot; strawberries, dust with sulphur or spray with dinocap against mildew. FLOWERS: spray with derris any that are attacked by caterpillars or aphids, spray roses with captan or maneb against black spot.

579. Miscellaneous. VEGETABLES: thin seedlings, earth up potatoes, stake peas, train and feed tomatoes and cucumbers coming into bearing, start to blanch early leeks, cut asparagus, prick off celery. FRUIT: mulch fruit trees with manure, disbud and thin peaches, nectarines, and vines under glass, train and feed melons, ring unfruitful apples and pears, straw strawberries, start to pick gooseberries at end of month, thin out new raspberry canes. FLOWERS: stop chrysanthemums according to growth, clear beds of spring bedding, heel in tulips, daffodils, hyacinths, etc., train sweet peas, thin and stake herbaceous plants, thin roses, apply lawn sand, feed plants in growth.

A lesson in thinning. The evils of over-crowding are evident on the right.

WORK FOR JUNE

580. Seeds to Sow Outdoors. VEGETABLES: french beans, shorthorn carrots, coleworts, cress, endive, lettuces, mustard, parsley, early peas, radishes, summer spinach, turnips. FLOWERS: tuberous anemones, *Alyssum saxatile*, aquilegias, aubrietas, Canterbury bells, campanulas and other miscellaneous hardy biennials, perennials, and rock plants, perennial coreopsis, double daisies, delphiniums, forget-me-nots, foxgloves, hollyhocks, lupins, Oriental poppies, Iceland poppies, Brompton stocks, sweet williams.

581. Seeds to Sow under Glass. Calceolarias, cinerarias, greenhouse primulas.

582. Planting Outdoors. VEGETABLES: french beans, runner beans, broccoli, brussels sprouts, cabbage, cauliflowers, celeriac, celery, ridge cucumbers, kale, leeks, vegetable marrow, savoys, tomatoes. FLOWERS: abutilons, auriculas, tuberous begonias, cannas, dahlias, heliotropes, flag irises (immediately flowers fade), maize, polyanthuses, primroses, ricinus, scarlet salvias, mossy saxifrages, bedding plants.

583. Potting under Glass. Auriculas, perpetual-flowering carnations, chrysanthemums, early-sown greenhouse primulas and cinerarias.

584. Pruning Outdoors. FRUIT: red and white currants, gooseberries. FLOWERS: brooms, *Clematis montana, Chaenomeles speciosa,* evergreen ceanothus (all as soon as possible after flowering). Remove faded flower trusses from rhododendrons and azaleas. Cut back aubrietas, arabis, and perennial candytufts. Trim hedges.

585. Pest Control Outdoors. VEGETABLES: spray onions and peas with dinocap against mildew, spray peas with BHC or malathion against thrips, spray with derris any vegetables attacked by caterpillars or aphids. FRUIT: spray or dust raspberries with derris when first fruits of Lloyd George start to colour, spray apples and plums with lime sulphur or captan against scab and mildew, spray pears with captan against scab, spray with derris any trees attacked by caterpillars or aphids. FLOWERS: spray roses with captan or maneb against black spot, spray with derris, lindane or malathion any plants attacked by aphids.

586. Miscellaneous. VEGETABLES: blanch leeks, earth up potatoes, train and feed cucumbers and tomatoes, thin seedlings, start to dig early potatoes, draw soil from shallot bulbs, pinch broad beans, stop cutting asparagus about middle of month. FRUIT: start to thin apples and pears, train and feed melons, complete thinning of peaches, nectarines, and vines, remove runners from strawberries. FLOWERS: remove runners from violets, disbud roses and border carnations, rest arums, cyclamens, and pot-grown roses and shrubs outdoors, bud roses, take cuttings of hardy pinks.

WORK FOR JULY

587. Seeds to Sow Outdoors. VEGETABLES: spring cabbage, shorthorn carrots, coleworts, cress, endive, lettuces, mustard, parsley, early peas, radishes, turnips. FLOWERS: forget-me-nots, Brompton stocks.

588. Seeds to Sow under Glass. Calceolarias, cinerarias, greenhouse primulas.

589. Planting Outdoors. VEGETABLES: broccoli, brussels sprouts, cabbage, cauliflowers, celery, kale, leeks, savoys. FLOWERS: seedlings of biennials and perennials raised from seed sown in June, colchicums, autumn-flowering crocuses, *Lilium candidum*, sternbergias.

590. Potting under Glass. Seedling greenhouse primulas, cinerarias, and calceolarias as soon as the smaller pots become filled with roots. Also pot the late spring-struck cuttings of pelargoniums.

591. Pruning Outdoors. FRUIT: apples, apricots, trained cherries, red and white currants, gooseberries, nectarines, peaches, pears, plums. FLOWERS: brooms, evergreen ceanothuses, deutzias, helianthemums, philadelphuses, hybrid tea roses, weigelas (diervillas), wisterias – all after flowering.

592. Cuttings to Root in a Frame or Cool Greenhouse. Hardy shrubs and shrubby alpine plants generally.

593. Propagation Outdoors. Bud roses and fruit trees, layer border carnations, shrubs, and clematises; peg down strawberry runners.

594. Pest Control Outdoors. VEGETABLES: spray potatoes with Bordeaux or Burgundy mixture against blight, dust peas with sulphur against mildew, spray peas with malathion against thrips, spray with derris any vegetables attacked by caterpillars or aphids, fumigate tomatoes under glass with lindane or spray with carbaryl against white fly. FRUIT: spray apples with captan against scab, dust vines with sulphur against mildew, saw off plum branches attacked by silver leaf, burn straw on strawberry beds. FLOWERS: spray roses with captan or maneb against black spot, spray with dinocap any plants attacked by mildew, with thiram plants attacked by other fungal disorders and with derris any plants attacked by caterpillars or aphids.

Layering a strawberry runner. Peg it down into a pot of soil sunk in the ground near the parent plant.

595. Miscellaneous. VEGETABLES: blanch leeks, lift and store shallots and autumn-sown onions, lift early potatoes as required, gather and dry herbs, commence to earth up celery, make outdoor mushroom beds, cut globe artichokes. FRUIT: allow atmosphere to dry in vineries carrying fruit starting to colour, begin to pick early apples and pears, pick cherries, plums, currants and gooseberries in season, remove unwanted runners from strawberries. FLOWERS: lift and store daffodils and bulbous irises, tulips and hyacinths, remove faded flowers from annuals and bedding plants, remove runners from violets, disbud dahlias and roses.

WORK FOR AUGUST

596. Seeds to Sow Outdoors. VEGETABLES: spring cabbage, pickling cabbage, cress, endive, lettuces (for transplanting later to a frame), mustard, onions, radishes, winter spinach, spinach beet, lawn grass seed.

597. Seeds to Sow under Glass. FLOWERS: cyclamen, mignonette (for pot culture), winter-flowering stocks, schizanthus.

598. Planting Outdoors. VEGETABLES: late broccoli, winter cabbage, coleworts, kale, savoys. FRUIT: strawberries. FLOWERS: *Lilium candidum, L. testaceum,* colchicums, autumn crocus, sternbergia.

599. Potting under Glass. Winter-flowering begonias, calceolarias, cinerarias, cyclamen (old corms), freesias, Roman and 'prepared' hyacinths, lachenalias, arum lilies, greenhouse primulas.

600. Pruning Outdoors. FRUIT: same as July. Also summer-fruiting raspberries. FLOWERS: show and regal pelargoniums, evergreen shrubs and hedges, hydrangeas.

601. Cuttings to Root in Frame or Cool Greenhouse. Hardy shrubs and shrubby alpines generally, fuchsias, hydrangeas, bedding pelargoniums (geraniums), show and regal pelargoniums, calceolarias, penstemons.

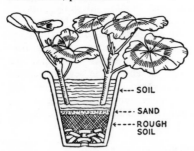

Potting pelargonium (geranium) cuttings. Note that the lower leaves have been removed.

602. Propagation Outdoors. As July. Also tip layer blackberries and loganberries.

603. Pest Control Outdoors. VEGETABLES: as July. FRUIT: spray gooseberries and currants with derris as soon as crop has been gathered, brush methylated spirits into white woolly patches on apples attacked by American blight. FLOWERS: as July. Also set traps or place poison bait for earwigs.

604. Miscellaneous. VEGETABLES: lift second early potatoes as required. Earth up leeks and early celery, bend over leaves of spring-sown onions, blanch early endive when well grown, lift and store early beetroot when large enough. FRUIT: as July. FLOWERS: remove faded flowers from annuals and bedding plants, remove runners from violets, disbud dahlias and roses, 'take' chrysanthemum buds, start nerines, cyclamen, and arum lilies.

WORK FOR SEPTEMBER

605. Seeds to Sow Outdoors. VEGETABLES: brussels sprouts, cauliflower (to a frame later). FLOWERS: annual alyssum, calendula, candytuft, clarkia, annual coreopsis, cornflower, godetia, larkspur, nigella, Shirley and cardinal poppies, annual scabious, viscaria, lawn grass seed.

606. Seeds to Sow under Glass. VEGETABLES: cress, endive, lettuces, mustard, radishes. FLOWERS: annuals for flowering in pots in the greenhouse.

607. Planting Outdoors. VEGETABLES: late winter and spring cabbages, late kales, savoys. FRUIT: strawberries. FLOWERS: anemones, rooted border carnation layers, crocuses, daffodils (narcissi), bulbous irises, lilies, muscaris, scillas, snowdrops, other spring-flowering bulbs, all herbaceous plants not actually in flower, evergreen shrubs.

608. Potting or Planting under Glass. VEGETABLES: parsley (seedlings raised outdoors). FLOWERS: as August. Also cyclamen seedlings, daffodils (narcissi), hyacinths, bulbous irises, lilies, tulips, violets (in frames).

609. Pruning Outdoors. FRUIT: blackberries, blackcurrants, loganberries, summer-fruiting raspberries (as soon as crop is gathered). FLOWERS: rambler roses (as soon as flowers are faded).

610. Cuttings to Root in a Frame or Cool Greenhouse. Bedding calceolarias, fuchsias, gazanias, mesembryanthemums, pansies, zonal pelargoniums (geraniums), penstemons, verbenas, violas, violets, and hardy evergreen shrubs generally (many hardy evergreen shrubs will root in a sheltered place in the open).

611. Pest Prevention Outdoors. Spray with dinocap any vegetables, fruits, or flowers attacked by mildew, fix greasebands around fruit trees.

612. Plants to be Removed to Shelter at First Sign of Frost. Agapanthus, Indian azaleas, camellias, perpetual-flowering carnations, greenhouse chrysanthemums, fuchsias, gazanias, genistas, heliotropes, hydrangeas, arum lilies, marguerites, mesembryanthemums, pelargoniums, double-flowered tropaeolums.

613. Miscellaneous. VEGETABLES: lift beetroots, carrots and potatoes for storing, continue to blanch leeks, celery and endive. FRUIT: allow grapes, peaches, melons, etc., to ripen as rapidly as possible. Continue to pick apples and pears as they part readily from the trees. ORNAMENTAL GARDEN: turf lawns, apply worm-killer if necessary.

WORK FOR OCTOBER

614. Seeds to Sow Outdoors. Sweet peas.

615. Planting Outdoors. VEGETABLES: spring cabbage, coleworts. FLOWERS: hardy perennials, biennials, and evergreen shrubs generally. Also spring bedding plants such as double daisies, forget-me-nots, polyanthuses, and wallflowers. Hardy bulbs as September. Also hyacinths, lily of the valley, and tulips.

616. Planting or Potting under Glass. VEGETABLES: box mint roots for forcing. FLOWERS: hardy plants, bulbs,

CALENDAR OF GARDEN OPERATIONS

hardy annuals and evergreen shrubs for the greenhouse. Calceolarias, cinerarias, greenhouse primulas.

617. Pruning Outdoors. Blackberries, currants, gooseberries, loganberries.

618. Cuttings to Root Outdoors. FRUIT: currants, gooseberries. FLOWERS: roses and deciduous shrubs generally.

619. Cuttings to Root in a Frame or Cool Greenhouse. As September.

620. Plants to be Lifted and Stored in a Frost-proof Place. Tuberous-rooted begonias, dahlias, gladioli, *Lobelia cardinalis*, choice montbretias and *Salvia patens*.

621. Miscellaneous. VEGETABLES: dig vacant ground, working in lime or manure where necessary. Lift and store potatoes, carrots, beetroots, turnips, and swedes. Cut back asparagus and globe artichokes, complete blanching of leeks and celery, blanch endive as required, protect cauliflowers. FRUIT: gather and store all remaining apples and pears, prepare sites for fruit trees. FLOWERS: prepare ground for trees and shrubs, including roses, turf and repair lawns, disbud perpetual-flowering carnations, stop feeding chrysanthemums.

WORK FOR NOVEMBER

622. Seeds to Sow Outdoors. Long-pod broad beans, hardy culinary peas.

623. Planting Outdoors. FRUIT: all the hardy kinds with the exception of strawberries. FLOWERS: hardy bulbs as October. Also hardy deciduous trees, shrubs, and climbers, including roses.

624. Potting under Glass. Azaleas, brooms, deutzias, hydrangeas, lilacs, roses, and other flowering shrubs required for the greenhouse. Also astilbes and other herbaceous perennials.

273

625. Pruning Outdoors. FRUIT: all hardy varieties, including canes if not already dealt with. FLOWERS: all deciduous hedges.

626. Cuttings to Root Outdoors. As October.

627. Pruning under Glass. Apricots, nectarines, peaches and vines as soon as they have lost their leaves.

628. Miscellaneous. VEGETABLES: dig and manure or lime all vacant ground, protect cauliflower and broccoli curds from frost, blanch endive as required, lift and store Jerusalem artichokes, horseradish, parsnips and salsify, lift chicory, rhubarb, and seakale for forcing. FRUIT: cut and store late grapes, ventilate vineries and peach houses freely, root prune excessively vigorous fruit trees. FLOWERS: tidy up herbaceous borders, cut back outdoor chrysanthemums and remove a few plants of each kind to a frame, bring early potted bulbs into the greenhouse, protect tender or woolly-leaved alpines with panes of glass.

WORK FOR DECEMBER

629. Cuttings to Take under Glass. Perpetual-flowering carnations, greenhouse chrysanthemums.

630. Planting Outdoors. As November, when weather and soil conditions are favourable.

631. Pruning Outdoors. As November. Also prune *Clematis jackmanii*.

632. Pruning under Glass. Vines, peaches, nectarines, and apricots. Lower vine rods to check flow of sap. Ventilate vineries freely.

633. Miscellaneous. VEGETABLES: continue to protect curds of broccoli and cauliflowers, continue to blanch endives, continue to force seakale, rhubarb, and chicory. FLOWERS: cut back chrysanthemums as they pass out of flower, pinch tips out of sweet pea seedlings, examine all plants and tubers in store.

SECTION EIGHT

PESTS, DISEASES, AND WEEDS

MISCELLANEOUS INFORMATION

634. Group Treatment. It is not always necessary to know precisely what pest or disease is attacking plants in order to apply effective remedies. Frequently it is sufficient to be able to fit it into one or other of a few main groups. First decide whether it is a pest, e.g. insect, or other creature, or a disease, e.g. fungus, or other low type of vegetable organism. Pests must be treated with insecticides or acaricides (mite killers); diseases mainly with fungicides.

If it is an insect which is attacking the plant above soil level, e.g. leaves, stems, flowers, or fruits, it is probable that an insecticide such as BHC (644) or derris (662) will give reasonable control because these are poisonous to a wide range of insects, though not always as effective against particular insects as other chemicals which are more specific in their action.

Soil pests, such as cutworms, leather-jackets, wireworms, and millepedes, cannot be destroyed by spraying but must be attacked with a soil insecticide such as gamma-BHC (644). Slugs can be controlled by metaldehyde (681) or methiocarb (683), either mixed with a suitable bait such as bran or in suspension in water.

Red spider mites, which are not insects, can be killed by using azobenzene (643) in various forms or with malathion (677), derris (662), or dicofol (666).

If the trouble is due to disease, decide whether this is caused by a fungus, e.g. black spot, rust, mildew, etc., or bacterium or virus, e.g. streak, mosaic, etc. Fungi usually cause dark, dampish spots, or patches of decay or outgrowths of mould, rusty coloured spots, etc. Bacterial and virus diseases usually cause drier spotting or streaking without obvious outgrowth (637), but are in general more difficult to identify. Fungal diseases may be treated by spraying with reliable

275

fungicides such as Bordeaux mixture (646) or other preparations containing copper (655), or with thiram (707), or by dusting with sulphur (702). Bacterial and virus diseases cannot as a rule be treated (636), (637).

635. Trapping. Rats and mice can be caught in spring or cage traps baited with cheese or fat. Moles may be caught with steel traps set across the burrows. Gloves must be worn while setting the traps to avoid leaving human scent on them. Soil removed to set the traps must be replaced so that burrows are dark. Traps should be set across main burrows and those leading to water. Cockroaches can be caught in proprietary traps baited with bran. Earwigs may be trapped in inverted flower pots stuffed with hay, hollow broad bean stalks, slightly opened matchboxes, or any other similar dark hiding place. Leather-jackets and slugs can be trapped under wet sacks or heaps of damp vegetable refuse laid on the soil. Millepedes and wireworms can be collected from sliced carrots and potatoes buried just beneath the surface of the soil. For tree bands, see (187).

636. Incurable Diseases. Not all diseases can be controlled as yet. In some cases the only way of preventing further damage is to remove and burn affected plants as soon as detected. Even with diseases that can be treated, it is generally advisable to remove and burn specially bad plants or portions of plants. On no account should these be placed on the compost heap or left lying about. This applies, among other diseases, to plum silver leaf, all collar and root rots, club root, aster wilts, and brown rot of fruits.

637. Virus Diseases. A large class of diseases caused by ultra-microscopic organisms which infect the sap. Symptoms vary from a slight mottling or rolling of the leaves to intense dry brown spotting or complete collapse. Such names as aucuba mosaic, bronze leaf, streak, leaf roll, yellow edge, etc., describe outstanding symptoms of different viruses. External

276

applications have not proved very satisfactory in controlling these diseases. Infection is carried largely by sucking insects, especially aphids, e.g. greenfly, blackfly, etc., and these must be kept down by spraying with suitable insecticides such as derris (662), dimethoate (667), formothion (672), menazon (679) or malathion (677). Virus may also be carried on knives, secateurs, etc. used in pruning, and these should be disinfected by dipping in a good household disinfectant. Badly infected plants should always be burned.

Some varieties of plants subject to virus disease are resistant to infection and some are tolerant, i.e. they show no adverse symptoms. Tolerant plants can become unnoticed sources of infection for sensitive plants.

638. Eelworms. Microscopic, transparent, eel-like creatures which often infest roots or stems of certain plants in great numbers, causing knots, goutiness, and distortion. Much larger, transparent nematode worms are frequently mistaken for them and are allied but are harmless, as they feed on decaying matter in the soil and are frequently found in manure, compost, or leafmould.

Eelworms are principally found in phloxes, chrysanthemums, narcissi, tomatoes, cucumbers, potatoes, and onions. Usually there is no satisfactory remedy and plants should be destroyed. Eelworms on potatoes form very small white cysts on the outside of the tubers and these can be washed off in plain water.

Infected narcissus bulbs can be cleared of eelworms and fly larvae by keeping the bulbs for three hours in water maintained at 110° F. followed by immediate cooling in cold water but special apparatus is required for this. Infected chrysanthemum stools from which all stems have been cut can be heated in a similar manner but for 20–30 minutes only. For strawberry runners the time is 5 to 6 minutes and the water temperature 115°. Clean stock of phlox can usually be obtained from root cuttings (454). It is always advisable to sterilize the soil if practicable with steam (639) or chemicals (657) and (671).

639. Sterilization by Heat. In addition to treatment with cresylic acid (657) or formaldehyde (671), soil can be sterilized by raising the temperature. Four methods may be employed, namely electrical heating, baking, steaming, and scalding.

ELECTRICAL sterilization requires special apparatus, and manufacturer's instructions must be followed in the use of this.

BAKING can be done by spreading soil thinly in an oven or in trays in a special apparatus. The danger is that soil may be charred. This risk can be lessened if the soil is thoroughly moistened first. The temperature of the soil should be raised slowly until it is between 205° and 210° F. and maintained at this for 15 minutes.

STEAM sterilization must be done with special apparatus. Steam under pressure is forced through the soil until the temperature is raised to between 200° and 205° F. It is maintained at this for ½ hour.

SCALDING is a simple method for home use. Soil is placed dry in a sack and this is suspended in a copper containing a little water. The water is then boiled rapidly for ½ hour.

Soil that has been sterilized by heat shows a falling off in fertility for a few months. This can be counteracted by using the John Innes formulae for seed and potting composts (501), (505).

640. Spreaders. If water is sprayed on a leaf or other smooth surface it tends to run into globules instead of spreading evenly. This renders sprays inefficient. To overcome the difficulty, soft soap, or some other substance which lowers the surface tension of water, is added to the spray.

PESTS, DISEASES, AND WEEDS

Soap is used at $\frac{1}{2}$ to 2 oz. per gallon according to the hardness of the water. It cannot be mixed with lime sulphur (675) or Bordeaux mixture (646), as it curdles them.

More efficient spreaders are now available which can be added to these fungicides. These include saponin, calcium caseinate, flour paste, and preparations of resin. Many are obtainable in proprietary brands ready for use according to makers' instructions, or household detergent may be used.

641. Systemic Chemicals. Some chemicals when applied to plants remain on the outside, on leaves, stems etc. They are known as non-systemic chemicals in contrast to systemic chemicals, which are absorbed by the plant and enter into its sap in which they may be carried from one part of the plant to another. Systemic insecticides, fungicides and weed-killers are known. Advantages are that it is not necessary to cover the whole plant with the chemical to get a good result; that the chemical is not removed by rain; and with insecticides, that it is less likely to harm useful insects since these do not feed on the plant. Drawbacks are that systemic chemicals cannot be wiped or washed off, that some persist for a considerable time and may render a crop unusable until they have been dispersed or decomposed.

INSECTICIDES AND FUNGICIDES

642. Alum. There are many alums, but as a pesticide it is aluminium sulphate that is used. It is used primarily for killing slugs and snails but can also be used to make plants or buds distasteful to birds. For killing slugs it can be applied dry, sprinkled in powder form round plants and renewed fairly often, or as a heavy drench by dissolving 4 oz. in 1 gal. of water and applying it from a watering-can or sprayer. To deter birds the same solution is sprayed finely on to plants. Adding a little household detergent to the water helps to spread it evenly and more effectively.

643. Azobenzene. An insecticide obtainable in proprietary formulations ready for use according to manufacturer's instructions. It is chiefly valuable for killing red spiders under glass, for which purpose it is used either as an aerosol (a suspension in air of very minute particles produced as a rule by forcing the azobenzene through a fine nozzle by means of the pressure of carbon dioxide released from a 'sparklet' bulb) or as a smoke. While treatment is being carried out, the temperature of the greenhouse should be maintained near 70° F. Azobenzene can damage some plants if used in bright sunshine or after plants have been sprayed with anything which contains oil.

644. BHC. The letters stand for benzene hexachloride. The best form is gamma-BHC and when 99% pure, this is known as lindane. It can be obtained in various proprietary forms for wet or dry application and also in smoke generators, for fumigating under glass, and all these should be used strictly in accordance with manufacturer's instructions.

Dusts are suitable for use against ants, earwigs, flea beetles, leather-jackets, mushroom flies, springtails and wireworms. Sprays can be used against any of these, also aphids, apple suckers, cabbage root fly, capsid bugs, raspberry cane midge, sawflies, symphalids, thrips and woolly aphid.

Crude BHC has a strong tainting effect and should not be used on blackcurrants or as a soil insecticide where any root crops are to be grown. Lindane (gamma-BHC) has far less tendency to taint, but even so cannot be recommended for potatoes, nor for grapes or blackcurrants after they have blossomed.

Edible crops should not be harvested for two weeks after use of BHC dusts or sprays or for two days after use of BHC smokes.

645. Borax. Sometimes used to kill ants and cockroaches for which purpose powdered borax is well mixed with an equal quantity of castor sugar and sprinkled where ants are seen.

646. Bordeaux Mixture. The most generally useful fungicide against potato disease (phytophthora). See (202).

STRONG SOLUTION: For use against potato disease (blight) and on other strong-leaved plants not liable to be scorched.

> 9 oz. of copper sulphate.
> 6 oz. of quicklime.
> 5 gals. of water.

STANDARD SOLUTION: For use against apple and pear scab and as a general fungicide.

> 6 oz. of copper sulphate.
> 6 oz. of quicklime.
> 5 gals. of water.

REDUCED SOLUTION: For use on tender-leaved plants liable to be scorched.

> $4\frac{1}{2}$ oz. of copper sulphate.
> 9 oz. of quicklime.
> 5 gals. of water.

Dissolve the copper sulphate in 4 gals. water. Put the quicklime in another vessel and slake it by adding water, a little at a time.

Make up to 1 gal. with water; add to the copper sulphate solution slowly and stir well. Use at once. Wooden or enamelled vessels should be used for mixing. It is advisable to test the strong solution with litmus paper before using. If blue paper turns pink, more lime should be added, till there is no such reaction.

Bordeaux mixture can also be purchased in powder or paste form ready for mixing with water, when manufacturer's instructions should be consulted regarding strength.

647. Burgundy Mixture. A little more powerful as a fungicide than Bordeaux mixture and often used instead of it.

This mixture is found especially serviceable against rusts.

8 oz. of copper sulphate.

10 oz. of washing soda.

5 gals. of water.

Dissolve the copper sulphate in 4 gals. of water and the washing soda in the other gallon. Pour the washing soda solution into the copper sulphate solution, stirring well. Prepare mixture in wooden or enamel vessels. Use at once.

648. Calomel. This is the commercial name for mercurous chloride. It is usually supplied as a ready-prepared dust containing 4% calomel. It is used to kill the eggs of the cabbage root fly and onion fly, and is scattered for about 2 in. on both sides of each row of seedlings at the rate of 1 lb. to 60 yd., or round individual plants at about 1 oz. to 10 plants. The most effective time for brassicas is when they have made the second or third rough leaf; for onions when the seedlings are $1\frac{1}{2}$ in. high. Second applications may be given 10 to 14 days later. May and June are danger periods. Calomel dust well watered in also controls many lawn diseases.

Calomel is also used to check club root, for which purpose a little of the dust is sprinkled into each hole prepared for a brassica plant or, alternatively, the roots of the plants are dipped into a thin paste prepared by mixing calomel dust with water. Calomel dust can also be raked into the seed bed prior to sowing.

To control onion white rot 4% calomel is dusted along the seed drills at 1 lb. to 50 yd. Calomel can also be used as a dip for diseased gladiolus corms. 1 oz. of pure calomel in 1 gal. of water; immerse corms for 5–10 minutes, keeping the mixture stirred so that the calomel does not settle.

649. Captan. A synthetic chemical used as a fungicide. It is particularly recommended for the control of apple and pear scab as it does not scorch leaves or russet or crack fruits; it is also used to control rose black spot. It is purchased as a powder which must be mixed in water according to the manufacturer's instructions and kept stirred while it is applied as a spray. Its effect does not last long and so it may be necessary to spray every 10 to 14 days from April to August to secure complete control. Captan is also used in seed dressings to protect seedlings from damping off and other soil-borne diseases.

Captan is harmful to fish.

650. Carbaryl. A synthetic insecticide effective against a fairly wide range of pests including caterpillars, codling moths, cutworms, leather-jackets, flea beetles, weevils, scale insects, white flies, thrips, pear leaf blister mite, earwigs and woodlice. It is available as a wettable powder for mixing with water according to manufacturer's instructions. The mixture should be continually agitated while the spray is being applied. It is also available as a dust ready for use and this is commonly called sevin dust. Carbaryl is harmful to bees and fish, so should not be used when plants are in flower and should be kept out of streams and ponds. It is moderately persistent and should not be used with alkaline mixtures such as Bordeaux or lime sulphur. When used on edible crops at least one week must elapse before they are harvested.

651. Caustic Soda. A winter fruit-tree cleanser which has been practically superseded by tar-oil wash. The old formula was as follows:

1 lb. of caustic soda (98% purity).
5 gals. of water.

Dissolve the soda in 1 gal. of water, stirring occasionally. Add the remainder of the water and stir again. Apply in the form of a coarse spray. It must only be used in winter when trees are dormant, and must be kept off skin and clothes.

652. Cheshunt Compound. A soil fungicide used for the prevention or check of damping-off disease, collar rot, and other soil-borne diseases. The formula for mixing is as follows:

2 parts of finely ground copper sulphate.

11 parts of ammonium carbonate (fresh).

Mix the copper sulphate and ammonium carbonate thoroughly and store in a stoppered glass jar for at least 24 hours. Dissolve 1 oz. of the dry mixture in a little hot water and add to 2 gals. of water. The solution should be used at once. It may be watered freely on the soil in which plants or even seedlings are growing.

This preparation can also be purchased ready for mixing with water.

653. Chlorbenside. A synthetic acaricide used to control red spider mite both outdoors and under glass. It kills the eggs but not the mites, so is a little slow in action, but after a few weeks does give complete control. It is purchased as a wettable powder to be mixed with water as advised by the manufacturer and applied as a spray. For fruit-tree red spider, one application in May or early June is usually sufficient. On other plants it can be used immediately red spider mites are observed, and further applications can be given if necessary.

654. Chlordane. This is a synthetic chemical used at present for the control of worms and leather-jackets in lawns. It is very persistent and will remain effective for at least a year. It is supplied as a liquid to be mixed with water, and can be applied with a watering-can, or sprayer; it must penetrate the turf thoroughly. The best times to apply it are the spring or autumn. It is poisonous to warm-blooded animals and should not be used on seedling grass or turf less than three months old. Livestock should not be allowed on treated turf for two weeks.

655. Copper. Various formulations of copper compounds, including copper oxide and copper oxychloride, are sold as 'copper fungicide' or under trade names. They may be employed for any of the purposes for which other copper sprays, such as Bordeaux or Burgundy mixtures (646), (647), might be used. The manufacturer's instructions regarding strength and application must be followed. Soap must not be used as a spreader, but saponin etc. (64) can be substituted.

656. Copper Sulphate Wash. A very powerful fungicide for winter use against fungi which are difficult to kill by other means, such as those causing rose rust and black spot.

1 oz. of copper sulphate.

1 gal. of water.

Dissolve the copper sulphate in the water and stir well. This wash must be used only in winter when all leaves have fallen.

657. Cresylic Acid. A powerful soil sterilizer for use against many insects and fungi. One gallon of 97 to 99% purity cresylic acid is diluted with 100 gals of water. This is applied with a water-pot; 7 gals. is sufficient for about 1 sq. yd. of soil. Treated soil should be covered with tarpaulins or wet sacks for a day or so to trap fumes, after which it should be uncovered and left for from three to five weeks before use. For cleansing woodwork in glasshouses, it should be applied from a spraying machine with as much force as possible and the house closed down for 24 hours. No plants must be cultivated in the house for at least a month.

658. Dazomet. A soil sterilizer used to control certain eelworms and some soil-borne diseases. It also checks growth of weed seedlings and couch grass. It is available as a proprietary dust to be sprinkled on the soil and immediately worked in to a depth of about 1 ft. The usual rate is 1 lb. per 100 sq. ft., or 7 oz. per cu. yd. of potting soil but manufacturer's instructions should be followed. Treated potting soil should be covered with sacks or tarpaulins for three weeks, then uncovered and turned several times over a period of four or five weeks to allow fumes to escape.

285

Nothing should be planted or sown on treated soil for at least eight weeks.

659. DD. An abbreviation for dichloropropane-dichloropropene, a chemical used to kill eelworms in the soil. It is a liquid and can be poured into dibber holes 6 in. deep and 12 in. apart, $\frac{1}{8}$ fl. oz. DD per hole, but because the chemical is strongly irritating to skin, eyes, nose and mouth, this can be a somewhat hazardous undertaking. A far better method is to use special injection apparatus. DD must not be used near growing plants and treated soil must be left vacant for at least six weeks.

669. DDT. (Dichloro-diphenyl-trichloroethane). This powerful synthetic insecticide is not available in the pure state, and even in proprietary formulation its use is limited because of its extreme persistence. It is prepared as a dust to be applied dry, wettable powder for use as sprays, oil emulsions, also for liquid application after dilution with water and in smoke generators for fumigating under glass. In all cases manufacturer's instructions regarding strength should be obtained, as different brands may vary greatly in this respect. It is particularly effective against weevils (including the apple-blossom weevil), beetles (including flea beetles), caterpillars, thrips, flies (including the mushroom flies), scale insects, white fly and mosquitoes.

661. Demeton-S-methyl. An organo-phosphorus insecticide used to kill aphids, red spider mites, apple and plum sawflies, leaf hoppers and woolly aphid. It is poisonous to warm-blooded animals, including man, so proper care should be taken in handling the concentrated chemical and rubber gloves and face shield worn when applying it.

This insecticide is systemic, being absorbed by the plant through its sap and being distributed throughout the whole plant. It should not be used on edible crops within three weeks of harvesting, nor on brassicas of any kind after the end of October. It is poisonous to bees and fish, and should not be used on plants that are in flower or are about to flower, nor should it be allowed to get into ponds or streams. It is sold as a liquid for dilution with water and application as a spray, and also as an aerosol much diluted and ready for immediate use, following manufacturer's instructions.

662. Derris. An insecticide that is effective against many pests including aphids, leaf hoppers, thrips, caterpillars of many kinds, apple-blossom weevil, pea and bean weevil, raspberry beetle, gooseberry sawfly, flea beetles and red spider mites. Though relatively harmless to human beings, warm-blooded creatures and bees, it is recommended that at least one day elapse between use on edible crops and harvesting. It is very poisonous to fishes.

Derris is available as a dust, ready for immediate use, and as a liquid to be diluted with water and used as a spray according to manufacturer's instructions. The effectiveness of derris depends on the percentage of rotenone it contains and this may diminish with age.

Derris can be mixed with lime sulphur or Bordeaux mixture, but in that case soft soap must not be used. One of the alternative spreaders (640) should be substituted.

663. Diazinon. An insecticide used primarily to kill aphids, capsid bugs, leaf miners, thrips, red spider mites, mealy bugs, scale insects, springtails and mushroom flies. It is poisonous to warm-blooded animals, including man, but provided reasonable care is taken in handling, no special clothing need be worn. It should not be used on cucumbers or tomatoes in early spring. Special care should be taken if other chemicals of the organo-phosphorus group, to which diazinon belongs, have been used, as accumulation of these chemicals within the body can be harmful.

It is available as an aerosol, as a liquid for dilution

with water, in granular form and as a wettable powder. In all cases manufacturer's instructions must be followed. Edible crops should not be harvested for two days after treatment with diazinon aerosol or for two weeks after treatment with any of the other formulations.

664. Dichlofluanid. A fungicide used primarily to control botrytis (grey mould) on strawberries, currants etc., and black spot on roses. It should not be used on strawberries grown under glass or polythene. At least two weeks must elapse between use on edible crops and harvesting. It is harmful to fish. Dichlofluanid is available as a wettable powder to be stirred into water as recommended by the manufacturers and kept agitated while being applied as a spray.

665. Dichloran. A fungicide primarily used to control botrytis on cyclamen, lettuce and tomato and tulip fire. It is available as a proprietary dust for application direct. At least three weeks should elapse before any treated edible crop is harvested.

666. Dicofol. An acaricide used to kill red spider mites and their eggs. It is available as an aerosol for immediate use and also as a liquid to be diluted with water and applied as a spray according to manufacturer's instructions. It should not be used on seedlings or young plants under glass before mid-May or on plants while they are exposed to strong sunshine. Edible crops sprayed with dicofol should not be harvested for seven days or for two days after treatment with dicofol aerosol.

667. Dimethoate. A systemic insecticide, i.e. one that is absorbed into the sap of plants. It is used primarily to control aphids, apple and pear sucker, plum sawfly, woolly aphid and red spider mites. It is available as a liquid for dilution with water and as a wettable powder which must be kept agitated when mixed with water. All should be used according to manufacturer's instructions. Edible crops treated with dimethoate should not be harvested for at least one week. Special care should be taken if other chemicals of the organophosphorus group, to which dimethoate belongs, are being used, as accumulations of these in the body can be harmful. Dimethoate should not be used on chrysanthemums.

668. Dinocap. A fungicide used primarily to control powdery mildews on many plants, though it will also help to control red spider mites. It is available as a liquid for dilution with water or as a wettable powder to be kept agitated when mixed with water and applied as a spray. Dinocap is not very poisonous to warm-blooded animals, including man, but care should be taken not to inhale it nor to get the concentrated chemical on the skin.

Edible crops treated with dinocap should not be harvested for at least one week. It should be kept out of pools and streams as it is harmful to fish.

669. DNOC. (Dinitro-ortho-cresol). This insecticide has been added to petroleum oil (692) in certain proprietary preparations to produce a winter wash for fruit trees which proves effective against the overwintering stages (including the eggs) of capsid bugs, apple sucker, aphids, winter moth caterpillar, tortrix moth, raspberry moth, scale insects, apple-blossom weevil and red spider mites. The wash is applied as a heavy spray while the trees are dormant (December–late February). The usual formula is $2\frac{1}{2}$ to 3 pints of combined petroleum and dinitro-ortho-cresol to 5 gals. of water, but manufacturer's instructions should be consulted wherever possible. It is poisonous to warm-blooded animals, including man, and to fish. Rubber gloves and face shield should be worn when mixing this chemical.

670. Endosulfan. An insecticide used primarily to control mites, including big-bud mite in blackcurrants. It is also effective against aphids and capsid bugs. It is available as a liquid to be diluted with water and applied as a spray according to manufacturer's instructions. It is poisonous to warm-blooded animals, including man, and to fish. Rubber gloves and face shield should be worn when mixing and applying it. Edible crops treated with endosulfan must not be used for at least six weeks. It can only be used on black-currants at first open blossom and then three weeks later, and on strawberries after the crop has been picked and before the next season's flowers open.

671. Formalin (Formaldehyde). A powerful soil sterilizer. Formalin is the preparation used horticulturally and it contains 38–40% pure formaldehyde. To prepare this for use, all that is necessary is to mix it with 49 times its own bulk of water (1 pt. in 49 pt.; 1 gal. in 49 gals., etc.). Ordinarily, 75 gals. of dilute formalin is sufficient to treat 1 ton of soil, or approximately 2 gals. per bushel of soil. Where possible remove the soil to a hard floor, spread it out thinly and thoroughly saturate with the solution. Throw into a heap and cover with tarpaulins to trap the fumes. After 48 hours, remove the covering and spread the soil out to dry. It must not be used for plants until it ceases to smell of formaldehyde, usually in about three or four weeks.

A 2% solution of formalin is sometimes used as a dip or wash for infected plants, e.g. arum lily tubers affected by bacterial soft rot may be soaked in it for four hours. A 6% solution of formalin may be used to water onion seed drills to prevent onion smut.

Formalin may also be used for sterilizing soil in glasshouses, in frames or in seedboxes and for disinfecting certain seeds, particularly celery, against leaf spot. The seed should be soaked for 3 hours in a solution made by adding 1 part of formalin to 300 parts of water.

672. Formothion. A systemic insecticide which kills aphids and red spider mites. It is absorbed by the plant and carried round in the sap and can, if desired, be applied from a watering-can to the soil, to be taken up through the roots. This method of application has the advantage that it eliminates all possible danger to bees and useful insects such as ladybirds and lacewing flies. It is poisonous to warm-blooded animals, including man, to bees and to fish but special protective clothing is not required. However, as it belongs to the organo-phosphorus group, special care should be taken if other allied chemicals containing phosphorus have been used because of the possibility of a cumulative effect. Edible crops should not be harvested within a week of the use of formothion. It is available as a liquid to be diluted with water according to manufacturer's instructions. Chrysanthemums, nasturtiums, African marigolds and possibly some other plants may be damaged, but it is completely safe on roses.

Gamma-BHC. See BHC (644).

673. Gishurst Compound. A proprietary insecticide for use against mealy bug on vines. Use in winter when the vines are dormant. Apply direct with a brush to the affected parts.

674. Lime. This is mainly of value to correct soil acidity for which purpose it can be of great use in the control of club root of cabbages and other brassicas, since this disease thrives in acid soils. It is also used as a slug and snail deterrent. Quicklime is occasionally used to kill soil pests but has been largely replaced for this purpose by more efficient chemicals such as BHC.

Quicklime is very caustic and difficult to handle. It must not come directly in contact with leaves and is best used in winter or on vacant ground. Rate of application is $\frac{1}{2}$ to 1 lb. per square yard well worked in.

Hydrated lime is much easier to handle and is most effective when fresh. It can also be applied at $\frac{1}{2}$ to 1 lb. per square yard either as a top dressing or worked into the soil. As a slug and snail deterrent it is sprinkled around plants and renewed occasionally, especially following a shower of rain.

675. Lime Sulphur. One of the most useful fungicides, especially for fruit trees. It is liable to damage the foliage and fruits of pears and certain varieties of apple (202). It must be purchased as a manufactured liquid. The strength is estimated by specific gravity, the standard being 1·3. For use on apples and pears mix this as follows:

WINTER APPLICATION: Up to pink bud stage in apples, white bud stage in pears: 11 fl. oz. of lime sulphur to 2 gals. of water.

SUMMER APPLICATION: 3 fl. oz. of lime sulphur to 2 gals. of water.

To control big bug on blackcurrants (258), lime sulphur is used at twice winter strength, i.e. 22 fl. oz. in 2 gals.

To control cane spot on raspberries, loganberries, and blackberries (227), lime sulphur is used in winter as for big bud (above) and in summer at double summer strength, i.e. 6 fl. oz. in 2 gals.

676. Lindane. The name given to the gamma-isomer of BHC at 99% purity. (644).

677. Malathion. An insecticide effective against many pests including aphids, leaf hoppers, thrips, suckers, scale insects, mealy bugs, leaf miners, white flies, mushroom flies, gooseberry sawfly, raspberry beetle, pollen beetles and red spider mites. It is poisonous to warm-blooded animals, including man, also to bees and fish but protective clothing is not necessary when it is used. As it belongs to the organo-phosphorus group special care should be exercised if other chemicals of this group are being used because of the danger of cumulative effect. Four days should elapse between use of malathion and harvesting of edible crops.

Malathion is available as an aerosol and a dust, both for immediate use and as a liquid for dilution with water and application as a spray according to manufacturer's instructions. It should not be used on antirrhinums, crassulas, ferns, fuchsias, gerberas, petunias, pileas, sweet peas or zinnias.

678. Maneb. A synthetic fungicide of the dithiocarbamate group, containing manganese, which is particularly good for the control of downy mildews, rose black spot, potato blight, tomato leaf mould and tomato stem rot (didymella). It is practically non-poisonous, but should not be inhaled and should be kept off the skin. At least one week should elapse between its use on outdoor edible crops and harvesting and two days between use and harvesting of edible greenhouse crops. It is available as a wettable powder to be stirred into water at the rates directed by the manufacturers and agitated while being applied as a spray.

679. Menazon. A systemic insecticide for use against aphids of all kinds including woolly aphid. It is poisonous to warm-blooded animals, including man, and to bees but no special clothing need be worn when mixing or applying it. Edible crops sprayed with menazon should not be harvested under three weeks. Extra care in handling should be observed if other chemicals of the organo-phosphorus group, to which menazon belongs, are being used because of the danger of accumulation in the body. Menazon is available as a liquid, for dilution with water and application as a spray, as a wettable powder which must be kept agitated after stirring into water and as a dry seed dressing. Manufacturer's instructions regarding use must be followed.

680. Mercuric Fungicide. Various organic compounds of mercury are offered under trade names as fungicides, particularly for the control of apple and pear scab or as a lawn disease eradicant. Unlike most other fungicides they are not simply preventive in action but have some effect in killing the fungus even after it has invaded the plant. Mercuric seed dressings are also available. All are poisonous to warm-blooded animals, including man, and to bees and fish. Edible crops sprayed with mercuric fungicide should not be harvested for at least six weeks. Treated seed must not be fed to humans or animals. The concentrated fungicide should be kept off the skin.

Mercuric fungicides are available as liquids for dilution with water and application as a spray or as dry dressings ready for immediate use. Manufacturer's instructions must be followed.

681. Metaldehyde (Meta). Used as a poison bait for slugs and snails at the rate of 1 oz. of finely powdered metaldehyde to 3 lb. of bran. Mix well with sufficient water to make a crumbly mash. Place in small heaps beneath slates or boards. Metaldehyde in specially prepared forms is also available both as pellets for immediate use and in liquid form for mixing with water and application from a watering-can fitted with a rose.

Metasystox. See Demeton-S-methyl (661).

682. Metham-sodium. Used as a soil sterilizer to kill eelworms and some soil-borne fungi. It is highly damaging to plants so can only be used on vacant land on which nothing will be sown or planted for at least ten weeks. It is a fluid to be diluted with water according to manufacturer's instructions and applied from a watering-can until the soil is thoroughly wetted. The soil should then be covered with sacks or tarpaulins for a few days, after which the soil should be uncovered so that fumes may escape.

683. Methiocarb. A chemical used to kill slugs and snails and said to be more efficient than metaldehyde under damp conditions. It is available, ready for use, as small pellets or tablets to be sprinkled around plants liable to be attacked, or wherever slugs or snails are likely to be. It is harmful to fish, and poultry should be kept off treated ground for at least seven days.

684. Mowrah Meal. This is obtained from the bean of a tropical tree and is used for destroying worms on lawns. The lawn should be dressed at the rate of 4 to 8 oz. per square yard and then watered copiously. The most effective times for treatment are from February to May and August to October, in damp, mild weather when worms are close to the surface. The worms come out and must then be swept up.

685. Naphthalene. Flaked or powdered naphthalene can be used as a soil insecticide to kill or drive out wireworms, millepedes, cutworms etc. as well as the maggots of the carrot fly, cabbage root fly and onion fly. The naphthalene is scattered over the surface at 2–6 oz. per square yard and forked in or, for fly maggots, is dusted along the rows of young plants in May and June.

Marble-like balls of naphthalene, usually sold as 'moth balls', are also a useful deterrent against moles which do not like the smell emitted by the balls. For this purpose they should be dropped into dibber holes 3 or 4 in. deep and 2 or 3 in. apart all round the area to be protected. They normally retain their effectiveness for several years.

686. Nicotine. An insecticide for use against sucking insects such as aphids, capsid bugs, apple sucker, apple sawfly, thrips, leaf hoppers and leaf miners. Nicotine is very poisonous to warm-blooded animals, including man, also to bees and fish, but it is volatile and so soon disappears from plants. Rubber gloves and face shield should be used when diluting the chemical for use but edible crops outdoors treated with nicotine spray can be harvested in two days and glasshouse crops treated with nicotine smoke can be harvested in one day.

Nicotine is available as a dust for immediate use, as a liquid for dilution with water and application as a spray according to manufacturer's instructions, or in smoke generators for fumigating greenhouses.

For use against apple sucker, nicotine must be applied immediately before the blossom opens, and for apple sawfly 7 to 14 days after it falls. Against other pests, use as soon as noted.

687. Paradichlorbenzene. Used as a soil fumigant for killing wireworms, millepedes, cutworms, leather-jackets, slugs, etc. The crystals should be broken up as finely as possible and be dropped into 8-in. deep dibber holes made every 9 to 12 in. Refill with soil at once to trap the fumes. A level teaspoonful of powdered crystals will be sufficient for six holes on vacant ground or twelve holes if crops are in growth.

688. Parathion. An organo-phosphorus insecticide which is very effective against a number of insects including aphids, thrips, scale insects, mealy bugs, leaf miners, white flies and red spider mites. As a soil drench it can also be used to kill cucumber root maggot, millepedes, root knot eelworm, springtails, symphalids and woodlice. It is a liquid which may be applied as a spray outdoors or under glass, but as it is very poisonous to human beings and warm-blooded animals generally and also to bees and fish, it must be used with care. It is essential that rubber clothing and a gas mask should be worn when using this insecticide. Special care must be exercised if other chemicals of the organo-phosphorus group, to which parathion belongs, are being used as these tend to accumulate in the body. Edible crops should not be harvested under four weeks after application of parathion. It can be mixed with lime sulphur, Bordeaux mixture, and other alkaline solutions.

689. Paris Green. An arsenical poison sometimes used in the preparation of poison baits for use against woodlice, leather-jackets, soil caterpillars, slugs, etc. There are two formulae:

(1) $\frac{1}{4}$ lb. of Paris Green.
  7 lb. of bran.

(2) 2 oz. of Paris Green.

7 lb. of dried blood.

In both formulae the two ingredients are mixed thoroughly and placed in small heaps where the pests can get at them, but out of reach of domestic animals, e.g. beneath boards or flat stones, etc. Mixture 1 may be moistened with water to make a crumbly mash which is particularly attractive to leather-jackets and soil caterpillars. Mixture 2 is specially recommended for woodlice. Paris Green is exceedingly poisonous to all warm-blooded animals, including man.

690. Pepper Dust. This may be sprinkled freely on the leaves and flowers of plants. It is chiefly useful to keep earwigs at bay, but is also of some service against slugs and cats.

691. Permanganate of Potash. This is sometimes used to kill or deter slugs and snails, for which purpose simply scatter a thin trail of crystals round the plants to be protected or where the pests are known to frequent. It is also employed as a mild fungicide to check damping-off disease of seedlings and to kill moss on lawns. For both purposes 1 oz. of permanganate of potash is dissolved in 1 gal. of water and applied from a watering-can fitted with a fine rose.

692. Petroleum Oil (White Oil). Proprietary insecticides manufactured from high-grade petroleum oils. Two grades are obtainable, one for winter, the other for summer application. In winter it is used chiefly to control capsid bug eggs and red spider mite winter eggs on fruit trees; in summer to control red spider mites, thrips, scale insects, and white fly on all plants. Summer petroleum is used on a wide variety of plants, particularly glasshouse plants, but may damage carnations, smilax and asparagus fern. Manufacturer's instructions regarding preparation and application must be followed.

693. Phosphorus Paste. This is sometimes used as a rat or mouse poison for which purpose it is spread on pieces of bread, cheese, fat, fish or any other attractive bait and placed where the rodents are likely to feed. Phosphorus paste is highly poisonous to all warm-blooded animals, including man, and must be kept out of reach of domestic animals.

694. Pyrethrum. An insecticide prepared from the flower heads of certain tropical plants. It is not very poisonous to warm-blooded animals, including man, but acts very rapidly on many insects, including aphids, capsid bugs, leaf hoppers and thrips, giving a knock-down effect but not always a complete kill, for which reason it is often combined with slower but more certain insecticides. Pyrethrum is available as a dust ready for use or as a liquid to be diluted with water and applied as a spray according to manufacturer's instructions.

695. Quassia. An old-fashioned, non-poisonous insecticide, chiefly used against aphids but now practically superseded by more efficient insect killers. It is intensely bitter and is sometimes used to make plants distasteful to birds.

Quassia extract can be purchased ready for dilution with water and application as a spray according to manufacturer's instructions. Alternatively it can be prepared by boiling 4 oz. of quassia chips for two hours in a gallon of water. After ten minutes' boiling, add 1 teaspoonful of carbonate of soda. Dissolve 8 oz. of soft soap in another gallon of water and add the quassia extract. The chips should be strained off and boiled again in a further gallon of water for an hour without carbonate of soda. Finally, add this liquor to that previously obtained, stir well, and make up to 5 gals. with cold water. Apply in the form of a heavy spray.

696. Quintozene. A fungicide primarily used for the control of soil-borne diseases such as damping off, wire stem, foot rot, root rot and grey bulb rot, and also of tulip fire and lawn diseases such as dollar spot, corticium (red thread) and fusarium patch (snow mould). It is supplied as a dust ready for use and may be worked into the soil, dusted on plants or over bulbs according to manufacturer's instructions. It is also available as a wettable powder to be stirred into water and kept agitated while being sprayed, watered on or used as a dip. It should not be used on soil intended for cucumbers, marrows or melons.

697. Red Lead. Ordinary red lead as sold for the preparation of paint can be used as a dressing for seeds to protect them from wireworms, mice and birds. Shake the seeds in a very little paraffin to damp them, then roll them in red lead.

698. Schradan. A systemic insecticide used mainly against aphids and red spider mites, though it is also effective against most sap suckers. It is very poisonous to all warm-blooded animals, including man, and also to fish. Rubber gloves and face shield should be worn when mixing and applying it. Special care should be taken if other chemicals of the organo-phosphorus group, to which schradan belongs, are being used because of the danger of accumulations in the body. The minimum harvesting time for edible crops sprayed with schradan is four weeks from April to July and six weeks from August to mid-September, after which no sprayed crops should be used. Supplied as a liquid to be diluted with water and applied as a spray according to manufacturer's instructions.

699. Soft Soap. Mainly used as a spreader (640) but has some insecticidal properties and is occasionally used to control aphids and red spider mites. For this purpose, use at 5 to 10 oz. to every 5 gals. of water.

700. Soot. In addition to its use as a fertilizer (81), soot is also employed as an insecticide. Fresh soot dug into vacant ground at 8 oz. per square yard has some effect in clearing it of slugs, cutworms, wireworms etc., but is rendered more efficient if fresh hydrated lime (674) is applied at the same time. Weathered soot can be dusted on the leaves of celery, chrysanthemums, etc., to ward off leaf-mining flies. It is best applied when the foliage is damp with dew.

701. Sulphate of Iron. Used to control some soil-borne diseases, notably fairy rings on lawns. The method is to spike the affected area fairly closely to a depth of 4 in., and then to apply a solution of sulphate of iron, mixed with water at the rate of 4 oz. per gallon. The solution is applied freely and can be repeated in six weeks' time if necessary.

702. Sulphur. A fungicide particularly useful against mildews and moulds, and also as a deterrent of red spider mites. It is available as a fine powder, often known as 'flowers of sulphur', for use direct or in various colloidal or wettable formulations to be mixed with water and applied as a spray according to manufacturer's instructions. Flowers of sulphur for garden use is often coloured green so that it does not look unsightly on foliage.

703. Tar-oil Wash. Proprietary sprays made from tar distillate and used to clear fruit trees of caterpillar and aphid eggs, scale insects, lichen, moss, etc. Can only be applied with safety while trees are completely dormant. Usually applied in late December or early January. Manufacturer's instructions should be obtained where possible. Standard strength is usually $2\frac{1}{2}$ pts. to 5 gals. of water, but different brands may vary slightly. Also obtainable as an emulsion for use in the same way. This has the advantage that it mixes with water better and so gives a more complete and economical covering of the branches. As tar-oil scorches foliage, care must be taken when applying it to trees underplanted with green crops.

704. Tecnazene. (TCNB). A fungicide used to control dry rot in potatoes, to check the premature sprouting of stored potatoes and to control grey mould (botrytis) on chrysanthemums, lettuces, tomatoes and other plants grown under glass. It is applied to potatoes as a dust, purchased ready for use at the rate of $\frac{1}{2}$ lb. per 1 cwt. The potatoes must be covered immediately with soil, straw or tarpaulins. To control grey mould (botrytis) tecnazene is obtained in a smoke generator to be ignited in the greenhouse according to manufacturer's instructions.

705. Tetrachlorethane (White Fly Vapour). Used as a fumigant in glasshouses against white fly. It is sold under various trade names and is a colourless fluid. Dose is from 3 to 5 fl. oz. per 1,000 cu. ft. (23) of house. The specified quantity is sprinkled on the floor towards evening and the house is shut for twelve hours. The fumes are poisonous to human beings and domestic animals, and are damaging to *Asparagus sprengeri*, azaleas, balsam, begonias, chrysanthemums, cinerarias, calceolarias, camellias, cannas, crassulas, dahlias, fuchsias, hydrangeas, lemon verbena (lippia), pelargoniums, salvias, and sweet peas. These should be removed while fumigating. A second fumigation should be given 14 days later, or three applications at intervals of seven days if an attack is very severe. Temperature of house during fumigation should be 70° or higher and the air should be rather dry.

706. Thiocyanate Winter Wash. Contains petroleum oil and beta-thiocyanodiethyl ether for application to fruit trees to control capsid bugs, red spider mites, woolly aphid and other aphids, caterpillars, apple sucker, etc. It is a fluid which must be diluted with water. Usual strength is $1\frac{1}{2}$ to $2\frac{1}{4}$ pts. to 5 gals. of water, but manufacturer's instructions should be obtained where possible. It should be applied when buds start to expand and each has a green tip (usually March). This wash may prove very useful when bad weather makes it impossible to complete the application of tar oil (703) while the trees are still dormant.

707. Thiram. A fungicide effective in controlling a wide range of diseases including rose black spot, grey mould (botrytis), tulip fire, some rusts, apple and pear scab, downy mildew, raspberry cane spot and tomato leaf mould, as

301

well as some soil-borne diseases such as damping off and pea and bean foot rot. It is available as a dust for treatment of seeds before they are sown and also as colloidal or wettable powders to be stirred into water and kept agitated while being applied as a spray. Manufacturer's instructions must be followed. Thiram should not be used on fruit intended for canning or deep freezing because of a tendency to taint and also to affect the lacquer used inside tins.

708. Trichlorphon. A synthetic insecticide of the organophosphorus group which is not highly poisonous to warm-blooded animals, including human beings, but is very effective in killing flies and fly larvae, leaf miners, caterpillars, cutworms, earwigs and ants. A minimum period of two days should be allowed between use and harvesting of edible crops. It is applied as a spray. Trichlorphon is harmful to fish.

709. Washing Soda. Sometimes used as a fungicide primarily for the control of gooseberry mildew, especially on varieties such as Careless, Early Sulphur, Golden Drop and Leveller that are liable to be injured by fungicides containing sulphur. 12 oz. of washing soda and 12 oz. of soft soap are dissolved in 5 gals. of water and applied as a spray every 10 to 14 days from the time the blossom falls until well into the summer.

710. Zineb. A dithiocarbamate fungicide containing zinc which is effective in giving protection against many plant diseases. including potato blight, tomato leaf mould, various mildews and rusts, blackcurrant and celery leaf spot, grey mould (botrytis) and tulip fire. It is virtually non-poisonous but should not be inhaled, should be kept off the skin and it is recommended that outdoor edible crops should not be harvested under one week after application of zineb, glasshouse crops not under two days. It is available as a dust for direct application, or as a wettable powder to be stirred into water, as directed by the makers, and kept agitated while being applied as a spray.

711. A Table of Pests and Diseases

Figures in brackets refer to paragraphs, plain figures months

Name	Notes	Treatment Month	Treatment Method
American blight	See Aphid, woolly		
Antirrhinum rust	See rust		
Ants	Soil disturbed, aphid encouraged	1–12	(644) (645) (708)
Aphids (blackfly, greenfly, greyfly, rosy apple aphid, etc.)	Lice suck juices, carry virus, and cripple young growth	12–1 5–10	(669) (703) (667) (672) (677) (679)
Aphid, root	Lice suck juices from roots of lettuces and auriculas	5–10	(644) (663)
Aphid, woolly	Lice, protected by white, woolly covering, on stems and roots. Paint with methylated spirits in summer	12–1	(703)
Apple blossom weevil	Grubs 'cap' and destroy blossom	4, 5	(650)
		1	(703)
Apple blossom wilt	Fungus kills blossom and spurs	4	(675)
Apple canker	Festering wounds encircle branches	1	(703)
		3–11	(655)
Apple codling moth	Caterpillars eat into fruits	5–6	(650) (187)
Apple sawfly	Maggots eat into fruits	5–6	(644)
Apple and pear scab	Black spots on leaves and fruits later cracked	4–7	(646) (649) (675)
Apple sucker	Lice deforms leaves and kill blossom	4–5	(644) (677)
Aster wilt	Annual asters rot at soil level	5–7	(639) (671)
Bacterial soft rot	Celery, etc., rots at the heart	6–10	(655) (671)
Bacterial canker (cherry and plum)	Round holes in leaves, gum oozes from bark. branches die	8–10	(646)
Bean anthracnose	Sunken black spots on pods	6–7	(646) (675)
Bean beetle	See Pea beetle		

A TABLE OF PESTS AND DISEASES—*continued*

Name	Notes	Treatment Month	Treatment Method
Bean chocolate spot	Leaves and stems of broad beans blotched	2–5	(646) (655)
Bean halo spot	Angular spots on leaves	4–8	(636)
Bean rust	See Rust		
Bean weevil	See Pea Weevil		
Blackfly	See Aphid		
Botrytis (Grey Mould)	Black decay followed by white mould	5–9	(665) (696) (702) (703)
Brown rot	Fruits of apples, plums, etc., mummified with rings of white mould	1	(703)
Brown scale	See scale		
Cabbage caterpillars	Leaves skeletonized	6–10	(644) (650) (662) (708)
Cabbage gall weevil	White maggots in galls at soil level	5–10	(648)
Cabbage root fly	White maggots eating roots	5–7	(644) (708)
Cabbage white blister	White blisters on stems and leaves	3–9	(646)
Cabbage white fly	Tiny white flies fouling leaves	9	(644) (677)
Cane spot	See Raspberry cane spot		
Canker	See Apple, Bacterial or Rose canker		
Capsid bug	Active lice on fruit trees. Leaves distorted, fruits marked	2–3 / 4–9	(669) (692) (644) (663) (667)
Carnation spot	Leaves yellow and curled	1–12	(649) (678) (710)
Carrot fly	Maggots eat roots	5–7	(644) (663) (685)
Caterpillars	Leaves and stems of many plants eaten	12–1 / 4–8	(669) (703) (644) (650) (662) (708)

Celery fly	See Leaf miners	
Celery heart rot	See Bacterial soft rot	(671)
Celery spot	Numerous spots on leaves	1–3 (655) (710)
		6–9 (685) (687)
		1–12
Chafers	White larvae attack roots of many plants	4–5 (646) (655)
Clematis wilt	Stems wither and die	1–12 (674)
Club root	Roots of cabbage tribe swell and decay	3–10 (648)
		1–12 (644) (645)
Cockroaches	Seedlings eaten	
Codling moth	See Apple codling moth	
Collar rot	See Aster wilt, Damping off, Tomato collar rot	
Cranefly larvae	See Leather-jackets	
Cuckoo spit (froghopper)	Lice covered with froth on leaves and stems of many plants	5–8 (644) (677)
Currant big-bud	Buds swollen by mites within	3–4 (670) (675)
Currant clear wing moth	Shoots tunnelled by caterpillars	6–10 (636)
Currant reversion	Leaf veins reduced in number, little fruit produced	1–12 (636)
Cutworms	Caterpillars in soil eat stems and roots of many plants	1–12 (644) (650)
		(685)
Damping off	Seedlings rot at soil level	1–12 (652)
Didymella	See tomato stem rot	
Die back	Stems of roses and gooseberries die, especially in winter	12–2 (87) (656)
		6–7 (646)
Earwigs	Flowers and young leaves of dahlias, etc., eaten	7–10 (644) (650)
Eelworms	Roots and stems infested by microscopic 'worms'	1–12 (638) (658)
		(659) (682)
Flea beetles	Leaves of cabbages, turnips, etc., riddled with small round holes	3–10 (644) (650)
		(662)
Foot rot	Stem decays at base	1–12 (649) (652)
		(707)
Frog flies (leaf hoppers)	Pale larvae suck juices from leaves	5–9 (662) (667)
		(672) (677)

305

A TABLE OF PESTS AND DISEASES—continued

Name	Notes	Treatment Months	Treatment Method
Gladiolus scab	Leaves decay at soil level, corms spotted and split	9–3	(648) (649)
Gladiolus dry rot	Leaves wither from tips, corms spotted	5–10	(648)
Gooseberry mildew, American	Felt-like mildew on leaves, stems and fruits	3–6	(675) (709)
Gooseberry mildew, European	See Mildew		
Gooseberry rust or cluster-cup	Reddish blister-like swellings on leaves and fruits	3–4	(646) (655)
Greenfly	See Aphid		
Grey Mould	See Botrytis		
Gumming	See Bacterial canker		
Gummosis	Cucumber fruits ooze gum and crack	6–9	(710)
Hollyhock rust	See Rust		
Honey fungus (armillaria)	Roots die, white fungus under bark	1–12	(671)
Iris rhizome rot	Plants rot at base	3–6	(655)
Lawn diseases (dollar spot, red thread and fusarium)	Grass develops pale or pinkish patches	3–10	(648)
Leaf hoppers	See Frog flies		
Leaf miners	Small maggots burrowing leaves	1–12	{ (644) (677) (708)
Lettuce grey mould	Stems rot and become mouldy	1–12	(665)
Leather-jackets	Blackish larvae in the soil eat roots and stems of many plants including grass	1–12	(644) (650) (654)
Lily disease	See Botrytis rot		
Lily mosaic	See Mosaic		
Mealy bug	Juice sucked from vines and other green-house plants	1–12 / 11–12	(662) (663) (677) (703)

PESTS, DISEASES AND WEEDS

Mice	Bulbs, corms and seeds eaten	1–12	(635) (693)
Mildew, Powdery	Powdery white outgrowth on stems and leaves of many plants	5–10	(697) (668) (702)
Downy	Leaves yellow, shrivelling, faintly powdered	5–9	(655) (710)
Millepedes	Whitish to black, many-legged soil pests which feed on the roots of the plants	1–12	(635) (644)
Mint rust	Rusty spots on leaves and stems	6–9	(636)
Moles	Tunnels in soil and mounds of soil	1–12	(635) (685)
Mosaic	Yellow mottling of leaves caused by virus	5–9	(637)
Mushroom maggots	Mushrooms holed and maggoty	1–12	(644) (685)
Mussel scale	See Scale		
Narcissus basal rot	Base of bulb decays	8–10	(696)
Narcissus fly	Maggots eat interior of bulb	7–8	(638) (644)
Nut weevil	Maggots feed in kernels	5–6	(660)
Onion fly	Maggots eat plants just beneath soil	5–7	(644) (650) (708)
Onion neck rot	Top of bulb decays	9–12	(636)
Onion smut	Black stripes on leaves	5–8	(671) (707)
Onion white rot	White mould and decay at base of bulb	6–8	(636)
Pea beetle	Seeds holed. Reject bad seeds		
Pea moth	Small caterpillars eat peas in pod	6–8	(660)
Pea and bean weevil	Holes eaten in leaf edge	5–7	(662)
Peach leaf curl	Leaves curled and red	2–3	(646) (655)
Pear leaf blister mite	Reddish blister on leaves	2	(692)
		4	(675)
Pear midge	Maggots eat interior of fruitlets	4	(660)
Pear sawfly	See Caterpillars		
Pear scab	See Apple and pear scab		
Potato blackleg	Black decay of stems from soil	6–9	(636)
Potato blight	Damp, black blotches on leaves, brown decay in tubers	7–9	(646) (655) (678) (710)
Potato eelworm	White cysts on tubers	8–12	(638) (658) (659)

307

A TABLE OF PESTS AND DISEASES—continued

Name	Notes	Treatment Month	Treatment Method
Potato scab (common)	Scabs on skin of tubers. Avoid liming soil. Diseased tubers keep and are fit for use. Dig in leaf-mould or peat		
Potato storage rot	Dry brown rot after lifting	9–10	(704)
Potato wart disease	Wart-like outgrowths which destroy tubers	7–10	(636)
Raspberry beetle	White maggots eat fruits, beetles eat flower buds	5–6	(662)
Raspberry cane blight	Canes wither and snap off near ground level	5	(644)
Raspberry cane spot	Purplish decay encircling canes. Also attacks blackberries and loganberries	3–5	(675)
Raspberry mosaic	See Mosaic		
Raspberry midge	Pink grubs in rind of young canes	5	(644)
Red spider mites	Minute reddish mites, suck juices from leaves of many plants	6–9	(643) (662) (666) (677); (692)
Rhododendron bud blast	Flower buds die	2–3	(644) (646)
Ring spot	Circular spots on leaves of cabbages and other brassicas	6–8 6–9	(707)
Root maggot	Small maggots in roots of chrysanthemums and lettuces	4–9	(644) (685)
Root rot	Roots and lower stems of many plants killed	1–12	(671)
Rose black spot	Circular black spots on leaves. See also (41)	5–9	(649) (662) (678)
Rose canker	Festering wounds encircling branches	12	(656)
Rose sawfly	Leaves curled	1–12	(636)
Rust	Rusty spots on under surface of leaves	5–7 6–9	(686) (707) (710)

Scale	Scale-covered insects on branches of fruit trees, etc.	1–12	(663) (677)
Silver leaf	Leaves of plum, apples, cherries, peaches, etc., silvered. Branches killed	12–1 6–7	(692) (357)
Slugs	Leaves, stems, and fruits of many plants eaten	1–12	(681) (683)
Slugworms	Black maggots eating leaf surface of fruit trees, roses, etc.	6–9	(644) (662) (677)
Snails	Damage and treatment, see Slugs		
Sooty mould	Black coating on leaves	1–12	(663) (677)
Spotted wilt	Plants stunted. Brown spots on leaves	1–12	(637)
Springtails	Minute white insects in soil	9–3	(644)
Strawberry leaf spot	Reddish spots on leaves	5–7	(668) (675)
Strawberry yellow edge	Virus, dwarfs and curls leaves and turns edges yellow	5–9	(637)
Streak (sweet pea, tomato)	Leaves and stems deformed and streaked	6–9	(637)
Tarsonemid mite	Mites suck juices from young leaves of strawberries, cyclamen, etc.	6–8	(666)
Thrips	Small active insects, deform leaves, flowers, etc., and cause silvery streaking of many plants	1–12	(644) (663) (677)
Tomato blossom end rot	Black decay of fruit at end opposite to stalk. Encouraged by underwatering	5–10	(68)
Tomato leaf-mould	Khaki mould on underside of leaves	6–9	(678) (710)
Tomato sleepy disease	Plant flags but recovers when temperature is raised above 75°F.	1–12	(636)
Tomato stem rot	Stems shrink and rot	3–8	(649) (678)
Tulip fire	Leaves and flowers scorched	3–5	(649) (678) (710)
Turnip flea beetle	See Flea Beetle		
Vine mildew	See Mildew		
Virus	See (637)		
Wasps	Ripening fruits eaten	7–9	(644) (662)
Weevils	Notches in leaves, grubs in roots	1–12	(644) (650)

A TABLE OF PESTS AND DISEASES—continued

Name	Notes	Treatment	
		Month	Method
White fly	Small white 'flies' on many plants	1–12	{ (644) (650) (677)
White rust	White 'felt' on stems and leaves of brassicas, wallflowers and stocks	1–12	(646) (707)
Winter moth	Caterpillars eat young leaves of apples, etc.	1 4–5 9	(703) (662) (187)
Wirestem	Stems of young brassicas wither	3–6	{ (649) (696) (707)
Wireworm	Yellow, hard-skinned larvae eating roots of many plants	1–12	(635) (644) (685)
Woodlice	Seedlings eaten	1–12	(650) (689)
Worms	Mainly beneficial but drainage of pot plants blocked and lawns fouled	4–5 9–10 }	(654) (684)

WEEDS AND WEED-KILLERS

712. Mechanical Destruction. All weeds can be killed in time by digging and hoeing. Frequently these are the best means, though laborious. Deep-rooted weeds such as bindweed, dock, coltsfoot, and ground elder cannot be destroyed readily by chemical means. If their roots are dug out to a depth of 18–24 in. and top growth is prevented for one whole spring and summer by hoeing, no further trouble is likely.

Annual and biennial weeds such as groundsel, chickweed, and common purple thistle can be exterminated quickly by hoeing only, if this is done before they ripen seeds.

Most surface-rooting weeds, e.g. creeping buttercup, nettles, and couch grass, can be killed by burying them 18 in. deep.

713. Types of Herbicide. Some chemicals kill almost all kinds of plants and are called 'total herbicides'. Some kill particular types of plant but are more or less harmless to other types and are called 'selective herbicides'. Some kill plants by being scattered or sprayed over them, some are applied to the soil and some are effective applied in either of these ways. Herbicides which kill only part of the plant they touch are known as 'contact herbicides' in contrast to 'translocated' or 'systemic herbicides', which enter the plant either by leaves or roots and are carried round in the sap. Herbicides which remain active in the soil for a considerable time, preventing the growth of seedlings or small plants, are known as 'residual herbicides'. Scientists prefer the term 'herbicide', meaning plant killer, to 'weed-killer' since no chemical can distinguish between a garden plant and a weed. The user, by selection of an appropriate chemical and choice of the right method and time for application, ensures that weeds, not garden plants, are killed.

714. Application of Herbicides. Both dry and liquid chemicals are available. Some of the forms are applied direct

311

to weeds, others are dissolved in water and applied as sprays or from sprinklers. Dry herbicides may be spread by hand but care is needed to ensure even distribution and correct dosage. Alternatively the various mechanical fertilizer distributors may be used to spread herbicides. Some manufacturers prepare lawn fertilizers blended with chemicals to kill lawn weeds, thus doing two jobs in one.

Liquid herbicides, after dilution with water, may be sprayed with any garden spraying equipment but there is often danger of spray drifting where it is not wanted. Herbicides are more safely applied from a watering-can or special applicator fitted with a fine rose or sprinkler bar, from which the liquid can be delivered almost in contact with the weeds or soil. Sprinkle bars of different widths are available to suit particular requirements, e.g. a very narrow (3-in.) bar for applying herbicides between garden plants or in awkward places and a wide (18-in.) bar for covering lawns or large areas of vacant ground.

All equipment should be well washed after use. It is best to keep equipment solely for application of herbicides, thus reducing the risk of the chemicals getting on to garden plants.

715. Calomel. (Mercurous chloride). Used either alone or in combination with sulphate of iron (731) as a moss killer, particularly on lawns. For this purpose it may be supplied as a liquid for spraying or sprinkling or as a powder for application direct according to manufacturer's instructions. It is rather slow in action but persistent, and is most effective in early autumn. It is harmful to fish.

716. Chlorpropham. A selective residual herbicide usually offered for garden use in mixture with other chemicals such as fenuron (722) and propham (727). It is available as a liquid or wettable powder to be applied to the soil as a spray and by itself is used mainly to prevent growth of weed seedlings in various bulb crops and around blackcurrants, gooseberries and strawberries. It is liable to cause damage to plants on light soils lacking in humus.

717. 2,4-D. A translocated selective weed-killer which will kill a good many weeds in lawns without injury to the grass. It is often mixed with other herbicides, such as mecoprop (725) to widen its band of efficacy. It is most effective if applied when grass and weeds are growing actively. Lawns should not be cut for a few days after application to give the chemical time to act. It is harmful to most garden plants other than grass and also to fish, so care should be taken to prevent drift. It is not persistent in the soil. It is available in various forms to be used according to manufacturer's instructions.

718. Dalapon. A translocated selective herbicide which will kill grass, including couch grass, also reeds, sedges and other monocotyledons but is much less toxic to dicotyledons. It is particularly useful for killing grass in orchards and around bush fruits. It should not be used near Apple Cox's Orange Pippin in winter. Sensitive plants should not be planted on treated ground under six weeks. Dalapon is sold as a powder to be dissolved in water according to manufacturer's instructions and applied as a spray or sprinkle to the weeds.

719. Dicamba. A translocated selective herbicide used either alone or in combination with other herbicides such as MCPA (724) for the control of weeds in lawns. It is supplied as a liquid to be diluted with water and applied as a spray or sprinkle to the lawn or weeds. It is harmful to most plants, other than grass, and also to fish.

720. Dichlobenil. A total residual herbicide which can be used to keep paths, drives etc. clean for many months or in carefully limited doses can also be used to prevent growth of seedlings and small weeds around established shrubs, trees, blackcurrants, gooseberries etc. It is purchased in granular form for application direct according to manufacturer's instructions.

721. Diquat. A total weed-killer which is inactivated by contact with the soil. It is not itself poisonous to plants but is changed into a poisonous substance in the plant leaf by photosynthesis. Light is therefore essential for its action which is most rapid in warm, bright weather. It is available as a liquid for dilution and can be used to clear ground for sowing or planting or to kill weeds around growing plants, provided care is taken to apply it to the leaves of the weeds and to keep it off the leaves or green stems of garden plants. It does not matter if it falls on the soil.

722. Fenuron. A residual herbicide which in large doses will kill most plants but in carefully regulated quantities can be selective. For garden use it is often combined with other herbicides such as chlorpropham (716) or propham (727). It is available as a liquid or wettable powder to be mixed with water and applied as a spray or sprinkle according to manufacturer's instructions, its principal garden use being the repression of seedling weeds among perennial plants, shrubs, etc.

723. Ioxynil. A translocated selective weed-killer primarily used to kill weeds in young seedling lawns. It must be used 7 to 10 days after the germination of the grass seed when each seedling grass plant has approximately two leaves. It is purchased as a powder to be dissolved in water according to manufacturer's instructions and applied as a spray or sprinkle.

Lawn Sand. See (108).

724. MCPA. A translocated selective herbicide used mainly in gardens for the control of weeds on lawns. For this purpose it may be used alone or in combination with other selective herbicides such as 2,4-D (717) or dicamba (719). Both it and these mixtures are used in the same way as 2,4-D.

725. Mecoprop. A translocated selective herbicide chiefly

314

used in gardens for the control of weeds in lawns. It is more effective than either 2,4-D (717) or MCPA (724) in killing clover and is often offered in mixture with 2,4-D to provide a weed-killer with a wide band of effectiveness. Method of use, either alone or in mixture, is the same as for 2,4-D.

726. Paraquat. A total herbicide allied to diquat (721) and with similar properties. It is a better grass killer than diquat and mixtures of the two are offered to provide a herbicide with the widest possible band of effectiveness. Method of use either alone or in this mixture is the same as for diquat.

727. Propham. A selective residual herbicide which is used either alone or in combination with other herbicides such as chlorpropham (716) and fenuron (722) to prevent the emergence of weed seedlings among certain plants and vegetable crops. It is available as a liquid or wettable powder for mixing with water and application as a spray or sprinkle according to manufacturer's instructions. Propham is not so effective on soils containing a high percentage of peat. It is dangerous to fish.

728. Simazine. A residual herbicide which in heavy doses will inhibit the growth of all plants and can be used to keep paths, drives, etc. clear of weeds for long periods. In smaller, carefully controlled doses it can be used selectively to prevent growth of weeds in rose beds, round ornamental trees and shrubs, in orchards, around bush and cane fruits, etc. It is available as a powder for dissolving in water and application as a spray or sprinkle direct to the soil according to manufacturer's instructions. It moves about very little in the soil.

729. Sodium Chlorate. A total herbicide which is both translocated in the plant and also effective in the soil. It is useful for clearing waste land and for keeping paths, drives, etc. clear of weeds. Drawbacks are its readiness to move about in the soil where it may easily be carried to places where it was not intended to be; the difficulty of knowing just how long it will remain effective, since it is easily washed out by rain yet may be retained for a long time in heavy soils or in dry weather; and its inflammability. To counter this last danger sodium chlorate is often mixed with a fire depressant. It is applied both as a powder (or granules) for use dry or for solution in water and application as a spray or sprinkle either to the weeds or to the soil. Clothing wetted with sodium chlorate may become inflammable.

730. Sodium Monochloroacetate. A contact herbicide that is used to kill seedling weeds among brassicas (cabbage, kale, etc.), also leeks and onions. It is harmful to bees and livestock including poultry. It is available as a powder to be dissolved in water according to manufacturer's instructions and applied as a spray.

731. Sulphate of Iron. This is sometimes used as a moss killer on lawns and elsewhere, either by itself at 2–4 oz. per gallon or more usually in combination with other chemicals such as sulphate of ammonia, to make lawn sand (108), or with chlorpropham (716). It kills moss more rapidly than chlorpropham but is not so persistent.

732. 2,4,5-T. A translocated selective herbicide used primarily as a nettle and brushwood killer. It is often mixed with 2,4-D (717) to make it effective where both herbaceous and woody plants are to be killed without injury to grass. It is available as a liquid to be diluted with water according to manufacturer's instructions and applied as a spray or sprinkle to the leaves and stems of plants to be destroyed. It has no effect in the soil. It is harmful to fish.

SECTION NINE
SPECIAL TECHNIQUES

733. Ring Culture. Some plants, notably tomatoes, chrysanthemums and carnations, grow well in bottomless 'pots' standing on a bed of gravel or ashes. Real pots with the bottoms knocked out can be used but most ring culture is carried out in special rings made of bituminised cardboard or 'whalehide'. Rings 9 inches in diameter and 9 inches deep are suitable for strong-growing plants. They are filled with ordinary potting soil and are stood on a bed of clean washed gravel or well-weathered boiler ashes at least 6 inches deep. The plants are raised in the normal way from seed or cuttings and are planted in the rings while still quite small. After planting they are well watered in so that the soil in the 'rings' is moist throughout. Subsequently all water is applied to the gravel or ash base from which it is drawn up into the soil by capillary attraction. Any solid or liquid food required is applied to the soil in the rings from which the plants derive all the chemicals they require.

The plants make two quite distinct root systems, one of fine feeding roots in the soil, the other much coarser, moisture-gathering roots, in the aggregate base. At the end of the season the plants and roots are removed (they come easily out of the aggregate), the soil is discarded, to be replaced by fresh soil the following year, and the aggregate is flushed with water, perhaps with the addition of a little disinfectant such as formalin (671).

734. Straw Bale Culture. A method of growing tomatoes, cucumbers and possibly some other plants in greenhouses on decomposing straw bales. Wheat straw is the best, although barley straw can be used. Oat straw is too soft. Soil in the greenhouse should be level and covered with sheets of polythene film to isolate the straw from possible soil-borne infection. When placed in position end to end the bales, well bound with wire, should be thoroughly soaked in stages, so that the water is completely absorbed, applying about 9 gals. per $\frac{1}{2}$-cwt. bale in all over a period of three days.

Apply to each bale $1\frac{1}{2}$ lb. of Nitro-chalk (75) and water in well. Give two more dressings at intervals of three days, of 1 lb. and $\frac{3}{4}$ lb. respectively, watering in each. To this last application of Nitro-chalk add 18 oz. of nitrate of potash (72) and 4 oz. of sulphate of magnesium. Maintain a minimum temperature of 50° F. Decomposition will result and when the temperature falls below 100° F., planting can take place into a shallow bed (2 or 3 in. deep) of JIP.2 potting compost (505) spread on top of the bales.

Cultivation is the same as for tomatoes or cucumbers in soil beds, except that heavy feeding is necessary at first, preferably with a liquid fertilizer. The bales will decompose slowly during the season and it will be necessary to loosen and readjust the supports for the plants to prevent their roots being pulled out as the straw sinks.

735. Mist Propagation. Various appliances are now available for keeping cuttings constantly moist and cool by automatically spraying them with water at fairly frequent intervals. Broadly these devices may be divided into two types, those that are controlled by the actual rate of water evaporation and those that work on a simple time basis. Rate of evaporation may be determined by electrical contacts placed in the cutting bed. As long as these contacts remain moist current flows between them. As soon as they become dry the flow of current ceases and a sensitive electronic control unit switches on more powerful current which operates a solenoid valve which itself turns on the water supply to the misting jets. These wet cuttings and electric contacts alike so that after a few seconds current flows between the contacts, the electronic control unit switches off the current to the solenoid valve and the water ceases to flow.

Time switches can as a rule be set to give any sequence of stop and flow desired but are not sensitive to changing conditions of evaporation. A third alternative is a device which measures the amount of light reaching the cuttings and controls the frequency of mist bursts accordingly. Other devices work purely mechanically, as by water dripping into a little 'bucket' which, when full, tips a valve to start the water flow and at the same time empty itself; or a tiny piece of sponge on the arm of a balance which, when dry, allows it to rise and turn on the water.

Mist propagation is most satisfactory in spring and summer. The cuttings are not kept close, as they are in a normal propagating frame, but are usually rooted on the floor or staging of a greenhouse. Coarse sand and peat is the most satisfactory rooting medium and the best results are obtained when this is warmed to about 65°–70° F. from below as, for example, with an electrical soil-warming cable. Cuttings should be removed to ordinary compost or soil, sand and peat as soon as they are rooted.

736. Tomato and Cucumber Grafting. Tomatoes and cucumbers can be grafted to provide a root system which is resistant to certain soil-borne diseases and pests such as wilt, corky root and eelworm. Various rootstocks are available and doubtless more will be produced. Rootstock K.N. is resistant to root knot eelworm and corky root, and Tomato Rootstock K.V.F. resists corky root, fusarium and verticillium wilt.

The rootstock seed should be sown and seedlings reared in the same way as those of ordinary tomatoes or cucumbers. Seedlings are ready for grafting when they are about 4 in. high. The rootstocks should have the tops cut off to leave one or two leaves only. A sloping downward cut is made in the stem just below the lowest leaf and a corresponding upward cut is made in the stem of the fruiting variety. The two tongues formed should be fitted together and kept in place by adhesive tape. The two joined plants are then potted into a 3½-in. pot with the two root systems together.

For plants to be grafted on tomato K.V.F. stock it is necessary to remove the roots of the fruiting variety before they are planted in the fruiting quarters. To do this easily the seedlings of rootstock should~be potted singly before they are grafted. The soil is shaken from the roots of the scion (fruiting variety) and, after grafting, the plants are kept warm and shaded until wanted when the roots of the scion can be cut off.

INDEX (*page nos.*)
The figures in parentheses refer to the line illustrations

321

INDEX

INDEX

INDEX

325

INDEX

326

INDEX

INDEX

INDEX

INDEX

335